"No other gui
a pleasure to

". . . Excellently organized for the casual traveler who is looking for a mix of recreation and cultural insight."
Washington Post

★★★★★ (5-star rating) "Crisply written and remarkably personable. Cleverly organized so you can pluck out the minutest fact in a moment. Satisfyingly thorough."
Réalités

"The information they offer is up-to-date, crisply presented but far from exhaustive, the judgments knowledgeable but not opinionated." *New York Times*

"The individual volumes are compact, the prose succinct, and the coverage up-to-date and knowledgeable . . . The format is portable and the index admirably detailed."
John Barkham Syndicate

". . . An abundance of excellent directions, diversions, and facts, including perspectives and getting-ready-to-go advice — succinct, detailed, and well organized in an easy-to-follow style." *Los Angeles Times*

"They contain an amount of information that is truly staggering, besides being surprisingly current."
Detroit News

"These guides address themselves to the needs of the modern traveler demanding precise, qualitative information . . . Upbeat, slick, and well put together."
Dallas Morning News

". . . Attractive to look at, refreshingly easy to read, and generously packed with information." *Miami Herald*

"These guides are as good as any published, and much better than most." *Louisville* (Kentucky) *Times*

Stephen Birnbaum Travel Guides

Acapulco
Bahamas, Turks & Caicos
Barcelona
Bermuda
Boston
Canada
Cancun, Cozumel, and Isla Mujeres
Caribbean
Chicago
Disneyland
Eastern Europe
Europe
Europe for Business Travelers
Florence
France
Great Britain
Hawaii
Ireland
Italy
Ixtapa & Zihuatanejo
London
Los Angeles
Mexico
Miami
New York
Paris
Portugal
Rome
San Francisco
South America
Spain
United States
USA for Business Travelers
Venice
Walt Disney World
Western Europe

CONTRIBUTING EDITORS

Frederick H. Brengelman
Kevin Causey
Melanie Falick
Harlan Feder
Wendy Luft
Frank Shiell
Melinda Tang
Carol Zaiser

MAPS Susan Hohl
SYMBOLS Gloria McKeown

A Stephen Birnbaum Travel Guide

Birnbaum's IXTAPA & ZIHUATANEJO 1992

Stephen Birnbaum
Alexandra Mayes Birnbaum
EDITORS

Lois Spritzer
EXECUTIVE EDITOR

Laura L. Brengelman
Managing Editor

Mary Callahan
Ann-Rebecca Laschever
Julie Quick
Beth Schlau
Dana Margaret Schwartz
Associate Editors

HarperPerennial
A Division of HarperCollins*Publishers*

FIRST EDITION

ISSN: 0749-2561 (Stephen Birnbaum Travel Guides)
ISSN: 1055-5676 (Ixtapa & Zihuatanejo)
ISBN: 0-06-278009-3 (pbk.)

91 93 94 95 96 CC/OPM 10 9 8 7 6 5 4 3 2 1

Contents

GETTING READY TO GO

All the practical travel data you need to plan your Mexican vacation to the final detail.

When and How to Go

Preparing

On the Road

Sources and Resources

USEFUL WORDS AND PHRASES

THE CITIES

A thorough, qualitative guide to one of Mexico's favorite Pacific resort areas. This is a comprehensive report on the most compelling attractions and amenities, designed to be used on the spot.

DIVERSIONS

A selective guide to more than ten active and/or cerebral theme vacations, including the best places in Mexico to pursue them.

For the Experience

For the Body

DIRECTIONS

Three major driving routes, from Mexico's beautiful Pacific beaches to nearby cities and ancient ruins.

A Word from the Editor

I came upon Zihuatanejo for the first time in the late afternoon. We'd been driving down the Pacific Coast of Mexico for more than a week, stopping only where the beaches looked most inviting. It was all part of the sort of nomadic exploration that only young people undertake when they are without any real responsibilities, and when unknown foreign villages are still more intriguing than frightening.

We were following what had come to be our daily ritual: a late breakfast followed by roamings in a generally southerly direction, with stops any time the water and sand looked particularly appealing. Lunch was purposefully planned for late in the day, so it could be combined with a little end-of-day libation that would be drunk to the health of the setting sun. The Zihuatanejo eatery into which we migrated was perfect for our needs.

We ordered the obligatory fish grilled over an open charcoal fire, served with thick wedges of lime, all washed down with cold local beer. The combination of food and place made the meal near-ambrosial, the sort of perfect marriage of vittles and venue that has kept me happily on the road all these years.

But unlike the unhurried, peaceful pace that had accompanied such meals in other, similar Mexican villages, the proprietress of the informal restaurant that we had chosen clearly couldn't wait to be rid of us. Where we previously had been able to linger from late afternoon to sunset everywhere else we had dined during the days immediately past — just as long as we continued to order *mas cerveza, por favor* — our hostess obviously couldn't wait for us to get our rumps out of her restaurant.

Well, sunset watching is no idle pastime in Mexico — to the true believer, it occupies a position only slightly less exalted than sacred rite — so we refused to be rushed. Each drink reorder brought new angst to the face of our waitress, and whatever the Mexican equivalent of toe-tapping had long since deteriorated into not very thinly veiled animosity. Still we lingered, waiting for the sun to finally fall into the Pacific.

But just as the rim of the sun touched the distant horizon, local patience evaporated. As if to say, "Good riddance!" the waitress forgot all about us (and our unpaid check) and grabbed an empty chair and headed out the door. As extraordinary as the impatience had been among Mexican restaurateurs in those days, the precipitous exit was even more atypical. It was so extraordinary that we abandoned our own twilight vigil to see what was driving our waitress out into the rapidly gathering evening.

Down the dusty main drag we followed, and we were quite happy that we had followed the waitress's example by each hauling a chair along with us. For the lure was flickering on the side of the building closest to the beach, where a 16mm film projector had been set up to show a film for the entire town. All you had to do was bring your own box or sack on which to sit, and you could see the flick free. I think the movie was *The Treasure of the Sierra Madre* (all I really remember is Humphrey Bogart), but I'll never forget the night.

This story (hopefully) evokes some of the old-days-type memories that made me less than exultant when I heard that Ixtapa (once Zihuatanejo's closest suburb) was to become one of Mexico's two spanking-new computer-generated resorts (the other is Cancún). But while it's certainly true that the creation of a new airport, high-rise hotels, a golf course, and other modern vacation amenities has robbed the local real estate of its innocence and most of its laid-back atmosphere, it is impossible to deny that what the computer has wrought has real appeal. This appeal is doubly alluring because the combination of Ixtapa's modern facilities and 21st-century technology dovetails surprisingly well with Zihuatanejo's mostly traditional fishing village orientation. But it is just this new/old contrast of pace and style that makes it so important to have an accurate, up-to-date guide to this increasingly popular, extremely diverse travel destination.

What's more, the broadening sophistication of contemporary travelers has made it essential that guidebooks evolve in very fundamental ways in order to keep pace with their readers. That's why we've tried to create a guide to Ixtapa and Zihuatanejo that's specifically organized, written, and edited for this more demanding, modern traveler headed to this increasingly complex country. This is a traveler for whom qualitative information is infinitely more desirable than mere quantities of unappraised data. We think that this book, along with the other guides in our series, represents a new generation of travel guides — one that is especially responsive to modern needs and interests.

For years, dating back as far as Herr Baedeker, travel guides have tended to be encyclopedic, seemingly much more concerned with demonstrating expertise in geography and history than with any real analysis of the sorts of things that genuinely concern a typical tourist. But today, when it is hardly necessary to tell a traveler where Mexico's Pacific Coast is located (in many cases, the traveler has been to that country nearly as often as the guidebook editors), it becomes the responsibility of those editors to provide new perceptions and to suggest new directions to make a guide genuinely valuable.

That's exactly what we've tried to do in this series. I think you'll notice a different, more contemporary tone to the text, as well as an organization and focus that are distinctive and more functional. And even a random reading of what follows will demonstrate a substantial departure from the standard guidebook orientation, for we've not only attempted to provide information of a different sort, but we also have tried to present it in a format that makes it particularly accessible.

Needless to say, it's difficult to decide what to include in a guidebook of this size — and what to omit. Early on, we realized that giving up the encyclopedic approach precluded the inclusion of every single route and restaurant, a realization that helped define our overall editorial focus. Similarly, when we discussed the possibility of presenting certain information in other than strict geographical order, we found that the new format enabled us to arrange data in a way that we feel best answers the questions travelers typically ask.

Large numbers of specific questions have provided the real editorial skeleton for this book. The volume of mail I regularly receive seems to emphasize that modern travelers want very precise information, so we've tried to organize our material in the most responsive way possible. Readers who want to learn where to find the best *coco loco* in Ixtapa or the most fascinating place to parasail will have no trouble whatever extracting that data from this guide.

Travel guides are, above all, reflections of personal taste, and putting one's name on a title page obviously puts one's preferences on the line. But I think I ought to amplify just exactly what "personal" means. I don't believe in the sort of personal guidebook that's a palpable misrepresentation on its face. It is, for example, hardly possible for any single writer to visit thousands of restaurants (and nearly as many hotels) in any given year and provide accurate appraisals of each one. And even if it *were* possible for one human being to survive such an itinerary, it would of necessity have to be done at a dead sprint and the perceptions derived therefrom would probably be less valid than those of any other intelligent individual visiting the same establishments. It is, therefore, impossible (especially in an annually revised and updated guidebook *series* such as we offer) to have only one person provide all the data on the entire world.

I also happen to think that such individual orientation is of substantially less value to readers. Visiting a single hotel for just one night or eating one hasty meal in a random restaurant hardly equips anyone to provide appraisals that are of more than passing interest. No amount of doggedly alliterative or oppressively onomatopoeic text can camouflage a technique that is essentially specious. We have, therefore, chosen what I like to describe as the "thee and me" approach to restaurant and hotel evaluation and, to a somewhat more limited degree, to the sites and sights we have included in the other sections of our text. What this really reflects is personal sampling tempered by intelligent counsel from informed local sources, and these additional friends-of-the-editors are almost always residents of the city and/or area about which they have been consulted.

Despite the presence of several editors, writers, researchers, and local correspondents, very precise editing and tailoring keep our text fiercely subjective. So what follows is the gospel according to the Birnbaums and represents as much of our own taste and instinct as we can manage. It is probable, therefore, that if you prefer chili peppers that leave the roof of your mouth largely intact, can't stand canned fruit juices, and won't tolerate fresh fish that is relentlessly overcooked, then we're likely to have a long and meaningful relationship. Readers with dissimilar tastes may be less enraptured.

I should also point out something about the person to whom this guidebook is directed. Above all, he or she is a "visitor." This means that such elements as restaurants have been specifically picked to provide the visitor with a representative, enlightening, stimulating, and, above all, pleasant experience. Since so many extraneous considerations can affect the reception and service accorded a regular restaurant patron, our choices can in no way be construed as an exhaustive guide to resident dining. We think we've listed all the best places in various price ranges, but they were chosen with a visitor's enjoyment in mind.

Other evidence of how we've tried to tailor our text to reflect modern travel habits is most apparent in the section we call DIVERSIONS. Where once it was common for travelers to spend a Mexican visit simply lying beside some pool or beachfront, the emphasis today is more likely to be directed toward pursuing some favorite activity while visiting foreign turf. So we've selected every activity we could reasonably evaluate and organized the material in a way that is especially accessible to activists of either athletic or cerebral bent. It is no longer necessary, therefore, to wade through a pound or two of superfluous prose just to find the most challenging dive spot or ancient ceremonial center within a reasonable distance of your hotel.

Although the sheer beauty of this unique spot along Mexico's Pacific Coast is reason enough to want to visit, there also are a number of added bonuses once you arrive. The entire adjacent coastline offers a veritable cornucopia of activities to challenge the imagination of any visitor. There is lots of undeveloped coastline to explore, as well as day trips (and longer rides) to cities and villages awash in colonial history.

If there is one single thing that best characterizes the revolution in and evolution of current holiday habits, it is that most travelers now consider travel a right rather than a privilege. Travel today translates as the enthusiastic desire to sample all of the world's opportunities, to find that elusive quality of experience that is not only enriching, but comfortable. For that reason, we've tried to make what follows not only helpful and enlightening, but the sort of welcome companion of which every traveler dreams.

Finally, I should point out that every good travel guide is a living enterprise; that is, no part of this text is carved in stone. In our annual revisions, we refine, expand, and further hone all our material to serve your travel needs even better. To this end, no contribution is of greater value to us than your personal reaction to what we have written, as well as information reflecting your own experiences while using the book. We earnestly and enthusiastically solicit your comments about this book *and* your opinions and perceptions about places you have recently visited. In this way, we will be able to provide the most current information — including the actual experiences of real travelers — and to make those experiences more readily available to others. So please write to us at 60 E. 42nd St., New York, NY 10165.

We sincerely hope to hear from you.

STEVE BIRNBAUM

How to Use This Guide

A great deal of care has gone into the special organization of this guidebook, and we believe it represents a real breakthrough in the presentation of travel information. Our aim is to create a new, more modern generation of travel books, and to make this guide the most useful and practical travel tool available today.

Our text is divided into five basic sections in order to present information in the most useful way possible on every aspect of a vacation to Ixtapa and Zihuatanejo. This organization itself should alert you to the vast and varied opportunities available, as well as indicating all the specific data necessary to plan a successful trip. You won't find much of the conventional "swaying palms and shimmering sands" type of text in this guide; we've chosen instead to deliver more useful and practical information. Prospective itineraries tend to speak for themselves, and with so many diverse travel opportunities, we feel our main job is to highlight what's where and to provide basic details — how, when, where, how much, and what's best (and what's not) — to assist you to make the most intelligent choices possible.

Here is a brief summary of the five sections of this book, and what you can expect to find in each. We believe that you will find both your travel planning and en route enjoyment enhanced by having this book at your side.

GETTING READY TO GO

This mini-encyclopedia of practical travel facts is meant to be a sort of know-it-all companion, with all the precise information necessary to create a successful visit to Ixtapa and Zihuatanejo. There are entries on more than 25 separate topics, including how to get where you're going, what the trip is likely to cost, and how to avoid prospective problems. The individual entries are specific, realistic, and where appropriate, cost-oriented.

We expect you to use this section most in the course of planning your trip, for its ideas and suggestions are intended to simplify this often confusing period. Entries are intentionally concise, in an effort to get to the meat of the matter. These entries are augmented by extensive lists of specific sources from which to obtain even more detailed data, plus some suggestions for obtaining travel information on your own.

USEFUL WORDS AND PHRASES

Though most resorts in Ixtapa and Zihuatanejo have English-speaking staff, at smaller establishments and on most stops along the attendant driving routes a little knowledge of Spanish will go a long way. This collection of often-used words and phrases will help you to make a hotel or dinner reservation, order a meal, mail a letter — and even buy toothpaste.

THE CITIES

The individual report on Ixtapa and Zihuatanejo has been created with the assistance of researchers, contributors, professional journalists, and experts who live in the area. Although useful at the planning stage, THE CITIES is really designed to be taken along and used on the spot. The reports offer a short-stay guide, including an essay introducing each city as a historic entity and as a contemporary place to visit. *At-a-Glance* material is actually a site-by-site survey of the most important, interesting (and sometimes most eclectic) sights to see and things to do. *Sources and Resources* is a concise listing of pertinent tourist information meant to answer a range of potentially pressing questions as they arise — from something simple like the address of the tourist office, how to get around, which sightseeing tours to take, and when special events and holidays occur to something more difficult like where to find the best nightspot, which are the shops that have the finest merchandise and/or the most irresistible bargains, and where the best golf, tennis, fishing, and swimming are to be found. *Best in Town* is our collection of cost-and-quality choices of the best places to eat and sleep on a variety of budgets.

DIVERSIONS

This very selective guide is designed to help travelers find the very best place in which to pursue a wide range of physical and cerebral activities, without having to wade through endless pages of unrelated text. With a host of activities, DIVERSIONS provides a guide to the special place where the quality of experience is likely to be highest. Whether you opt for golf or tennis, surfing, sport fishing, or bullfights, each category is the equivalent of a comprehensive checklist of the absolute best in the area.

DIRECTIONS

Here are 3 driving itineraries, from Ixtapa and Zihuatanejo's superb beaches to more beaches and the exciting nightlife of Acapulco, farther southeast to the serene strands along the Bays of Huatulco, and inland to the historic city of Oaxaca. Though they cover a considerable distance, portions of the itineraries in the Ixtapa area can be done as day trips, using Ixtapa and Zihuatanejo as a base, while others can be "connected" for longer drives or used individually for short, intensive explorations along the way.

Each entry includes a guide to sightseeing highlights; a cost-and-quality guide to accommodations along the road; hints and suggestions for activities; and detailed driving maps of the route, noting points of interest described in the text.

Although each of the book's sections has a distinct format and a special function, they have been designed to be used together to provide a complete inventory of travel information. To use this book to full advantage, take a few minutes to read the table of contents and random entries in each section to give you an idea of how it all fits together.

Pick and choose needed information from different sections. Assume, for example, that your idea of a dream vacation has always been to play golf or just bask on a beach in Ixtapa or Zihuatanejo, see a bullfight in Acapulco, visit the "manmade" tourist development at Huatulco, and explore the ruins at Monte Albán, but you never really knew how to put such a trip together. Since your vacation will include driving, start by reading the short, informative section on traveling by car in GETTING READY TO GO. This will provide all the factual information needed to organize and prepare a road trip. It will alert you to insurance needs (and direct you to the insurance chapter in the same section of the book) and other equally detailed potential problems and pleasures of a driving vacation. But where to go and what to see? Turn to DIVERSIONS: *Scuba and Skin Diving,* for the best dive spots in the waters around Ixtapa and Zihuatanejo; *Good Golf,* for information on Ixtapa's *Club de Golf Ixtapa; Natural Wonderlands,* for the best places to see wildlife — without straying too far from the beach. Then turn to DIRECTIONS for our explicit suggested driving routes from Ixtapa and Zihuatanejo to the various destinations along the coast and north to Oaxaca.

In other words, the sections of this book are building blocks to help you put together the best possible trip. Use them selectively as a tool, a source of ideas, a reference work for accurate facts, and a guide to the best buys, the most exciting sights and sites, the most pleasant accommodations, and the tastiest food — *the best travel experience* that you can have.

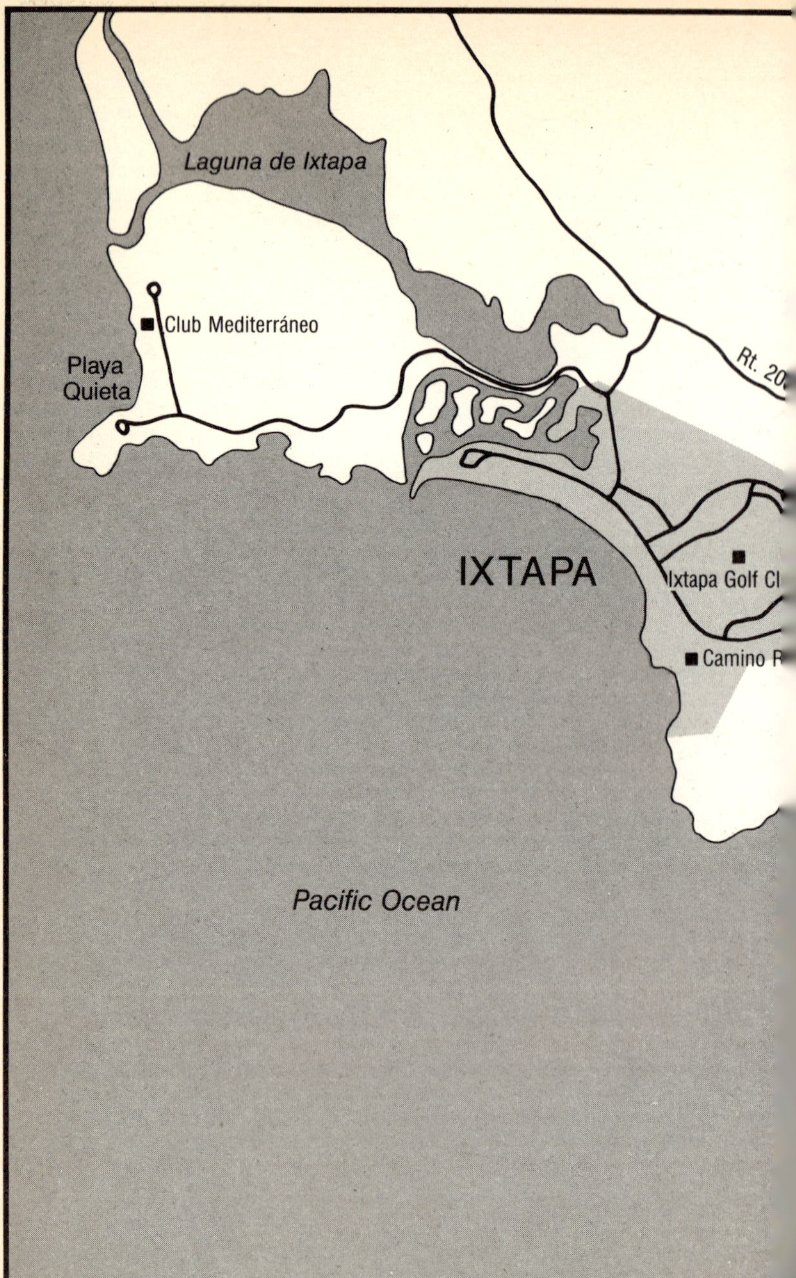
Laguna de Ixtapa
Club Mediterráneo
Playa
Quieta
Rt. 20
IXTAPA
Ixtapa Golf Cl
Camino R
Pacific Ocean

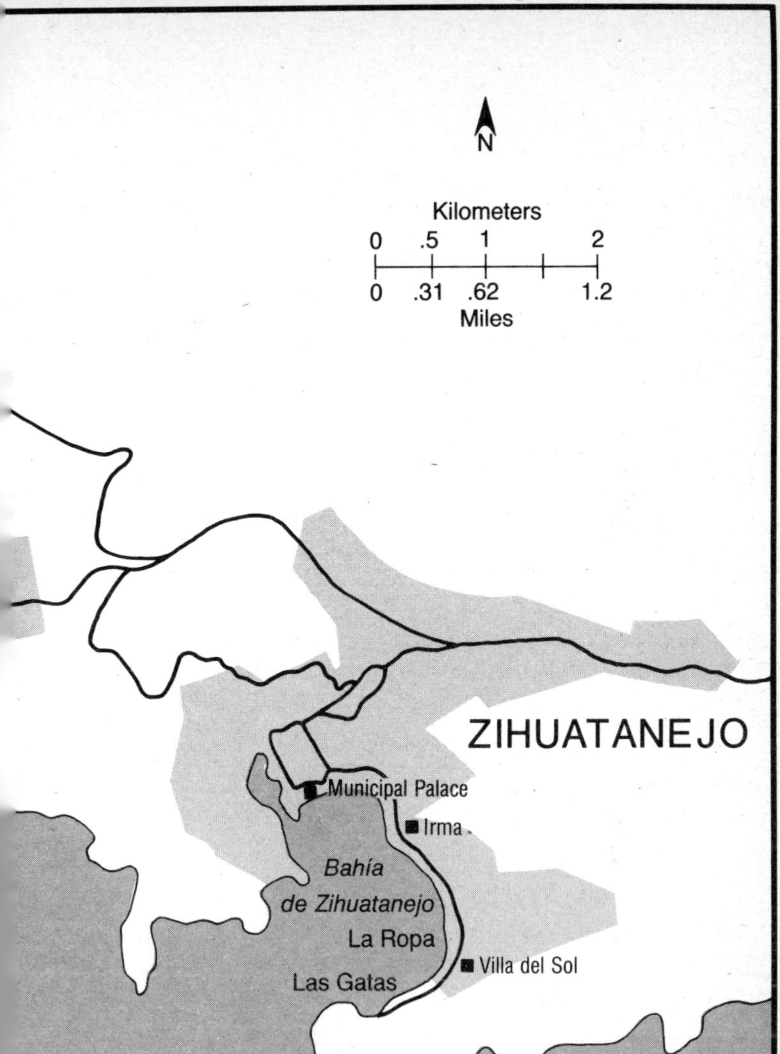
N
Kilometers
0 .5 1 2
0 .31 .62 1.2
Miles
ZIHUATANEJO
Municipal Palace
Irma
Bahía
de Zihuatanejo
La Ropa
Las Gatas
Villa del Sol

GETTING READY TO GO

When and How to Go

What's Where

Between the foothills of the Sierra Madre del Sur and Mexico's Pacific Coast, 130 miles (208 km) north of the better-known resort of Acapulco, Ixtapa and Zihuatanejo are nestled side by side, almost as two sides of a different coin. Ixtapa was developed into an upscale resort area after the Mexican government conducted a series of computerized feasibility studies, while Zihuatanejo still retains the charm and flavor of a traditional Mexican fishing village.

The combined resort area of Ixtapa-Zihuatanejo is poised at the edge of the state of Guerrero, which, along with Oaxaca, stretches to the Sierra Madre de Oaxaca. The state of Oaxaca — cool forested mountains, lush tropical valleys, and the humid coastline — is still inhabited by descendants of the ancient Zapotec and Mixtec Indian civilizations, and is famous for its red soil, which yields a variety of agricultural produce, as well as clay for pottery.

East of Ixtapa and Zihuatanejo, also on the coast, are posh Acapulco, unspoiled and unsophisticated Puerto Escondido, and the up-and-coming resort area of Huatulco. Inland from there is the Indian and colonial city of Oaxaca, a center for regional crafts (particularly ceramics and textiles), as well as a base for visits to the nearby magnificent ruins of Monte Albán and Mitla, among others.

When to Go

Most people associate Ixtapa and Zihuatanejo with winter suntans and beautiful seaside resorts. They aren't wrong. Mexico's Pacific Coast is one of the all-time favorite escapes for Americans trapped in snow and icy slush. (The winter season begins on December 15, when Mexicans traditionally take their annual 2-week, year-end vacation. It ends around the middle of April, after *Easter.*)

The destinations covered in this book are blessed with year-round tourism seasons, so there really isn't a "best" time to visit them. But it is important to emphasize that more and more travelers are enjoying the substantial advantages of off-season travel — that is, late spring, summer, and fall at most of the coastal resorts. Getting there and staying there are less expensive during the off-season as airfares, hotel rooms, and car rental rates go down, and less expensive package tours become available; the independent traveler can go farther on less, too. What's more, major tourist attractions, beaches, and other facilities tend to be less crowded, and — throughout Mexico — life proceeds at a more leisurely pace.

It should also be noted that what the travel industry refers to as shoulder seasons — the 1½ to 2 months before and after the peak season — often are sought out because they offer fair weather and somewhat smaller crowds. But be aware that very near high-season prices still can prevail.

CLIMATE AND CLOTHES: Mexico's Pacific Coast is, for good reason, one of the most popular winter vacation areas in North America. In sunny Ixtapa and Zihuatanejo, the weather is warm except when it is hot, with temperatures generally in the 80s or 90s during the day and in the 70s or 80s at night. It often is humid, but there tends to be a breeze after sundown. It may be slightly cooler and windy at times, and the rainy season, which lasts from June through September, drops a couple of hours of refreshing rain in the afternoons. Sailors be warned that the coastal waters have frequent gales and are subject to hurricanes during the summer and fall. In Ixtapa and Zihuatanejo, daytime wear is casual, but nothing shocking (although people are now less conservative in this respect). Upscale resortwear is worn in most restaurants and nightclubs in the evening.

Travelers can get current readings and 3-day Accu-Weather forecasts through *American Express Travel Related Services'* Worldwide Weather Report number. By dialing 1-900-WEATHER and punching in IXT for Ixtapa, you will hear an up-to-date recording of the current temperature, sky conditions, wind speed and direction, heat index, relative humidity, local time, and beach and boating report. This 24-hour service can be accessed from any Touch-Tone phone in the US and costs 75¢ per minute. The charge will show up on your phone bill. For a listing of other areas covered and the corresponding access codes, send a self-addressed, stamped envelope to *1-900-WEATHER,* 261 Central Ave., Farmingdale, NY 11735.

Traveling by Plane

The quickest, most efficient way to get to Ixtapa and Zihuatanejo is by air. Among the airlines offering flights to Mexico, almost all sell seats at a variety of prices under a vast spectrum of requirements and restrictions. You probably will spend more for your airfare than for any other single item in your travel budget. In order to take advantage of the lowest available fare, you should know what kinds of flights are available, the rules and regulations pertaining to air travel, and all the special package options.

SCHEDULED FLIGHTS: At the time of this writing, although there were no direct flights between the US and Ixtapa and Zihuatanejo, *Aeroméxico* and *Mexicana* do offer connecting flights — passengers must change planes in Mexico City. These flights depart from Chicago, Dallas, Houston, Los Angeles, Miami, New York, San Antonio, and San Francisco.

An alternative is to take one of the many regularly scheduled flights between the US and Mexico City — offered by such leading US airlines as *American, Continental, Delta, Pan American,* and *United* — and then connect to one of *Aeroméxico*'s or *Mexicana*'s domestic flights to Ixtapa-Zihuatanejo. These flights depart from Chicago, Dallas, Houston, Miami, New York, San Francisco, and Washington, DC, with connections available from most other US gateways.

Tickets – A full-fare ticket provides maximum travel flexibility (although at considerable expense) because there are no advance booking requirements. This "open reservation" system means that a prospective passenger can buy a ticket for a flight right up to the minute of takeoff — if a seat is available. If your ticket is for a round trip, you can make the return reservation any time you wish and you can cancel your flight at any time without penalty. These tickets are good for a year, but can be renewed if not used. However, while it is true that this category of ticket can be purchased at the last minute, it is advisable to reserve well in advance during popular vacation periods and around holiday times.

Fares – Perhaps the most common misconception about fares on scheduled airlines is that the cost of the ticket determines how much service will be provided on the flight. This is true only to a certain extent. A far more realistic rule of thumb is that the less you pay for your ticket, the more restrictions and qualifications are likely to come into play *before* you board the plane (as well as after you get off). These qualifying aspects relate to the months (and the days of the week) during which you must travel, how far in advance you must purchase your ticket, the minimum and maximum amount of time you may or must remain away, your willingness to decide on a return date at the time of booking — and your ability to stick to that date. It is not uncommon for passengers sitting side by side on the same wide-body jet to have paid fares varying by hundreds of dollars, and all too often the traveler paying more would have been equally willing (and able) to accept the terms of the less expensive ticket.

In general, the great variety of fares to Ixtapa and Zihuatanejo can be reduced to four basic categories. These include first class, business class, coach (also called economy or tourist class), and excursion or discount fares.

A **first class** ticket is your admission to the special section of the aircraft — larger seats, more legroom, sleeperette seating on some wide-body aircraft, better (or more elaborately served) food, free drinks and headsets for movies and music channels, and, above all, personal attention. First class fares are about twice those of full-fare economy, although both first class passengers and those paying full-fare economy fares are entitled to reserve seats and are sold tickets on an open reservation system.

Not too long ago, there were only two classes of air travel, first class and all the rest, usually called economy or tourist. Then **business class** came into being. Business class passengers usually sit in a separate cabin or cabins toward the front of the plane. While standards of comfort and service are not as high as in first class, they represent a considerable improvement over conditions in the rear of the plane, with roomier seats, more leg and shoulder space between passengers, and fewer seats abreast. Free liquor and headsets, a choice of meal entrées, and a separate counter for speedier check-in are other inducements. As in first class, business class passengers are sold seats on an open reservation system, and neither booking restrictions nor cancellation penalties apply. Note that airlines often have their own names for their business class services — such as *Aeroméxico*'s Premier Class, which is offered on flights between New York and Ixtapa-Zihuatanejo (via Mexico City).

The terms of the **coach** or **economy** fare may vary slightly from airline to airline, and, in fact, from time to time airlines may be selling more than one type of economy fare. Coach or economy passengers sit more snugly, as many as 10 in a single row on a wide-body jet, behind the first class and business class sections. Normally, alcoholic drinks are not free, nor are the headsets. If there are two economy fares on the books, one (often called "regular economy") still may include free stopovers. The other, less expensive (often called "special economy"), may limit stopovers to one or two, usually with a charge for each one. Like first class, there are no advance booking requirements, no minimum or maximum stay requirements, and no cancellation penalties; tickets are sold on an open reservation system. The cost of economy and business class tickets on flights between the US and Mexican coastal resort areas generally varies from a basic (low-season) price in effect most of the year to a peak (high-season) price in winter.

Excursion and other **discount** fares are the airlines' equivalent of a special sale and usually apply to round-trip bookings only. These fares generally differ according to the season and the number of travel days permitted. They are only a bit less flexible than full-fare economy tickets and are, therefore, often useful for both holiday and business travelers. Most round-trip excursion tickets include strict minimum and maximum stay requirements — generally a minimum of 3 to 7 days and a maximum of 2 months.

Reservations can be changed only within the prescribed time limits. So don't count on extending a ticket beyond the prescribed time of return or staying less time than required. The ticket must be purchased a certain number of days — usually no fewer than 7 or 14 days — in advance of departure, and the return reservation usually has to be made at the time of the original ticketing and cannot be changed later than a certain number of days (again, usually 7 or 14) before the return flight. If events force a passenger to change the return reservation to a date less than the minimum stay or more than the maximum stay, the difference between the round-trip excursion rate and the round-trip coach rate probably will have to be paid. Last, cancellation penalties of up to 50% of the full price of the ticket have been assessed — check the specific penalty in effect when you purchase your discount/excursion ticket.

The availability of these reduced-rate seats is most limited at busy times, such as holidays. Discount or excursion fare ticket holders sit with the coach passengers and, for all intents and purposes, are indistinguishable from them. They receive all the same basic services, even though they may have paid anywhere between 30% and 55% less for the trip. Obviously, it's wise to plan early enough to qualify for this less expensive transportation, if possible.

Of even greater risk — and bearing the lowest price of all the current discount fares — is the ticket where no change at all in departure and/or return flights is permitted, and where the ticket price is totally nonrefundable. If you do buy a nonrefundable ticket, you should be aware that for a fee — set by the airline and payable at the airport when checking in — you *may* be able to change the time or date of a return flight on a nonrefundable ticket. However, if the nonrefundable ticket price for the replacement flight is higher than that of the original (as is generally the case when trading in a weekday for a weekend flight), you will have to pay the difference. Any such change must be made a certain number of days in advance — in some cases as little as 2 days — of either the original or the replacement flight, whichever is earlier; restrictions are set by the individual carrier. (Travelers holding a nonrefundable or other restricted ticket who must change their plans due to a family emergency should know that some carriers may make special allowances in such situations; for further information, see *Medical and Legal Aid and Consular Services,* in this section.)

Standby fares, at one time the rock-bottom price at which a traveler could fly, recently have become rather elusive. While the definition of standby varies somewhat from airline to airline, it generally means that you make yourself available to buy a ticket for a flight (usually no sooner than the day of departure), then literally stand by on the chance that a seat will be empty. Once aboard, however, a standby passenger has the same meal service and frills (or lack of them) enjoyed by others in the economy class compartment.

Something else to check is the availability of a **GIT** (Group Inclusive Travel) fare, which requires that a specified dollar amount of ground arrangements be purchased, in advance, along with the ticket. The requirements vary as to the number of travel days and stopovers permitted, and the minimum number of passengers in a group. (The last can be as few as two full fares.) The actual fares also vary, but the cost will be spelled out in brochures distributed by the tour operators handling the ground arrangements. In the past, GIT fares typically were among the least expensive in the fare schedules of the established carriers. But although very attractive group fares still may appear from time to time, the advent of discount fares has caused group fares to all but disappear from some air routes, or their price tags have become the equivalent of all the other discount fares. Travelers reading brochures on group package tours to Ixtapa and Zihuatanejo will find that, in almost all cases, the applicable airfare given as a sample (to be added to the price of the land package to obtain the total tour price) is the same discount fare available to the independent traveler.

The major airlines serving Ixtapa and Zihuatanejo from the US sometimes also offer individual fare excursion rates similar to GIT fares, which are sold in conjunction with ground accommodation packages. Previously called ITX, these fares generally are offered as part of "air/hotel/car transfer packages," and can reduce the cost of an economy fare by more than a third. They are booked for a specific amount of time, with return dates specified; rescheduling and cancellation restrictions and penalties vary from carrier to carrier. These fares most often are offered to popular resort areas — such as Ixtapa and Zihuatanejo — and may include a stopover of day or more in Mexico City. (For further information on fly/drive packages, see *Package Tours,* in this section.)

Travelers looking for the least expensive airfares possible should, finally, scan the pages of their hometown newspapers (especially the Sunday travel sections) for announcements of special promotional fares. Most airlines traditionally have offered their most attractive special fares to encourage travel in slow seasons, and to inaugurate and publicize new routes. Even if none of these factors apply, prospective passengers can be fairly sure that the number of discount seats per flight at the lowest price is strictly limited, or that the fare offering includes a set expiration date — which means it's absolutely necessary to move fast to obtain the lowest possible price.

Among other special airline promotional deals for which you should be on the lookout are discount or upgrade coupons sometimes offered by the major carriers. They are good for either a percentage discount or an upgrade on domestic and international airline tickets — including flights to Mexico. There may be minimum airfare restrictions before the coupon is redeemable, but in general these are worthwhile offers. Restrictions often include certain blackout days (when the coupon cannot be used at all), usually imposed during peak travel periods. These coupons are particularly valuable to business travelers who tend to buy full-fare tickets, and while the coupons are issued in the buyer's name, they can be used by others who are traveling on the same itinerary.

It's always wise to ask about discount or promotional fares and about any conditions that might restrict booking, payment, cancellation, or changes in plans. Check the prices from other neighboring cities. A special rate may be offered in a nearby city but not in yours, and it may be enough of a bargain to warrant your leaving from that city. Ask if there is a difference in price for midweek versus weekend travel, or if there is a further discount for traveling early in the morning or late at night. Also be sure to investigate package deals, which are offered by virtually every airline. These may include car rentals, accommodations, and dining and/or sightseeing features in addition to the basic airfare, and the combined cost of packaged elements usually is considerably less than the cost of the exact same elements when purchased separately.

If in the course of your research you come across a deal that seems too good to be true, keep in mind that logic may not be a component of deeply discounted airfares — there's not always any sane relationship between miles to be flown and the price to get there. More often than not, the level of competition on a given route dictates the degree of discount, and don't be dissuaded from accepting an offer that sounds irresistible just because it also sounds illogical. Better to buy that inexpensive fare while it's being offered and worry about the sense — or absence thereof — while you're flying to your desired destination.

When you're satisfied that you've found the lowest possible price for which you can conveniently qualify (you may have to call the airline more than once, because different airline reservation clerks have been known to quote different prices), make your booking. Then, to protect yourself against fare increases, purchase and pay for your ticket as soon as possible after you've received a confirmed reservation. Airlines generally will honor their tickets, even if the operative price at the time of your flight is higher than the price you paid; if fares go up between the time you *reserve* a flight and the time you *pay* for it, you likely will be out of luck. Finally, with excursion or discount fares, it is important to remember that when a reservation clerk says that you must purchase a ticket by a specific date, this is an absolute deadline. Miss it and the airline may automatically cancel your reservation without telling you.

- **Note:** Another wrinkle in the airfare scene is that if the fares go *down* after you purchase your ticket, you *may* be entitled to a refund of the difference. However, this is possible only in certain situations — availability and advance purchase restrictions pertaining to the lower rate are set by the airline. If you suspect that you may be able to qualify for such a refund, check with your travel agent or the airline.

Frequent Flyers – The leading US carriers serving Mexico — *American, Continental, Delta, Pan American,* and *United* — offer a bonus system to frequent travelers. After the first 10,000 miles, for example, a passenger might be eligible for a first class seat for the coach fare; after another 10,000 miles he or she might receive a discount on his or her next ticket purchase. The value of the bonuses continues to increase as more miles are logged.

Bonus miles also may be earned by patronizing affiliated car rental companies or hotel chains, or by using one of the credit cards that now offers this reward. In deciding whether to accept such a credit card from one of the issuing organizations that tempt you with frequent flyer mileage bonuses on a specific airline, first determine whether the interest rate charged on the unpaid balance is the same as (or less than) possible alternate credit cards, and whether the annual "membership" fee is also equal or lower. If these charges are slightly higher than those of competing cards, weigh the difference against the potential value in airfare savings. Also ask about any bonus miles awarded just for signing up — 1,000 is common, 5,000 generally the maximum.

For the most up-to-date information on frequent flyer bonus options, you may want to subscribe to the monthly newsletter *Frequent.* Issued by Frequent Publications, it provides current information about frequent flyer plans in general, as well as specific data about promotions, awards, and combination deals to help you keep track of the profusion — and confusion — of current and upcoming availabilities. For a year's subscription, send $33 to Frequent Publications, 4715-C Town Center Dr., Colorado Springs, CO 80916 (phone: 800-333-5937).

There also is a monthly magazine called *Frequent Flyer,* but unlike the newsletter mentioned above, its focus is primarily on newsy articles of interest to business travelers and other frequent flyers. Published by Official Airline Guides (PO Box 58543, Boulder, CO 80322-8543; phone: 800-323-3537), *Frequent Flyer* is available for $24 for a 1-year subscription.

Taxes and Other Fees – Travelers who have shopped for the best possible flight at the lowest possible price should be warned that a number of extras will be added to that price and collected by the airline or travel agent who issues the ticket. There is also a $6 International Air Transportation Tax — a departure tax paid by all passengers flying from the US to a foreign destination.

Still another fee is charged by some airlines to cover more stringent security procedures, prompted by recent terrorist incidents. The 8% federal US Transportation Tax, which applies to travel within the US or US territories (such as the US Virgin Islands or Puerto Rico), is already included in advertised fares and in the prices quoted by reservations clerks. It does not apply to passengers flying between US cities or territories en route to a foreign destination, unless the trip includes a stopover of more than 12 hours at a US point. Someone flying from Boston to Ixtapa and stopping in Dallas for more than 12 hours before boarding a connecting flight to Ixtapa, for instance, would pay the 8% tax on the domestic portion of the trip.

Reservations – For those who don't have the time or patience to investigate personally all possible air departures and connections for a proposed trip, a travel agent can be of inestimable help. A good agent should have all the information on which flights go where and when, and which categories of tickets are available on each. Most have computerized reservation links with the major carriers, so that a seat can be reserved and confirmed in minutes. An increasing number of agents also possess fare-comparison computer programs, so they often are very reliable sources of detailed competitive price data. (For more information, see *How to Use a Travel Agent,* in this section.)

When making plane reservations through a travel agent, ask the agent to give the airline your home phone number, as well as your daytime business phone number. All too often the agent uses the agency number as the official contact for changes in flight plans. Airlines are fairly reliable about getting information about drastically delayed flights to passengers if they can reach them; diligence does little good at 10 PM if the airline has only the agency's or an office number.

Reconfirmation is strongly recommended for all international flights. Some (though increasingly fewer) reservations to and from international destinations are automatically canceled after a required reconfirmation period (typically 72 hours) has passed — even if you have a confirmed, fully paid ticket in hand. It is always a good idea to call ahead to make sure that the airline did not slip up in entering your original reservations, or in registering any changes you may have made since, and that it has your seat reservation and/or special meal request in the computer. Although policies vary from carrier to carrier, some recommend that you reconfirm your return flight 48 to 72 hours in advance. If you look at the printed information on your ticket, you'll see the airline's reconfirmation policy stated explicitly. Don't be lulled into a false sense of security by the "OK" on your ticket next to the number and time of the return flight. It only means that a reservation has been entered; a reconfirmation still may be necessary. If in doubt — call.

If you plan not to take a flight on which you hold a confirmed reservation, by all means inform the airline. Because the problem of "no-shows" is a constant expense for airlines, they are allowed to overbook flights, a practice that often contributes to the threat of denied boarding for a certain number of passengers (see "Getting Bumped," below).

Seating – For most types of tickets, airline seats usually are assigned on a first-come, first-served basis at check-in, although some airlines make it possible to reserve a seat at the time of ticket purchase. Always check in early for your flight, even with advance seat assignments. A good rule of thumb for international flights is to arrive at the airport *at least* 2 hours before the scheduled departure to give yourself plenty of time in case there are long lines.

Most airlines furnish seating charts, which make choosing a seat much easier, but in general, there are only a few basics to consider. You must decide whether you prefer a window, aisle, or middle seat. On flights where smoking is permitted, you also should indicate if you prefer the smoking or nonsmoking section.

There is a quarterly publication called the *Airline Seating Guide* that publishes seating charts for most major US airlines and many foreign carriers as well. Your travel agent should have a copy, or you can buy the US edition for $39.95 per year and the international edition for $44.95. Order from Carlson Publishing Co., Box 888, Los Alamitos, CA 90720 (phone: 800-728-4877 or 213-493-4877).

Simply reserving an airline seat in advance, however, actually may guarantee very little. Most airlines require that passengers arrive at the departure gate at least 1 hour (sometimes more) ahead of time to hold a seat reservation, and *ask* travelers to check in at least 2 hours before international flights. It pays to read the fine print on your ticket carefully and plan ahead.

A far better strategy is to visit an airline ticket office (or one of a select group of travel agents) to secure an actual boarding pass for your specific flight. Once this has been issued, airline computers show you as checked in, and you effectively own the seat you have selected (although some carriers may not honor boarding passes of passengers arriving at the gate less than 10 minutes before departure). This is also good — but not foolproof — insurance against getting bumped from an overbooked flight and is, therefore, an especially valuable tactic at peak travel times.

Smoking – One decision regarding choosing a seat has been taken out of the hands of many travelers who smoke. Effective February 25, 1990, the US government imposed a smoking ban that prohibits smoking on all flights scheduled for 6 hours or less within the US and its territories. The regulation applies to both domestic and international carriers serving these routes.

In the case of flights to Ixtapa and Zihuatanejo, these rules do not apply to nonstop flights going directly from the US to Mexico or those with a continuous flight time of over 6 hours between stops in the US or its territories. Smoking is not permitted on segments of international flights where the flight time between US landings is under 6 hours — for instance, flights that include a stopover (even with no change of plane) or connecting flights.

On those flights that do permit smoking, the US Department of Transportation has determined that nonsmoking sections must be enlarged to accommodate all passengers who wish to sit in one. The airline does not, however, have to shift seating to accommodate nonsmokers who arrive late for a flight. Cigar and pipe smoking are prohibited on all flights, even in the smoking sections.

For a wallet-size guide that notes in detail the rights of nonsmokers according to these regulations, send a self-addressed, stamped envelope to ASH (Action on Smoking and Health), Airline Card, 2013 H St. NW, Washington, DC 20006 (phone: 202-659-4310).

Meals – If you have specific diet requirements, be sure to let the airlines know well before departure time. The available meals include vegetarian, seafood, kosher, Muslim, Hindu, high-protein, low-calorie, low-cholesterol, low-fat, low-sodium, diabetic, bland, and children's menus. There is no extra charge for this option. It usually is necessary to request special meals when you make your reservations — check-in time is too late. It's also wise to reconfirm that your request for a special meal has made its way into the airline's computer — the time to do this is 24 hours before departure.

Baggage – Travelers from the US face two different kinds of rules. When you fly on a US airline or on a major international carrier, US baggage regulations will be in effect. Though airline baggage allowances vary slightly, in general all passengers are allowed to carry on board, without charge, one piece of luggage that will fit easily under a seat of the plane or in an overhead bin, and whose combined dimensions (length, width, and depth) do not exceed 45 inches. (Most airlines will allow you to check this bag in the hold if you prefer not to carry it with you.) A reasonable amount of reading material, camera equipment, and a handbag are also allowed. In addition, all passengers are allowed to check two bags in the cargo hold: one usually not to exceed 62 inches when length, width, and depth are combined, the other not to exceed 55 inches in combined dimensions. Generally, no single bag may weigh more than 70 pounds.

On domestic Mexican flights (aboard such carriers as *Aeroméxico* and *Mexicana*), baggage allowances may be subject to a different weight determination, under which each economy cabin passenger is allowed only a total of 55 pounds (or less) of luggage without additional charge. First class or business class passengers may be allowed a total of 66 pounds. (If you are flying from the US to Mexico and connecting to a domestic flight, you generally will be allowed the same amount of baggage as on the international flight. If you break your trip and then take a domestic flight, the local carrier's weight restrictions apply.)

Charges for additional, oversize, or overweight bags usually are made at a flat rate; the actual dollar amount varies from carrier to carrier. If you plan to travel with any special equipment or sporting gear, be sure to check with the airline beforehand. Most have specific procedures for handling such baggage, and you may have to pay for transport regardless of how much other baggage you have checked. Golf clubs may be checked through as luggage (most airlines are accustomed to handling them), but tennis rackets should be carried onto the plane. Aqualung tanks, depressurized and appropriately packed with padding, and surfboards (minus the fin and padded) also may go as baggage. Snorkeling gear should be packed in a suitcase, duffel, or tote bag. Some airlines require that bicycles be partially dismantled and packaged.

Airline policies regarding baggage allowances for children vary and are usually based on the percentage of full adult fare paid. Although on many US carriers children who are ticket holders are entitled to the same baggage allowance as a full-fare passenger, some carriers allow only one bag per child. Often there is no luggage allowance for a child traveling on an adult's lap or in a bassinet. Particularly for international carriers, it's wise to check ahead. (For more information on flying with children, see *Hints for Traveling with Children,* in this section.)

To reduce the chances of your luggage going astray, remove all airline tags from previous trips, label each bag inside and out — with your business address rather than your home address on the outside, to prevent thieves from knowing whose house might be unguarded. Lock everything and double-check the tag that the airline attaches, to make sure that it is coded correctly for your destination: ZIH for Ixtapa-Zihuatanejo.

If your bags are not in the baggage claim area after your flight, or if they're damaged, report the problem to airline personnel immediately. Keep in mind that policies regarding the specific time limit within which you have to make your claim vary from carrier to carrier. Fill out a report form on your lost or damaged luggage and keep a copy of it and your original baggage claim check. If you must surrender the check to claim a damaged bag, get a receipt for it to prove that you did, indeed, check your baggage on the flight. If luggage is missing, be sure to give the airline your destination and/or a telephone number where you can be reached. Also take the name and number of the person in charge of recovering lost luggage.

Most airlines have emergency funds for passengers stranded away from home without their luggage, but if it turns out that your bags are truly lost and not simply delayed, do not then and there sign any paper indicating you'll accept an offered settlement. Since the airline is responsible for the value of your bags within certain statutory limits ($1,250 per passenger for lost baggage on a US domestic flight; $9.07 per pound or $20 per kilo for checked baggage, and up to $400 per passenger for unchecked baggage, on an international flight), you should take some time to assess the extent of your loss (see *Insurance,* in this section). It's a good idea to keep records indicating the value of the contents of your luggage. A wise alternative is to take a Polaroid picture of the most valuable of your packed items just after putting them in your suitcase.

Be aware that airport security is increasingly an issue worldwide, and in Mexico is taken very seriously. Police patrol the airports, and unattended luggage of any description may be confiscated and quickly destroyed. Passengers checking in at an airport may undergo at least two separate inspections of their tickets, passports, and luggage by courteous, but serious, airline personnel — who ask passengers if their baggage has been out of their possession between packing and the airport, or if they have been given gifts or other items to transport — before checked items are accepted.

Airline Clubs – US carriers often have clubs for travelers who pay for membership. These clubs are not solely for first class passengers, although a first class ticket *may* entitle a passenger to lounge privileges. Membership (which, by law, requires a fee) entitles the traveler to use the private lounges at airports along their route, to refreshments served in these lounges, and to check-cashing privileges at most of their counters. Extras include special telephone numbers for individual reservations, embossed luggage tags, and a membership card for identification. Airlines that offer membership in such clubs (and fly to Mexico City — for connecting flights to Ixtapa and Zihuatanejo) include the following:

American: The *Admiral's Club.* Single yearly membership $175 for the first year; $125 yearly thereafter; spouse an additional $70 per year.

Continental: The *President's Club.* Single yearly membership $140 for the first year; $90 yearly thereafter; spouse an additional $25 per year.

Delta: The *Crown Club.* Single yearly membership $150; spouse an additional $50 per year.

Pan American: The *Clipper Club.* Single yearly membership $150 (plus a onetime $25 initiation fee); spouse an additional $45 per year; 3-year and lifetime memberships also available.

United: The *Red Carpet Club.* Single yearly membership $200 for the first year; $100 yearly therafter; spouse an additional $50 per year; 3-year and lifetime memberships also available.

Note that such companies do not have club facilities in all airports; other airlines also offer a variety of special services in many airports.

Getting Bumped – A special air travel problem is the possibility that an airline will accept more reservations (and sell more tickets) than there are seats on a given flight. This is entirely legal and is done to make up for "no-shows," passengers who don't show up for a flight for which they have made reservations and bought tickets. If the airline has oversold the flight and everyone does show up, there simply aren't enough seats. When this happens, the airline is subject to stringent rules designed to protect travelers.

In such cases, the airline first seeks ticket holders willing to give up their seats voluntarily in return for a negotiable sum of money or some other inducement, such as an offer of upgraded seating on the next flight or a voucher for a free trip at some other time. If there are not enough volunteers, the airline may bump passengers against their wishes.

Anyone inconvenienced in this way, however, is entitled to an explanation of the criteria used to determine who does or does not get on the flight, as well as compensation if the resulting delay exceeds certain limits. If the airline can put the bumped passengers on an alternate flight that is *scheduled to arrive* at their original destination within 1 hour of their originally scheduled arrival time, no compensation is owed. If the delay is more than 1 hour — but less than 2 hours on a domestic US flight or less than 4 hours on an international flight — they must be paid denied-boarding compensation equivalent to the one-way fare to their destination (but not more than $200). If the delay is more than 2 hours after the original arrival time on a domestic flight or more than 4 hours on an international flight, the compensation must be doubled (but not more than $400). The airline may also offer bumped travelers a voucher for a free flight instead of the denied-boarding compensation. The passenger may be given the choice of either money or the voucher, the dollar value of which may be no less than the monetary compensation to which the passenger would be entitled. The voucher is not a substitute for the bumped passenger's original ticket; the airline continues to honor that as well. Keep in mind that the above regulations and policies are for only flights leaving the US and do *not* apply to charters or to inbound flights from Ixtapa-Zihuatanejo, even on US carriers.

To protect yourself as best you can against getting bumped, arrive at the airport extra early. If the flight is oversold, ask immediately for the written statement explaining the airline's policy on denied-boarding compensation and its boarding priorities. If the airline refuses to give you this information, or if you feel it has not handled the situation properly, file a complaint with both the airline and the appropriate government agency (see "Consumer Protection," below).

Delays and Cancellations – The above compensation rules also do not apply if the flight is canceled or delayed, or if a smaller aircraft is substituted because of mechanical problems. Each airline has its own policy for assisting passengers whose flights are delayed or canceled or who must wait for another flight because their original one was overbooked. Most airline personnel will make new travel arrangements if necessary. If the delay is longer than 4 hours, the airline may pay for a phone call or telegram, a meal, and in some cases, a hotel room and transportation to it.

■ **Caution:** If you are bumped or miss a flight, be sure to ask the airline to notify other airlines on which you have reservations or connecting flights. When your name is taken off the passenger list of your initial flight, the computer automatically cancels all of your reservations unless *you* take steps to preserve them.

CHARTER FLIGHTS: By booking a block of seats on a specially arranged flight, charter operators offer travelers air transportation for a substantial reduction over the full coach or economy fare. These operators may offer air-only charters (selling transportation alone) or charter packages (the flight plus a combination of land arrangements such as accommodations, meals, tours, or car rental). Charters are especially attractive to people living in smaller cities or out-of-the-way places, because they frequently leave from nearby airports, saving travelers the inconvenience and expense of getting to a major gateway.

From the consumer's standpoint, charters differ from scheduled airlines in two main respects: You generally need to book and pay in advance, and you can't change the itinerary or the departure and return dates once you've booked the flight. In practice, however, these restrictions don't always apply. Today, most of the charter flights to Mexico have the most popular resort areas, such as Ixtapa and Zihuatanejo, as their prime destinations, and although most still require advance reservations, some permit last-minute bookings (when there are unsold seats available), and some even offer seats on a standby basis.

Though charters almost always are round-trip, and it is unlikely that you would be sold a one-way seat on a round-trip flight, on rare occasions one-way tickets on charters are offered. Although it may be possible to book a one-way charter in the US, giving you more flexibility in scheduling your return, note that US regulations pertaining to charters may be more permissive than the charter laws of other countries. For example, if you want to book a one-way charter back to the US, you may find advance booking rules in force.

Some things to keep in mind about the charter game:

1. If you are forced to cancel your trip, you can lose much (and possibly all) of your money unless you have cancellation insurance, which is a must (see *Insurance,* in this section). Frequently, if the cancellation occurs far enough in advance (often 6 weeks or more), you may forfeit only a $25 or $50 penalty. If you cancel only 2 or 3 weeks before the flight, there may be no refund at all unless you or the operator can provide a substitute passenger.
2. Charter flights may be canceled by the operator up to 10 days before departure for any reason, usually underbooking. Your money is returned in this event, but there may be too little time to make new arrangements.
3. Most charters have little of the flexibility of regularly scheduled flights regarding refunds and the changing of flight dates; if you book a return flight, you must be on it or lose your money.
4. Charter operators are permitted to assess a surcharge, if fuel or other costs warrant it, of up to 10% of the airfare up to 10 days before departure.
5. Because of the economics of charter flights, your plane almost always will be full, so you will be crowded, though not necessarily uncomfortable. (There is, however, a new movement among charter airlines to provide flight accommodations that are more comfort-oriented, so this situation may change in the near future.)

To avoid problems, *always* choose charter flights with care. When you consider a charter, ask your travel agent who runs it and carefully check the company. The Better Business Bureau in the company's home city can report on how many complaints, if any, have been lodged against it in the past. Protect yourself with trip cancellation and interruption insurance, which can help safeguard your investment if you or a traveling companion is unable to make the trip and must cancel too late to receive a full refund from the company providing your travel services. (This is advisable whether you're buying a charter flight alone or a tour package for which the airfare is provided by charter or scheduled flight.)

Bookings – If you do fly on a charter, read the contract's fine print carefully and pay particular attention to the following:

Instructions concerning payment. To ensure that the charter company can't spend your money until your flight has safely returned, make out your check to the company's escrow account. By law, the name of the depository bank and the account number must appear on the operator-participant contract (all too often on the back, in minuscule print). Write the details of the charter, including the destination and dates, on the face of the check; on the back, print "For Deposit Only." Your travel agent may prefer that you make out your check to the agency, saying that it will then pay the tour operator the fee minus commission. It is perfectly legal to write the check as we suggest, however, and if your agent objects too vociferously (he or she should trust the tour operator to send the proper commission), consider taking your business elsewhere. If you don't make your check out to the escrow account, you lose the protection of that escrow. Furthermore, even the protection of escrow may not be enough to safeguard your investment, and trip cancellation insurance is strongly advised. Payment by credit card has become popular, since it offers some additional safeguards.

Specific stipulations and penalties for cancellations. Most charters allow you to cancel up to 45 days in advance without major penalty, but some cancellation dates are 50 to 60 days before departure.

Stipulations regarding cancellation and major changes made by the charterer. US rules say that charter flights may not be canceled within 10 days of departure except when circumstances — such as natural disasters or political upheavals — make it physically impossible to fly. Charterers may make "major changes," however, such as in the date or place of departure or return, but you are entitled to cancel and receive a full refund if you don't wish to accept these changes. A price increase of more than 10% at any time up to 10 days before departure is considered a major change; no price increase at all is allowed during the last 10 days immediately before departure. The charter company should be bonded (usually by an insurance company), and if you want to file a claim against it, the claim should be sent to the bonding agent. The contract will set a time limit within which a claim must be filed.

At the time of this writing, the following companies regularly offered charter flights to Ixtapa and Zihuatanejo. As indicated, one of these companies sells charter flights directly to clients, while the other two are wholesalers and must be contacted through a travel agent.

Apple Vacations West (25 NW Point Blvd., Elk Grove Village, IL 60007; phone: 800-365-2775). This agency is a wholesaler, so use a travel agent.

Latur (500 Fifth Ave., Suite 424, New York, NY 10110; phone: 212-599-2203). This agency is a wholesaler, so use a travel agent.

Suntrips (2350 Paragon Dr., San Jose, CA 95131; phone: 800-444-7866 in California; 800-937-0747 elsewhere in the US). Retails to the general public.

For the most current information on charter flight options, the travel newsletter *Jax Fax* regularly features a list of charter companies and packagers offering seats on charter flights. For a year's subscription send a check or money order for $12 to *Jax Fax* (397 Post Rd., Darien, CT 06820; phone: 203-655-8746).

DISCOUNTS ON SCHEDULED FLIGHTS: Promotional fares often are called discount fares because they cost less than what used to be the standard airline fare — full-fare economy. Nevertheless, they cost the traveler the same whether they are bought through a travel agent or directly from the airline. Tickets that cost less if bought from some outlet other than the airline do exist, however. While it is likely that the vast majority of travelers flying to Mexico in the near future will be doing so on a promotional fare or charter rather than on a "discount" air ticket of this sort, it still is a good idea for cost-conscious consumers to be aware of the latest developments in the budget airfare scene. Note that the following discussion makes clear-cut distinctions among the types of discounts available based on how they reach the consumer; in actual practice, the distinctions are not nearly so precise.

Net Fare Sources – The newest notion for reducing the costs of travel services comes from travel agents who offer individual travelers "net" fares. Defined simply, a net fare is the bare minimum amount at which an airline or tour operator will carry a prospective traveler. It doesn't include the amount that normally would be paid to the travel agent as a commission. Traditionally, such commissions amount to about 10% on domestic fares and 8% to 20% on international fares — not counting significant additions to these commission levels that are payable retroactively when agents sell more than a specific volume of tickets or trips for a single supplier. At press time, at least one travel agency in the US was offering travelers the opportunity to purchase tickets and/or tours for a net price. Instead of making its income from individual commissions, this agency assesses a fixed fee that may or may not provide a bargain for travelers; it requires a little arithmetic to determine whether to use the services of a net travel agent or those of one who accepts conventional commissions. One of the potential drawbacks of buying from agencies selling travel services at net fares is that some airlines refuse to do business with them, thus possibly limiting your flight options.

Travel Avenue is a formula fee-based agency that rebates its ordinary agency commission to the customer. For domestic flights, an agent will find the lowest retail fare, then rebate 7% to 10% (depending on the airline) of that price minus a $10 ticket-writing charge. The rebate percentage for international flights varies from 5% to 16% (again, depending on the airline), and the ticket-writing fee is $25. The ticket-writing charge is imposed per ticket; if the ticket includes more than eight separate flights, an additional $10 or $25 fee is charged. Customers using free flight coupons pay the ticket-writing charge, plus an additional $5 coupon-processing fee.

Travel Avenue will rebate its commissions on all tickets, including heavily discounted fares and senior citizen passes. Available 7 days a week, reservations should be made far enough in advance to allow the tickets to be sent by first class mail, since extra charges accrue for special handling. It's possible to economize further by making your own airline reservation, then asking *Travel Avenue* only to write/issue your ticket. For travelers outside the Chicago area, business may be transacted by phone and purchases charged to a credit card. For information, contact *Travel Avenue* at 641 W. Lake, Suite 201, Chicago, IL 60606-1012 (phone: 312-876-1116 in Illinois; 800-333-3335 elsewhere in the US).

Consolidators and Bucket Shops – Other vendors of travel services can afford to sell tickets to their customers at an even greater discount because the airline has sold the tickets to them at a substantial discount (usually accomplished by sharply increasing commissions to that vendor), a practice in which many airlines indulge, albeit discreetly, preferring that the general public not know they are undercutting their own "list" prices. Airlines anticipating a slow period on a particular route sometimes sell off a certain portion of their capacity to a wholesaler, or consolidator. The wholesaler sometimes is a charter operator who resells the seats to the public as though they were charter seats, which is why prospective travelers perusing the brochures of charter operators with large programs frequently see a number of flights designated as "scheduled service." As often as not, however, the consolidator, in turn, sells the seats to a travel agency specializing in discounting. Airlines can also sell seats directly to such an agency, which thus acts as its own consolidator. The airline offers the seats either at a net wholesale price, but without the volume-purchase requirement that would be difficult for a modest retail travel agency to fulfill, or at the standard price, but with a commission override large enough (as high as 50%) to allow both a profit and a price reduction to the public.

Travel agencies specializing in discounting sometimes are called "bucket shops," a term once fraught with connotations of unreliability in this country. But in today's highly competitive travel marketplace, more and more conventional travel agencies are selling consolidator-supplied tickets, and the old bucket shop's image is becoming respectable. Agencies that specialize in discounted tickets exist in most large cities, and usually can be found by studying the smaller ads in the travel sections of Sunday newspapers.

Before buying a discounted ticket, whether from a bucket shop or a conventional, full-service travel agency, keep the following considerations in mind: To be in a position to judge how much you'll be saving, first find out the "list" prices of tickets to your destination. Then do some comparison shopping among agencies. Also bear in mind that a ticket that may not differ much in price from one available directly from the airline may, however, allow the circumvention of such things as the advance purchase requirement. If your plans are less than final, be sure to find out about any other restrictions, such as penalties for canceling a flight or changing a reservation. Most discount tickets are non-endorsable, meaning that they can be used only on the airline that issued them, and they usually are marked "nonrefundable" to prevent their being cashed for a list price refund.

A great many bucket shops are small businesses operating on a thin margin, so it's a good idea to check the local Better Business Bureau for any complaints registered against the one with which you're dealing — before parting with any money. If you still do not feel reassured, consider buying discounted tickets only through a conventional travel agency, which can be expected to have found its own reliable source of consolidator tickets — some of the largest consolidators, in fact, sell only to travel agencies.

A few bucket shops require payment in cash or by certified check or money order, but if credit cards are accepted, use that option. Note, however, if buying from a charter operator selling seats for both scheduled and charter flights, that the scheduled seats are not protected by the regulations — including use of escrow accounts — governing the charter seats. Well-established charter operators, nevertheless, may extend the same protections to their scheduled flights, and when this is the case consumers should be sure that the payment option selected directs their money into the escrow account.

Listed below are some of the consolidators frequently offering discount fares to Ixtapa and Zihuatanejo:

Maharaja Consumer Wholesale (393 Fifth Ave., New York, NY 10016; phone: 212-213-2020 in New York; 800-223-6862 elsewhere in the US).

TFI Tours International (34 W. 37th St., 12th Floor, New York, NY 10001; phone: 212-736-1140).

25 West Tours (2490 Coral Way, Miami, FL 33145; phone: 305-856-0810; 800-423-6954 in Florida; 800-252-5025 elsewhere in the US).

■ **Note:** Although rebating and discounting are becoming increasingly common, there is some legal ambiguity concerning them. Strictly speaking, it is legal to discount domestic tickets but not international tickets. On the other hand, the law that prohibits discounting, the Federal Aviation Act of 1958, is consistently ignored these days, in part because consumers benefit from the practice and in part because many illegal arrangements are indistinguishable from legal ones. Since the line separating the two is so fine that even the authorities can't always tell the difference, it is unlikely that most consumers would be able to do so, and in fact it is not illegal to *buy* a discounted ticket. If the issue of legality bothers you, ask the agency whether any ticket you're about to buy would be permissible under the above-mentioned act.

OTHER DISCOUNT TRAVEL SOURCES: An excellent source of information on economical travel opportunities is the *Consumer Reports Travel Letter,* published monthly by Consumers Union. It keeps abreast of the scene on a wide variety of fronts, including package tours, rental cars, insurance, and more, but it is especially helpful for its comprehensive coverage of airfares, offering guidance on all the options from scheduled flights on major or low-fare airlines to charters and discount sources. For a year's subscription, send $37 ($57 for 2 years) to *Consumer Reports Travel Letter,* PO Box 53629, Boulder, CO 80322-3629 (phone: 800-999-7959). For information on other travel newsletters, see *Sources and Resources,* in this section.

Last-Minute Travel Clubs – Still another way to take advantage of bargain airfares is open to those who have a flexible schedule. A number of organizations, usually set up as last-minute travel clubs and functioning on a membership basis, routinely keep in touch with travel suppliers to help them dispose of unsold inventory at discounts of between 5% and 50%. A great deal of the inventory consists of complete tour packages and cruises, but some clubs offer air-only charter seats and, occasionally, seats on scheduled flights.

Members pay an annual fee and receive a toll-free hotline number to call for information on imminent trips. In some cases, they also receive periodic mailings with information on bargain travel opportunities for which there is more advance notice. Despite the suggestive names of the clubs providing these services, last-minute travel does not necessarily mean that you cannot make plans until literally the last minute. Trips can be announced as little as a few days or as much as 2 months before departure, but the average is from 1 to 4 weeks' notice.

Among such organizations offering discounted travel opportunities to Ixtapa and Zihuatanejo are the following:

Discount Club of America (61-33 Woodhaven Blvd., Rego Park, NY 11374; phone: 800-321-9587 or 718-335-9612). Annual fee: $39 per family.
Discount Travel International (Ives Building, 114 Forrest Ave., Suite 205, Narberth, PA 19072; phone: 215-668-7184 in Pennsylvania; 800-543-0110 elsewhere in the US). Annual fee: $45 per household.
Encore Short Notice (4501 Forbes Blvd., Lanham, MD 20706; phone: 301-459-8020; 800-638-0930 for customer service). Annual fee: $48 per family.
Last-Minute Travel (1249 Boylston St., Boston, MA 02215; phone: 800-LAST-MIN or 617-267-9800). No fee.
Moment's Notice (425 Madison Ave., New York, NY 10017; phone: 212-486-0503). Annual fee: $19.95 per family.
Spur-of-the-Moment Tours and Cruises (10780 Jefferson Blvd., Culver City, CA 90230; phone: 213-839-2418 in California; 800-343-1991 elsewhere in the US). No fee.
Traveler's Advantage (3033 S. Parker Rd., Suite 1000, Aurora, CO 80014; phone: 800-548-1116). Annual fee: $49 per family.
Vacations to Go (2411 Fountain View, Suite 201, Houston, TX 77057; phone: 800-338-4962). Annual fee: $19.95 per family.
Worldwide Discount Travel Club (1674 Meridian Ave., Miami Beach, FL 33139; phone: 305-534-2082). Annual fee: $40 per person; $50 per family.

Generic Air Travel – Organizations that apply the same flexible-schedule idea to air travel only and sell tickets at literally the last minute also exist. The service they provide sometimes is known as "generic" air travel, and it operates somewhat like an ordinary airline standby service, except that the organizations running it offer seats on not one but several scheduled and charter airlines.

One pioneer of generic flights is *Airhitch* (2790 Broadway, Suite 100, New York, NY 10025; phone: 212-864-2000), which arranges flights to Ixtapa and Zihuatanejo from various US cities at relatively low prices. Prospective travelers register by paying a fee (applicable toward the fare) and stipulate a range of acceptable departure dates and their desired destination, along with alternate choices. The week before the date range begins, they are notified of at least two flights that will be available during the time period, agree on one, and remit the balance of the fare to the company. If they do not accept any of the suggested flights, they lose their deposit; if, through no fault of their own, they do not ultimately get on any agreed-on flight, all of their money is refunded. Return flights are arranged the same way. The company's Sunhitch program is available for week-long stays in Ixtapa and Zihuatanejo from December through April. Their slightly more expensive Target program offers greater certainty regarding destinations and is available throughout the year.

BARTERED TRAVEL SOURCES: Suppose a hotel buys advertising space in a newspaper. As payment, the hotel gives the publishing company a number of hotel rooms in lieu of cash. This is barter, a common means of exchange among hotels, airlines, car rental companies, cruise lines, tour operators, restaurants, and other travel service companies. When a bartering company finds itself with empty airline seats (or excess hotel rooms or cruise ship cabin space, and so on) and offers them to the public, considerable savings can be enjoyed.

Bartered-travel clubs often offer discounts of up to 50% to members who pay an annual fee, which entitles them to select the flights, cruises, hotel rooms, or other travel services that the club obtained by barter. Members usually present a voucher, club credit card, or scrip (a dollar-denomination voucher negotiable only for the bartered product) to the travel service supplier, which in turn subtracts the dollar amount from the bartering company's account.

Selling bartered travel is a perfectly legitimate means of retailing. One advantage to club members is that they don't have to wait until the last minute to obtain flight or room reservations.

Among the companies specializing in bartered service, those that frequently offer members travel services to Ixtapa and Zihuatanejo include the following:

The Travel Guild (18210 Redmond Way, Redmond, WA 98052; phone: 206-885-1213). Annual fee: $48 per family.

Travel World Leisure Club (225 W. 34th St., Suite 2203, New York, NY 10122; phone: 800-444-TWLC or 212-239-4855). Annual fee: $50 per family.

CONSUMER PROTECTION: Consumers who feel that they have not been dealt with fairly by an airline should make their complaints known. Begin with the customer service representative at the airport where the problem occurs. If he or she cannot resolve your complaint to your satisfaction, write to the airline's consumer office. In a businesslike, typed letter, explain what reservations you held, what happened, the names of the employees involved, and what you expect the airline to do to remedy the situation. Send copies (never the originals) of the tickets, receipts, and other documents that back your claims. Ideally, all correspondence should be sent via certified mail, return receipt requested. This provides proof that your complaint was received.

Passengers with consumer complaints — lost baggage, compensation for getting bumped, smoking and nonsmoking rules, deceptive practices by an airline, charter regulations — who are not satisfied with the airline's response should contact the US Department of Transportation (DOT), Consumer Affairs Division (400 Seventh St. SW, Washington, DC 20590; phone: 202-366-2220). DOT personnel stress, however, that consumers should initially direct their complaints to the airline that provoked them.

Travelers with an unresolved complaint involving a foreign carrier also can contact the US Department of Transportation. DOT personnel will do what they can to help resolve all such complaints, although their influence may be limited.

Although Mexico does not have a specific government bureau that deals with airline complaints, consumers with complaints against other travel-related services can contact the tourist office in Mexico, or write to Lic. Gilberto Calderon Romo., Director

General de Auxilio Turístico, Presidente Masaryk No. 172, 2nd Floor, Ler. Nivel., México, DF.

To avoid more serious problems, *always* choose charter flights and tour packages with care. When you consider a charter, ask your travel agent who runs it and carefully check out the company. The Better Business Bureau in the company's home city can report on how many complaints, if any, have been lodged against it in the past. As emphasized above, protect yourself with trip cancellation and interruption insurance, which can help safeguard your investment in case you or a traveling companion is unable to make the trip and must cancel too late to receive a full refund from the company providing your travel services. (This is advisable whether you're buying a charter flight alone or a tour package for which the airfare is provided by charter or scheduled flight.) Some travel insurance policies have an additional feature, covering the possibility of default or bankruptcy on the part of the tour operator or airline, charter or scheduled.

Remember, too, that the federal Fair Credit Billing Act permits purchasers to refuse to pay charges if they do not receive the travel services for which they've been billed, so the onus of dealing with the receiver for a bankrupt airline falls on the credit card company. Do not rely on another airline to honor the ticket you're holding, since the days when virtually all major carriers subscribed to a default protection program that bound them to do so are long gone. Some airlines may voluntarily step forward to accommodate the stranded passengers of a fellow carrier, but this is now an entirely altruistic act.

The deregulation of US airlines has meant that travelers must find out for themselves what they are entitled to receive. The Department of Transportation's informative consumer booklet *Fly Rights* is a good place to start. To receive a copy, send $1 to the Superintendent of Documents, US Government Printing Office (Washington, DC 20402-9325; phone: 202-783-3238). Specify its stock number, 050-000-00513-5, and allow 3 to 4 weeks for delivery.

■ **Note:** Those who tend to experience discomfort due to the change in air pressure while flying may be interested in the free pamphlet *Ears, Altitude and Airplane Travel;* for a copy send a self-addressed, stamped, business-size envelope to the *American Academy of Otolaryngology* (One Prince St., Alexandria, VA 22314; phone: 703-836-4444). And for when you land, *Overcoming Jet Lag* offers some helpful tips on minimizing post-flight stress; it is available from Berkeley Publishing Group (PO Box 506, Mail Order Dept., East Rutherford, NJ 07073; phone: 800-631-8571) for $6.95, plus shipping and handling.

Traveling by Ship

There was a time when traveling by ship was extraordinarily expensive, time-consuming, utterly elegant, and utilized almost exclusively for getting from one point to another. No longer primarily pure transportation, cruising is riding a new wave of popularity as a leisure activity in its own right.

Among the destinations favored by cruise ship passengers, Mexico, with stops at Ixtapa and Zihuatanejo, ranks extremely high. From eastern US ports, cruise ships sail through the Panama Canal and call at popular resorts along Mexico's Pacific Coast. Sailings from US West Coast docks may reverse the trans-canal route, but by far the best-known cruise course to Mexico runs from Los Angeles down the west coast of Mexico and docks at coastal resort areas such as Ixtapa-Zihuatanejo. A variation on this cruise itinerary was made famous on TV by that oceanic icon, the "Love Boat."

Many modern-day cruise ships seem much more like motels-at-sea than the classic liners of a couple of generations ago, but they are consistently comfortable and passengers are often pampered. Cruise prices can be quite reasonable, and since the single cruise price covers all the major items in a typical vacation — transportation, accommodations, all meals, entertainment, a full range of social activities, sports, and recreation — a traveler need not fear any unexpected assaults on the family travel budget.

Generally, people take a cruise ship to Mexico for the sheer pleasure of being at sea, because it's part of a far broader itinerary, or because of a special interest in a particular area that is best visited by ship. Cruise lines promote sailings to Mexico as "get away from it all" vacations. But the prospective cruise ship passenger will find that the variety of cruises is tremendous, and the quality, while generally high, varies depending on shipboard services, the tone of shipboard life, the cost of the cruise, and operative itineraries. Prices vary greatly in the cruise ship category, depending on levels of luxury, accommodations, and length of the journey. Although there are less expensive ways to see Mexico, the romance and enjoyment of a sea voyage remain irresistible for some. Such sojourners should find out as much as possible before signing on for a seagoing vacation (after all, it's hard to get off in mid-ocean).

CRUISES TO MEXICO: Several cruise lines include Ixtapa and Zihuatanejo as part of their Mexican itineraries. These lines either sail only to Mexico or offer passengers the option of joining a leg of longer cruises — such as cruises through the Panama Canal to or from the Caribbean — that stop over in Ixtapa-Zihuatanejo.

Below is a list of cruise lines and ships sailing to Mexico from the US:

Clipper Cruises (7711 Bonhomme Ave., St. Louis, MO 63105; phone: 800-325-0010). The *Yorktown Clipper* makes 14-day sailings between San Diego and Acapulco that stop in Ixtapa and Zihuatanejo.

Crystal Cruises (2121 Ave. of the Stars, Los Angeles, CA 90067; phone: 800-446-6645). The *Crystal Harmony* makes 10-day sailings from Los Angeles along the Mexican Riviera, stopping in Zihuatanejo. This ship also makes 23-day trans-canal sailings between San Francisco and New York that stop in Ixtapa-Zihuatanejo.

Princess Cruises (10100 Santa Monica Blvd., Santa Monica, CA 90067; phone: 800-421-0522). This is it, folks, the "Love Boat" — or perhaps we should say the Love Boats — in person. The *Dawn Princess* and the *Fair Princess* sail from Los Angeles along the Mexican Riviera, stopping in Ixtapa-Zihuatanejo and other well-known west coast resort areas.

Royal Cruise Line (One Maritime Plaza, San Francisco, CA 94111; phone: 800-227-5628 or 415-956-7200). The *Crown Odyssey* makes 9-day cruises from Los Angeles along the Mexican Riviera that stop in Zihuatanejo.

A monthly newsletter that may be of interest to those planning to cruise Mexican waters is *Ocean and Cruise News,* which offers comprehensive coverage of the latest on the cruise ship scene. A year's subscription costs $24. Contact *Ocean and Cruise News,* PO Box 92, Stamford, CT 06904 (phone: 203-329-2787).

■ **A final note on picking a cruise:** A "cruise-only" travel agency can best help you choose a cruise ship and itinerary. Cruise-only agents are best equipped to tell you about a particular ship's "personality," the kind of person with whom you'll likely be traveling on a particular ship, what dress is appropriate (it varies from ship to ship), and much more. Travel agencies that specialize in booking cruises usually are members of the *National Association of Cruise Only Agencies (NACOA).* For a listing of the agencies in your area (requests are limited to three states), send a self-addressed, stamped envelope to *NACOA,* PO Box 7209, Freeport, NY 11520, or call 516-378-8006.

Traveling by Car

Driving is the best way to explore out-of-the-way regions of Mexico on the way to or from your stay in Ixtapa and Zihuatanejo. The privacy, comfort, and convenience of touring by car can't be matched by any other form of transportation. A car provides maximum flexibility, allowing visitors to cover large amounts of territory, to visit major cities and sites, or to move from one small town to the next while exploring the countryside.

Mexico's highways and roads are renowned for their scenery. Sudden, unexpected glimpses of tropical flowers, desert plants, pine trees, mountains, and aquamarine waters form the moving backdrop of the road as you drive. The distances between cities and towns are usually reasonable, and a visitor can use a car's flexibility to maximum advantage.

When planning your route, be realistic in calculating the amount of ground you can cover, and make plans on the conservative side when you have any doubts. Road incidents involving assaults and robberies of tourists, though relatively infrequent, are on the rise, and usually befall ill-advised travelers who have underestimated the distances between towns — or the time it takes to cover these distances. Try to avoid driving after dark, and *never* stop and spend the night in the car or on some deserted stretch of beachfront. Our choices of the most interesting driving itineraries, described in DIRECTIONS, include approximate distances to help in your calculations.

Most roads are well surfaced, but you will find few of the multi-lane highways found in the US, except around the larger cities. In general, secondary and lesser roads also are kept in reasonably good condition, although this may not always be the case, particularly during the rainy season. If you are planning to explore off the beaten track, consider renting a four-wheel-drive vehicle. Either way, there is plenty to see en route.

As the only road often goes through the middle of the town or resort area, be prepared to slow down as you pass through busy, populated centers. The speed limit on the best highways is 110 kilometers per hour (approximately 69 miles per hour). Speeds always are given in kilometers per hour and distances in kilometers (a kilometer is equal to approximately .62 miles); major highway signs use international symbols, which are quite easy to understand.

License – Any valid US driver's license is acceptable in Mexico. (You do not need an International Driving Permit.) Your US license also will be required for renting a car, and in most cases, you will need to present a major credit card. If you are driving across the border from the US, remember that a driver's license cannot be used as proof of citizenship. For information on valid proof of citizenship, see *Entry Requirements and Documents,* in this section.

Maps – Consult road maps. A number of the automobile clubs listed below offer their members (and members of affiliated clubs) free or inexpensive maps. Maps also are available at service stations on both sides of the border.

A company with more than half a century of experience in maps of Mexico is *Guía Roji* (31 J. Moran, México, DF 11850; phone: 5-277-2307). They publish road maps of all Mexican states and wall maps of several Mexican cities. Their road atlas, called *Atlas de Carreteras,* costs about $2.65 and is extremely useful for the motorist. It also is available from several US offices of *Sanborn's Mexican Insurance Service* (2009 S. 10th St., McAllen, TX 78502; phone: 512-686-7011; and 2212 Santa Ursula, Laredo, TX 78040-3122; phone: 512-722-0931).

Another wall map, the *Rand McNally Cosmopolitan Map of Mexico* ($2.95), indicates each Mexican state in a different color. All major highways are indicated, and there is no problem figuring out what is near what. For use on the road, the *Rand McNally Road Atlas: US, Canada and Mexico* ($7.95 paperback; $11.95 hardcover) is excellent. Both of these books may be found in bookstores or can be ordered directly from *Rand McNally* (150 E. 52nd St., New York, NY 10022; phone: 212-758-7488); call for information on charges for postage and handling.

An up-to-date road map of Mexico, published by the Mexican Ministry of Tourism, is available free from its offices (see *Mexican Consulates and Tourist Offices in the US,* in this section). Perhaps the most detailed series of maps available from the Mexican government are those published by Mexico's *Dirección General de Geografía.* A broad selection of maps of Mexico is available, with the emphasis ranging from topography to tourism. Numerous bookstores in Mexican cities carry these maps. A variety of Mexican maps also is available by writing to the *Servicio Meteorológico Nacional* (192 Av. Observatorio, Tacubaya, México, DF 11860).

A good source for most of the maps listed above, and just about any other kind of map of just about anywhere in the world, including Mexico, is *Map Link* (25 E. Mason St., Suite 201, Santa Barbara, CA 93101; phone: 805-965-4402). They carry the particularly useful *Pemex Mexican Road Atlas* ($11.95), which includes city plans of Ixtapa and Zihuatanejo, as well as maps of the broader *International Travel Maps (ITM)* series. If they don't stock a map of the area in which you are interested, they will do their best to get it for you.

Automobile Clubs – Most Mexican automobile clubs offer emergency service to any breakdown victim, whether a club member or not; however, only members of these clubs or affiliated clubs may have access to certain information services and receive discounted or free towing and repair services.

Members of the *American Automobile Association (AAA)* often are entitled automatically to a number of services from foreign clubs. With over 31 million members in chapters throughout the US and Canada, the *AAA* is the largest automobile club in North America. *AAA* affiliates throughout the US provide a variety of travel services to members, including a travel agency, trip planning, fee-free traveler's checks, and roadside assistance. They will help plan an itinerary, send a map with clear routing directions, and even make hotel reservations; these services apply to traveling in both the US and Mexico. Although *AAA* members receive maps and other brochures for no charge or at a discount (depending on the publication and branch), non-members also can order from an extensive selection of highway and topographical maps. You can join the *AAA* through local chapters (listed in the telephone book under *AAA*) or contact the national office, 1000 AAA Dr., Heathrow, FL 32746-5063 (phone: 407-444-8544).

The *American Automobile Association* also is affiliated with a Mexican automobile association, the *Asociación Mexicana Automovilística* (*AMA;* Mexican Automobile Association), with branches in the metropolitan Mexico City area, Cuernavaca, and Puebla. *AMA*'s main office is at 7 Calle Orizaba, México, DF 06700 (phone: 5-209-8329 or 5-511-6285). The association provides a variety of maps in English at no charge and, in some parts of Mexico, *AAA* members can call the *AMA* for emergency service.

The *Asociación Nacional Automovilística (ANA),* perhaps the most widely based in Mexico, also can be helpful to *AAA* members, as well as members of other automobile associations belonging to the *International Federation of Automobile Associations* (ask if a club is a member before joining). The association also sells a useful road map for about 50¢. The main offices are at 140 Calle Miguel E. Schultz, México, DF 06470 (phone: 5-705-0258).

Breakdowns – If you break down on the road, immediate emergency procedure is to get the car off the road. Some roads may have narrower shoulders than you're used to, so make sure you get all the way off, even if you have to hang off the shoulder a bit. The universal signal for help is raising the hood, and tying a white handkerchief or rag to the door handle or radio antenna. Don't leave the car unattended, and don't try any major repairs on the road.

The major Mexican highways are patrolled by the government's **Green Angel** fleet of emergency service trucks. They are manned by English-speaking crews and carry equipment for a modest range of on-the-road repairs. (Don't expect miracles, just an adequate, average repair job for a common emergency.) The Green Angels (called *Angeles Verdes*) know how to change tires, give first aid, and take care of minor problems. They also carry gasoline and oil and provide information on road conditions. Except for parts and fuel, the service is free. That's why they're called "angels" — they literally cruise the main highways looking for motorists to rescue. Sooner or later, if you break down on a main road, one of the Green Angels will get to you, as crews patrol every day (from 8 AM to 8 PM). Supplementing their efforts are the following hotline emergency numbers for tourists needing guidance or help: 915-250-4817 (24 hours), 915-250-0123, 915-250-8601, 915-250-8419, or 915-250-8221. (When calling within the Mexico City area, do *not* dial 915.)

Gasoline – *Pemex* (an acronym for *Petróleos Mexicanos*) is the only brand of gasoline and oil sold in Mexico since the petroleum industry was nationalized. Gasoline is sold in liters (approximately 3.7 liters equal 1 gallon), and two grades of gas are available: Nova (or regular) from the blue pump, and higher-priced Extra (or premium) from the silver pump (though Extra often is difficult if not impossible to find). Both grades come in leaded and unleaded varieties; ask the gas station attendant for "*con plomo*" if you want *leaded* gas or "*sin plomo*" for *unleaded.*

Gas prices everywhere rise and fall, depending on the world supply of oil. US visitors generally will find gasoline to be slightly less expensive than they are accustomed to paying in the US. Be prepared to pay for gas in cash (American oil company credit cards aren't accepted by *Pemex*). And if you request the attendants to check your oil and water or coolant in your radiator, or wipe your windshield, be sure to tip them between 500 and 1,000 pesos. We recommend tipping gas station attendants even if you are only filling up.

Particularly when traveling in rural areas, fill up whenever you come to a gas station. It may be a long way to the next station. You *don't* want to get stranded on an isolated stretch — so it is a good idea to bring along an extra few gallons in a steel container. Also note that in rural areas, gasoline may be diluted with water or kerosene. So if the car stops after you have just filled up, it could be due to impure gasoline.

Also note that rental cars usually are delivered with a full tank of gas (this is not always the case, however, so check the gas gauge when picking up the car, and have the amount of gas noted on your rental agreement if the tank is not full). Refill the tank before you return the car or you will have to pay to have the rental company fill it, and gasoline at the car rental company's pump always is much more expensive than at a service station. This policy may vary for smaller local and regional companies; ask when picking up the vehicle.

RENTING A CAR: Most visitors who want to drive in Mexico rent a car through a travel agent or international rental firm before leaving home, or from a local company once in Mexico. Another possibility, also arranged before departure, is to rent the car as part of a larger package of travel services.

Renting is not inexpensive, but it is possible to economize by determining your own needs and then shopping around among the car rental companies until you find the best deal. As you comparison shop, keep in mind that rates vary considerably, not only from city to city, but also from location to location within the same city. For instance, it might be less expensive to rent a car from an office in the center of a city rather than at the airport. Ask about special rates or promotional deals, such as weekend or weekly rates, bonus coupons for airline tickets, or 24-hour rates that include gas and unlimited mileage. It also should be noted that the general condition of rental cars in Mexico — even the most expensive ones — is tangibly worse than similar cars in most other parts of the world.

Rental car companies operating in Mexico can be divided into three basic categories: large national or international companies, regional companies, and local companies. Because of aggressive local competition, the cost of renting a car can be less expensive once a traveler arrives in Mexico, compared to the prices quoted in advance from the US. Local companies usually are less expensive than the international giants (although travelers who do not speak fluent Spanish may have to rule out smaller local companies that rent primarily to natives).

Given this situation, it's tempting to wait until arriving to scout out the lowest-priced rental from the company located the farthest from the airport high-rent district and offering no pick-up services. But if your arrival coincides with a holiday or peak travel period, you may be disappointed to find that even the most expensive car in town was spoken for months ago. Whenever possible, it is best to reserve in advance, anywhere from a few days in slack periods to a month or more during the busier seasons.

If you can read and speak Spanish, and decide to wait until after you arrive in Mexico and let your fingers do the walking through the local phone books, you'll often find a surprising number of small companies listed. Often the best guide to sorting through the options is the local tourist board, which usually can provide recommendations and a list of reputable firms.

Travel agents can arrange rentals for clients, but it is just as easy to call and rent a car yourself. Listed below are several national Mexican rental companies, as well as the major international rental companies represented in Ixtapa and Zihuatanejo:

Avis Rent-A-Car (phone: 800-331-1212). Has 1 location at the airport.
Budget Rent-A-Car (phone: 800-472-3325). Has 1 location at the airport and 1 in Zihuatanejo.
Dollar Rent-A-Car (phone: 800-800-4000). Has 1 location at the airport and 1 in Ixtapa.
Hertz (phone: 800-654-3001). Has 1 location at the airport and 1 in Ixtapa.

For further information on local car rental companies, see *Sources and Resources,* THE CITIES.

Requirements – Whether you decide to rent a car in advance from a large international rental company with Mexican branches or wait to rent from a local company, you should know that renting a car is rarely as simple as signing on the dotted line and roaring off into the night. If you are renting for personal use, you must have a valid driver's license and will have to convince the renting agency that (1) you are personally creditworthy; and (2) you will bring the car back at the stated time. This will be easy if you have a major credit card; most rental companies accept credit cards in lieu of a cash deposit, as well as for payment of your final bill. If you prefer to pay in cash, leave your credit card imprint as a "deposit," then pay your bill in cash when you return the car.

If you are planning to rent a car once in Mexico, *Avis, Budget, Hertz,* and other US rental companies usually will rent to travelers paying in cash and leaving either a credit card imprint or a substantial amount of cash as a deposit. This is not necessarily standard policy, however, as some of the other international chains, and a number of regional and local Mexican companies, will *not* rent to an individual who doesn't have a valid credit card. In this case, you may have to call around to find a company that accepts cash.

Also keep in mind that although the minimum age to drive a car in Mexico is 18 years, the minimum age to rent a car is set by the rental company. Many firms have a minimum age requirement of 21 years, some raise that to 24 or 25 years, and for some models of cars it rises to 30 years. The upper age limit at many companies is between 69 and 75; others have no age limit or may make drivers above a certain age subject to special conditions.

Costs – Finding the most economical car rental will require some telephone shopping on your part. As a *general* rule, expect to hear lower prices quoted by the smaller, strictly local companies than by the well-known international names, with those of the national Mexican companies falling somewhere between the two. Comparison shopping always is advisable, however, because the company that has the least expensive rentals in one city may not have the least expensive cars in another, and even the international giants offer discount plans whose conditions are easy for most travelers to fulfill.

If driving short distances for only a day or two, the best deal may be a per-day, per-mile (or per-kilometer) rate: You pay a flat fee for each day you keep the car, plus a per-mile (or per-kilometer) charge. An increasingly common alternative is to be granted a certain number of free miles or kilometers each day and then be charged on a per-mile or per-kilometer basis over that number.

A better alternative for Mexican touring is a flat per-day rate with unlimited free mileage; this certainly is the most economical rate if you plan to drive over 100 miles. (*Note:* When renting a car in Mexico, the term "mileage" may refer to either miles or kilometers.) Make sure that the low, flat daily rate that catches your eye, however, is indeed a per-day rate: Often the lowest price advertised by a company turns out to be available only with a minimum 3-day rental — fine if you want the car that long, but not the bargain it appears if you really intend to use it no more than 24 hours. Flat weekly rates also are available, as well as some flat monthly rates that represent a further saving over the daily rate.

Another factor influencing cost is the type of car you rent. Rentals generally are based on a tiered price system, with different sizes of cars — variations of budget, economy, regular, and luxury. Charges may increase by only a few dollars a day through several classes of subcompact and compact cars — where most of the competition is — then increase by great leaps through the remaining classes of full-size and luxury cars and passenger vans. The larger the car, the more it costs to rent and the more gas it consumes, but for some people the greater comfort and extra luggage space of a larger car (in which bags and sporting gear can be safely locked out of sight) may make it worth the additional expense.

Electing to pay for collision damage waiver (CDW) protection also will add to the cost of renting a car; however, buying the offered coverage (for about $11 to $13 a day) will relieve you of responsibility for the value of the vehicle being rented. Before making any decisions about optional collision damage waivers, first determine if you already are adequately covered by your personal automobile insurance policy or by a credit card company if you charge the rental to that card. (For further information, see *Insurance,* in this section.)

Another cost to be added to the price tag is drop-off charges or one-way service fees. The lowest price quoted by any given company may apply only to a car that is returned to the same location from which it was rented. A slightly higher rate may be charged if the car is to be returned to a different location.

Fly/Drive – Airlines, charter companies, car rental companies, and tour operators have been offering fly/drive packages for years, and even though the basic components of the package have changed somewhat — return airfare, a car waiting at the airport, and perhaps a night's lodging all for one inclusive price used to be the rule — the idea remains the same. You rent a car *here* for use *there* by booking it along with other arrangements for the trip. These days, the very minimum arrangement possible is the result of a tie-in between a car rental company and an airline, which entitles customers to a rental car for less than the company's usual rates, provided they show proof of having booked a flight on that airline. For information on available packages, check with the airline or your travel agent.

Package Tours

If the mere thought of buying a package for travel to Mexico conjures up visions of a trip spent marching in lockstep with a horde of frazzled fellow travelers, remember that packages have come a long way. For one thing, not all packages necessarily are escorted tours, and the one you buy does not have to include any organized touring at all — nor will it necessarily include traveling companions. If it does, however, you'll find that people of all sorts — many just like yourself — are taking advantage of packages today because they are economical and convenient, save you an immense amount of planning time, and exist in such variety that it's virtually impossible not to find one that fits at least the majority of your travel preferences. Given the high cost of travel these days, packages have emerged as a particularly wise buy.

In essence, a package is just an amalgam of travel services that can be purchased in a single transaction. A package (tour or otherwise) to or around Mexico may include any or all of the following: transportation from your home to Mexico, local transportation (and/or car rentals), accommodations, some or all meals, sightseeing, entertainment, transfers to and from the hotel at each destination, taxes, tips, escort service, and a variety of incidental features that might be offered as options at additional cost. In other words, a package can be any combination of travel elements, from a fully escorted tour offered at an all-inclusive price to a simple fly/drive booking allowing you to move about totally on your own. Its principal advantage is that it saves money: The cost of the combined arrangements invariably is well below the price of all of the same elements if bought separately. A package provides more than economy and convenience: It releases the traveler from having to make individual arrangements for each separate element of a trip.

Tour programs generally can be divided into two categories — "escorted" (or locally hosted) and independent. An escorted tour means that a guide will accompany the group from the beginning of the tour through to the return flight; a locally hosted tour means that the group will be met upon your arrival by a local host. On independent tours, there generally is a choice of hotels, meal plans, and sightseeing trips, as well as a variety of special excursions. The independent plan is for travelers who do not want a totally set itinerary, but who do prefer confirmed hotel reservations. Whether choosing an escorted or independent tour, always bring along complete contact information for your tour operator in case a problem arises, although tour operators often have local affiliates who can give additional assistance or make other arrangements on the spot.

To determine whether a package — or, more specifically, *which* package — fits your travel plans, start by evaluating your interests and needs, deciding how much and what you want to spend, see, and do. Gather whatever package tour information is available for your schedule. Be sure that you take the time to read the brochure *carefully* to determine precisely what is included. Keep in mind that travel brochures are written to entice you into signing up for a package tour. Often the language is deceptive and devious. For example, a brochure may quote the lowest prices for a package tour based on facilities that are unavailable during the off-season, undesirable at any season, or just plain nonexistent. Information such as "breakfast included" or "plus tax" (which can add up) should be taken into account. Note, too, that prices quoted in brochures almost always are based on double occupancy: The rate listed is for each of two people sharing a double room, and if you travel alone the supplement for single accommodations can raise the price considerably (see *Hints for Single Travelers,* in this section).

In this age of erratic airfares, the brochure most often will *not* include the price of an airline ticket in the price of the package, though sample fares from various gateway cities usually will be listed separately, to be added to the price of the ground arrangements. Before figuring your actual cost, check the latest fares with the airlines, because the samples invariably are out of date by the time you read them. If the brochure gives more than one category of sample fares per gateway city — such as an individual tour-basing fare, a group fare, an excursion, or other discount ticket — your travel agent or airline tour desk will be able to tell you which one applies to the package you choose, depending on when you travel, how far in advance you book, and other factors. When the brochure does include round-trip transportation in the package price, don't forget to add the cost of round-trip transportation from your home to the departure city to come up with the total cost of the package.

Finally, read the general information regarding terms and conditions and the responsibility clause (usually in fine print at the end of the descriptive literature) to determine the precise elements for which the tour operator is — and is not — liable. Here the tour operator frequently expresses the right to change services or schedules as long as equivalent arrangements are offered. This clause also absolves the operator of responsibility for circumstances beyond human control, such as hurricanes or floods, or injury to you or your property. While reading, ask the following questions:

1. Does the tour include airfare or other transportation, sightseeing, meals, transfers, taxes, baggage handling, tips, or any other services? Do you want all these services?
2. If the brochure indicates that "some meals" are included, does this mean a welcoming and farewell dinner, two breakfasts, or every evening meal?
3. What classes of hotels are offered? If you will be traveling alone, what is the single supplement?
4. Does the tour itinerary or price vary according to the season?
5. Are the prices guaranteed; that is, if costs increase between the time you book and the time you depart, can surcharges unilaterally be added?
6. Do you get a full refund if you cancel? If not, be sure to obtain cancellation insurance.
7. Can the operator cancel if too few people join? At what point?

One of the consumer's biggest problems is finding enough information to judge the reliability of a tour packager, since individual travelers seldom have direct contact with the firm putting the package together. Usually, a retail travel agent is interposed between customer and tour operator, and much depends on his or her candor and cooperation. So ask a number of questions about the tour you are considering. For example:

- Has the agent ever used a package provided by this tour operator?
- How long has the tour operator been in business? Check the Better Business Bureau in the area where the tour operator is based to see if any complaints have been filed against it.
- Is the tour operator a member of the *United States Tour Operators Association* (*USTOA;* 211 E. 51st St., Suite 12B, New York, NY 10022; phone: 212-944-5727)? The *USTOA* will provide a list of its members upon request; it also offers a useful brochure, *How to Select a Package Tour.*
- How many and which companies are involved in the package?

- If air travel is by charter flight, is there an escrow account in which deposits will be held; if so, what is the name of the bank?

This last question is very important. US law requires that tour operators place every charter passenger's deposit and subsequent payment in a proper escrow account, and money paid into such an account cannot legally be used except to pay for the costs of a particular package or as a refund if the trip is canceled. To protect your investment, you should either make your check payable to the escrow account or use a credit card. (As this procedure follows the same guidelines as payments for charter flights, see our discussion in *Traveling by Plane.*)

■ **A word of advice:** Purchasers of vacation packages who feel they're not getting their money's worth are more likely to get a refund if they complain in writing to the operator — and bail out of the whole package immediately. Alert the tour operator or resort manager to the fact that you are dissatisfied, that you will be leaving for home as soon as transportation can be arranged, and that you expect a refund. They may have forms to fill out detailing your complaint; otherwise, state your case in a letter. Even if the availability of transportation home detains you, your dated, written complaint should help in procuring a refund from the operator.

Following is a list of many of the major US operators who provide escorted or independent packages to Ixtapa and Zihuatanejo. Note that although the majority of these packages are centered in Ixtapa, Zihuatanejo is just a short drive away. Most tour operators offer several departure dates, depending on the length of the tour and areas visited. As indicated, some operators are wholesalers only, and will deal only with a travel agent.

Adventure Tours (9818 Liberty Rd., Randallstown, MD 21133; phone: 301-922-7000 in Baltimore; 800-638-9040 elsewhere in the US). Offers week-long air/hotel packages.

American Express Travel Related Services (300 Pinnacle Way, Norcross, GA 30071; phone: 800-327-7737 or 404-368-5100). Offers all-inclusive packages, for 3 days or longer in Ixtapa and Zihuatanejo. The tour operator is a wholesaler, so use a travel agent.

Apple Vacations East (7 Campus Blvd., Newtown Sq., PA 19073; phone: 800-727-3400). Offers land packages in Ixtapa. This agency is a wholesaler, so use a travel agent.

Asti Tours (21 East 40th St., New York, NY 10016; phone: 800-535-3711 in New York; 800-223-7728 elsewhere in the US). Offers air/hotel packages in Ixtapa. The tour operator is a wholesaler, so use a travel agent.

Cavalcade Tours (450 Harmon Meadow Blvd., PO Box 1568, Secaucus, NJ 07096-1568; phone: 800-521-2319 or 201-617-7100). Offers 3- to 14-day air/hotel packages in Ixtapa.

Creative Leisure (951 Transport Way, Petaluma, CA 94954; phone: 800-4-CONDOS in the US and Canada). Offers air/hotel packages (as well as independent rentals) in Ixtapa.

Fishing International (4010 Montecito Ave., PO Box 2132, Santa Rosa, CA 95405; phone: 800-950-4242). This fishing and hunting specialist books customized fishing packages.

Funway Holidays (PO Box 1460, Milwaukee, WI 53201-1460; phone: 800-558-3050). Offers land packages in Ixtapa. This agency is a wholesaler, so use a travel agent.

Liberty Travel (contact the central office for the nearest location: 69 Spring St., Ramsey, NJ 07446; phone: 201-934-3500). Offers customized, independent packages in Ixtapa.

Maya Route Tours (Box 1948, Murray Hill Station, New York, NY 10156; phone: 212-683-2136). This agency offers walking tours centered in Ixtapa and Zihuatanejo that explore Maya ruins.

Sunmakers (15375 SE 30th Place, Suite 350, Bellevue, WA 98007; phone: 800-841-4321). Offers customized packages in Ixtapa, ranging from weekend getaways to month-long tours. This operator is a wholesaler, so use a travel agent.

Preparing

Calculating Costs

DETERMINING A BUDGET: A realistic appraisal of travel expenses is the most crucial bit of planning required before any trip. It is also, unfortunately, one for which it is most difficult to give precise, practical advice.

In Mexico, estimating travel expenses depends on the mode of transportation you choose, how long you will stay, and, in some cases, what time of year you plan to travel. In addition to the basics of transportation, hotels, meals, and sightseeing, you have to take into account seasonal price changes.

When calculating costs, start with the basics, the major expenses being transportation, accommodations, and food. However, don't forget such extras as local transportation, shopping, and such miscellaneous items as laundry and tips. Package programs can reduce the price of a vacation in Mexico, because the rates obtained by the tour packager are usually lower than the tariffs for someone traveling on a free-lance basis, that is, paying for each element — airfare, meals, car rental — separately. And keep in mind, particularly when calculating the major expenses, that costs vary according to fluctuations in the exchange rate — that is, how much of a given foreign currency the dollar will buy.

Other expenses, such as the cost of local sightseeing tours and other excursions, will vary depending on the tour and the guide you select. The tourist information office and most of the better hotels will have someone at the front desk to provide a rundown on the cost of local tours and full-day excursions in and out of the city. Travel agents also can provide this information.

In planning a travel budget, it also is wise to allow a realistic amount for both entertainment and recreation. Are you planning to spend time sightseeing and visiting local tourist attractions? Do you intend to rent a sailboat or take parasailing lessons? Is daily golf or tennis a part of your plan? Finally, don't forget that if haunting discotheques or other nightspots is an essential part of your vacation or you feel that one dinner show may not be enough, allow for the extra cost of nightlife. This one item alone can add a great deal to your daily expenditures.

If at any point in the planning process it appears impossible to estimate expenses, consider this suggestion: The easiest way to put a ceiling on the price of all these elements is to buy a package tour. A totally planned and escorted tour, with almost all transportation, rooms, meals, sightseeing, local travel, tips, and a dinner show or two included and prepaid, provides a pretty exact total of what the trip will cost beforehand, and the only surprise will be the one you spring on yourself by succumbing to some irresistible, expensive souvenir.

■ **Note:** The combination of rapid peso devaluation and Mexico's inflation rate has led the government to authorize increases in hotel rates of as much as 35% from time to time. Between the time you originally make your hotel reservations and your arrival, the price in US dollars may vary substantially from the price originally quoted. To avoid paying more than you expected, it's wise to confirm rates by writing directly to hotels or by calling their representatives in the US.

Planning a Trip

123 Travelers fall into two categories: those who make lists and those who do not. Some people prefer to plot the course of their trip to the finest detail, with contingency plans and alternatives at the ready. For others, the joy of a voyage is its spontaneity; exhaustive planning only lessens the thrill of anticipation and the sense of freedom.

For most travelers, any week-plus trip to Ixtapa and Zihuatanejo can be too expensive for an "I'll take my chances" type of attitude. Even perennial gypsies and anarchistic wanderers have to take into account the time-consuming logistics of getting around, and even with minimal baggage, they need to think about packing. Hence at least some planning is crucial.

This is not to suggest that you work out your itinerary in minute detail before you go; but it's still wise to decide certain basics at the very start: where to go, what to do, and how much to spend. These decisions require a certain amount of consideration. So before rigorously planning specific details, you might want to establish your general travel objectives:

1. How much time will you have for the entire trip, and how much of it are you willing to spend getting where you're going?
2. What interests and/or activities do you want to pursue while on vacation? Do you want to visit one, a few, or several different places?
3. At what time of year do you want to go?
4. Do you want peace and privacy or lots of activity and company?
5. How much money can you afford to spend for the entire vacation?

There is an abundance of travel information on Mexico, including Ixtapa and Zihuatanejo. You can seek the assistance of travel agents, turn to travel clubs such as *AAA* and other motoring organizations, or use general travel sources such as guidebooks, brochures, and maps. Mexican tourist offices in ths US and Mexico have brochures and extensive material on all parts of Mexico, and there's a 24-hour information hotline in Mexico City (phone: 5-250-0123, 5-250-0493, 5-250-0151, or 5-250-0589). The US Department of State's brochure *Travel to Mexico* is another source of general information to the country. It can be obtained free from the Washington Passport Agency, 1425 K St. NW, Washington, DC 20524 (phone: 202-647-0518).

You now can make almost all of your own travel arrangements if you have time to follow through with hotels, airlines, tour operators, and so on. But you'll probably save considerable time and energy if you have a travel agent make arrangements for you. The agent also should be able to advise you of alternative arrangements of which you may not be aware. Only rarely will a travel agent's services cost a traveler any money, and they may even save you some (see *How to Use a Travel Agent,* below).

If you are traveling by plane and want to benefit from savings offered by a charter flight to Ixtapa and Zihuatanejo (see *Traveling by Plane,* in this section), you may need reservations as much as 3 months in advance. In the high season, hotel reservations also are required months in advance. Many hotels in Ixtapa and Zihuatanejo require deposits before they will guarantee reservations, and this most often is the case during peak travel periods. (Be sure to request a receipt for any deposit.) Travel during *Easter*

Week, the *Christmas/New Year* period, and local festival and holiday times also requires reservations well in advance.

Make a list of any valuable items you are carrying with you, including credit card numbers and the serial numbers of your traveler's checks. Put copies in your purse or pocket and leave other copies at home. Put a label with your name and home address on the inside of your luggage for identification in case of loss. Put your name and business address — *never your home address* — on a label on the outside of your luggage. (Those who run businesses from home should use the office address of a friend or relative.)

Review your travel documents. If you are traveling by air, check to see that your ticket has been filled in correctly. The left side of the ticket should have a list of each stop you will make (even if you are only stopping to change planes), beginning with your departure point. Be sure that the list is correct, and count the number of copies to see that you have one for each plane you will take. If you have confirmed reservations, be sure that the column marked "status" says "OK" beside each flight. Have in hand vouchers or proof of payment for any reservation for which you've paid in advance; this includes hotels, transfers to and from the airport, sightseeing tours, car rentals, and special events. Although policies vary from carrier to carrier, it's still smart to reconfirm your flight 48 to 72 hours before departure, both going and returning.

Finally, you always should bear in mind that despite the most careful plans, things do not always occur on schedule — especially in Mexico, where *ahora* ("now") means anytime between today and tomorrow, and *ahorita* ("right now") means anytime within the next few hours. If you maintain a flexible attitude and try to accept minor disruptions as less than cataclysmic, you will enjoy yourself a lot more.

How to Use a Travel Agent

T.A. A reliable travel agent remains your best source of service and information for planning a trip abroad, whether you have a specific itinerary and require an agent only to make reservations or you need extensive help in sorting through the maze of airfares, tour offerings, hotel packages, and the scores of other arrangements that may be involved in a trip to Ixtapa and Zihuatanejo.

Know what you want from a travel agent so that you can evaluate what you are getting. It is perfectly reasonable to expect your agent to be a thoroughly knowledgeable travel specialist, with information about your destination and, even more crucial, a command of current airfares, ground arrangements, and other wrinkles in the travel scene.

Most travel agents work through computer reservations systems (CRS). These are used to assess the availability and cost of flights, hotels, and car rental firms, and through them they can book reservations. Despite reports of "computer bias," in which a computer may favor one airline over another, the CRS should provide agents with the entire spectrum of flights available to a given destination, as well as the complete range of fares, in considerably less time than it takes to telephone the airlines individually — and at no extra charge to the client.

Make the most intelligent use of a travel agent's time and expertise; understand the economics of the industry. As a client, traditionally you pay nothing for the agent's services; with few exceptions, it's all free, from hotel bookings to advice on package tours. Any money the travel agent makes on the time spent arranging your itinerary — booking hotels, resorts, or flights, or suggesting activities — comes from commissions paid by the suppliers of these services — the airlines, hotels, and so on. These commissions generally run from 10% to 15% of the total cost of the service, although suppliers often reward agencies that sell their services in volume with an increased commission, called an override. In most instances, you'll find that travel agents make their time and experience available to you at no charge, and you do not pay more for an airline ticket, package tour, or other product bought from a travel agent than you would for the same product bought directly from the supplier.

Exceptions to the general rule of free service by a travel agency are the agencies beginning to practice net pricing. In essence, such agencies return their commissions and overrides to their customers and make their income by charging a flat fee per transaction instead (thus adding a charge after a reduction for the commission has been made). Net fares and fees are a growing practice, though hardly widespread.

Even a conventional travel agent sometimes may charge a fee for special services. These chargeable items may include long-distance telephone or cable costs incurred in making a booking, for reserving a room in a place that does not pay a commission (such as a small, out-of-the-way hotel), or for special attention such as planning a highly personalized itinerary. A fee also may be assessed in instances of deeply discounted airfares.

Choose a travel agent with the same care with which you would choose a doctor or lawyer. You will be spending a good deal of money on the basis of the agent's judgment, so you have a right to expect that judgment to be mature, informed, and interested. At the moment, unfortunately, there aren't many standards within the travel agent industry to help you gauge competence, and the quality of individual agents varies enormously.

At present, only nine states have registration, licensing, or some other form of travel agent–related legislation on their books. Rhode Island licenses travel agents; Florida, Hawaii, Iowa, and Ohio register them; and California, Illinois, Oregon, and Washington have laws governing the sale of transportation or related services. While state licensing of agents cannot absolutely guarantee competence, it can at least ensure that an agent has met some minimum requirements.

Perhaps the best-prepared agents are those who have completed the CTC Travel Management program offered by the *Institute of Certified Travel Agents (ICTA)* and carry the initials CTC (Certified Travel Counselor) after their names. This indicates a relatively high level of expertise. For a free list of CTCs in your area, send a self-addressed, stamped, #10 envelope to *ICTA,* 148 Linden St., Box 82-56, Wellesley, MA 02181 (phone: 617-237-0280 in Massachusetts; 800-542-4282 elsewhere in the US).

An agent's membership in the *American Society of Travel Agents (ASTA)* can be a useful guideline in making a selection. But keep in mind that *ASTA* is an industry organization, requiring only that its members be licensed in those states where required; be accredited to represent the suppliers whose products they sell, including airline and cruise tickets; and adhere to its Principles of Professional Conduct and Ethics code. *ASTA* does not guarantee the competence, ethics, or financial soundness of its members, but it does offer some recourse if you feel you have been dealt with unfairly. Complaints may be registered with *ASTA* (Consumer Affairs Dept., PO Box 23992, Washington, DC 20026-3992; phone: 703-739-2782). First try to resolve the complaint directly with the supplier. For a list of *ASTA* members in your area, send a self-addressed, stamped, #10 envelope to *ASTA,* Public Relations Dept., at the address above.

There also is the *Association of Retail Travel Agents (ARTA),* a smaller but highly respected trade organization similar to *ASTA.* Its member agencies and agents similarly agree to abide by a code of ethics, and complaints about a member can be made to *ARTA*'s Grievance Committee, 1745 Jeff Davis Hwy., Arlington, VA 22202-3402 (phone: 800-969-6069 or 703-553-7777).

Perhaps the best way to find a travel agent is by word of mouth. If the agent (or agency) has done a good job for your friends over a period of time, it probably indicates a certain level of commitment and competence. Always ask not only for the name of the company, but for the name of the specific agent with whom your friends dealt, for it is that individual who will serve you, and quality can vary widely within a single agency. There are some superb travel agents in the business, and they can facilitate vacation or business arrangements.

You may decide to use a travel agent within Mexico to set up tours for the duration or for portions of your stay. Among the leading travel agencies that have offices in Ixtapa are *American Express Travel Related Services* (in the lobby of the *Westin Resort Ixtapa,* hotel zone; phone: 753-30853) and *Turismo Caleta* (Centro Comercial, La Puerda, Ixtapa; phone: 753-30504, 753-30384, or 753-30444).

Entry Requirements and Documents

Regardless of the transportation you use, you will need a tourist card to enter Mexico. The only exception to this rule is that if you intend to visit border towns (those within approximately 12½ miles/20 km of the Mexican border) and not to travel any farther into Mexico, you can do so without a tourist card for a stay of up to 72 hours.

In order to obtain a tourist card, you must have proof of your US citizenship. This proof may consist of an original or certified copy of a birth certificate, a voter's registration certificate, or a valid passport. A driver's license, credit card, or military papers will not suffice. A naturalized citizen must present at least one of the following documents: naturalization papers, a US passport, or an affidavit of citizenship.

A tourist card can be obtained from a number of sources, including any Mexican Ministry of Tourism office or Mexican consulate in the US; the Mexican government border offices at any port of entry; and some travel agencies. Regardless of where you obtain the card, when you cross the border you must sign it in the presence of the Mexican immigration official, who also may ask to see proof of your citizenship. For those arriving by plane, the card can be obtained from any airline ticket office. It also must be presented along with proof of citizenship when you land in Mexico. The tourist card allows you to stay in Mexico for a specified number of days; if you request one for 90 days — the maximum is 6 months — you don't have to stay that long, but you are covered for that period of time.

In order to be issued a tourist card, minors under 18 who are traveling alone must present a passport or a notarized copy of a letter signed by both parents or legal guardians indicating permission. If the minor is traveling with only one parent or a guardian, an individual passport and a letter signed by the other parent or legal guardian (or proof that this person is the sole legal guardian) will be needed.

During your stay in Mexico, you always should carry your tourist card with you, although you aren't likely to be asked for it after the border crossing. If you happen to lose your card, you should report it immediately to the nearest office of the Secretaría de Gobernación. They should be able to replace it for you.

US citizens will not need any vaccination certificates in order to enter Mexico for a short period of time. There are, however, a number of vaccinations that travelers to Mexico would be well advised to have before leaving and medicines that should be brought along. (See *Staying Healthy,* in this section, for our recommendations and other information on health concerns and precautions.)

Although other forms of identification (such as those cited above) will suffice, a valid passport is the best identification and proof of US citizenship to carry when traveling through Mexico. While abroad, you should carry your passport with you at all times, and if you lose it, immediately report the loss to the nearest US consulate or embassy (for locations in Mexico, see *Medical and Legal Aid and Consular Services,* in this section). It's likely to speed up the replacement process if you have a record of your passport number and the place and date of its issue (a photocopy of the first page of your passport is perfect). Keep this information separate from your passport — you might want to give it to a traveling companion to hold.

DUTY AND CUSTOMS: As a general rule, the requirements for bringing the majority of items *into Mexico* is that they must be quantities small enough not to imply commercial import.

If you are accustomed to certain American brands of bourbon or whiskey (although imported brands are increasingly available, they are very costly), you are allowed to bring 3 liters of liquor into Mexico duty-free — any amount over this will be taxed. And if you prefer American cigarettes, be advised that the limit is 1 carton (20 packs). Each person also may bring in one still and one video camera, plus 12 rolls of film and 3 video cartridge tapes. For further information on Mexican customs regulations, contact the Mexican Ministry of Tourism offices or Mexican consulates in the US (see *Sources and Resources,* in this section, for addresses).

If you are bringing along a computer, camera, or other electronic equipment for your own use that you will be taking back to the US, you should register it with the US Customs Service in order to avoid being asked to pay duty both entering and returning from Mexico. (Also see *Customs and Returning to the US,* in this section.) For information on this procedure, as well as for a variety of informative pamphlets on US Customs regulations, contact the local office of the US Customs Service or the central office, PO Box 7407, Washington, DC 20044 (phone: 202-566-8195).

- **One rule to follow:** When passing through customs, it is illegal not to declare dutiable items; penalties range from stiff fines and seizure of the goods to prison terms. So don't try to sneak anything through — it just isn't worth it.

Insurance

It is unfortunate that most decisions to buy travel insurance are impulsive and usually made without any real consideration of the traveler's existing policies. Therefore, the first person with whom you should discuss travel insurance is your own insurance broker, not a travel agent or the clerk behind the airport insurance counter. You may discover that the insurance you already carry protects you adequately while you travel or that you need no more than excess value insurance for baggage, or trip cancellation insurance.

TYPES OF INSURANCE: To make insurance decisions intelligently, however, you first should understand the basic categories of travel insurance and what they cover. Then you can decide what you should have in the broader context of your personal insurance needs, and you can choose the most economical way of getting the desired protection: through riders on existing policies; with onetime short-term policies; through a special program put together for the frequent traveler; through coverage that's part of a travel club's benefits; or with a combination policy sold by insurance companies through brokers, automobile clubs, tour operators, and travel agents.

There are seven basic categories of travel insurance:

1. Baggage and personal effects insurance
2. Personal accident and sickness insurance
3. Trip cancellation and interruption insurance

4. Default and/or bankruptcy insurance
5. Flight insurance (to cover injury or death)
6. Automobile insurance (for driving your own or a rented car)
7. Combination policies

Baggage and Personal Effects Insurance – Ask your insurance agent if baggage and personal effects are included in your current homeowner's policy, or if you will need a special floater to cover you for the duration of a trip. The object is to protect your bags and their contents in case of damage or theft anytime during your travels, not just while you're in flight and covered by the airline's policy. Furthermore, only limited protection is provided by the airline (see *Traveling by Plane,* in this section).

If you are carrying goods worth more than the maximum protection offered by the airline, consider excess value insurance. Additional coverage is available from the airlines at an average, currently, of $1 to $2 per $100 worth of coverage, up to a maximum of $5,000. This insurance can be purchased at the airline counter when you check in, though you should arrive early to fill out the necessary forms and to avoid holding up other passengers.

Major credit card companies also provide coverage for lost or delayed baggage — and this coverage often also is over and above what the airline will pay. The basic coverage is automatic for all cardholders who use the credit card to purchase tickets, but to qualify for additional coverage, cardholders generally must enroll in advance.

American Express: Provides $500 coverage for checked baggage; $1,250 for carry-on baggage; and $250 for valuables, such as cameras and jewelry.

Carte Blanche and Diners Club: Each provides $1,250 worth of free insurance for checked or carry-on baggage that's lost or damaged.

Discover Card: Offers $500 insurance for checked baggage and $1,250 for carry-on baggage — but to qualify for this coverage, cardholders first must purchase additional flight insurance (see "Flight Insurance," below).

MasterCard and Visa: Baggage insurance coverage is set by the issuing institution.

Additional baggage and personal effects insurance also is included in certain of the combination travel insurance policies discussed below.

■ **A note of warning:** Be sure to read the fine print of any excess value insurance policy; there often are specific exclusions, such as cash, tickets, furs, gold and silver objects, art, and antiques. And remember that insurance companies ordinarily will pay only the depreciated value of the goods rather than their replacement value. The best way to protect the items you're carrying in your luggage is to take photos of your valuables and keep a record of the serial numbers of such items as cameras, laptops, radios, and so on. This will establish that you do, indeed, own the objects. If your luggage disappears or is damaged en route, deal with the situation immediately.

Personal Accident and Sickness Insurance – This covers you in case of illness during your trip or death in an accident. Most policies insure you for hospital and doctor's expenses, lost income, and so on. In most cases, it is a standard part of existing health insurance policies, though you should check with your insurance broker to be sure that your policy will pay for any medical expenses incurred abroad. If not, take out a separate vacation accident policy or an entire vacation insurance policy that includes health and life coverage.

One company offering such comprehensive health and life insurance policies is *Wallach & Co.* Both their HealthCare Global and HealthCare Abroad programs may be bought in combination with trip cancellation and baggage insurance at extra cost.

For information, write to *Wallach & Co.,* 243 Church St. NW, Suite 100-D, Vienna, VA 22180 (phone: 703-281-9500 in Virginia; 800-237-6615 elsewhere in the US).

Trip Cancellation and Interruption Insurance – Most charter and package tour passengers pay for their travel well before departure. The disappointment of having to miss a vacation because of illness or any other reason pales before the awful prospect that not all (and sometimes none) of the money paid in advance might be returned. So cancellation insurance for any package tour is a must.

Although cancellation penalties vary (they are listed in the fine print in every tour brochure, and before you purchase a package tour you should know exactly what they are), rarely will a passenger get more than 50% of this money back if forced to cancel within a few weeks of scheduled departure. Therefore, if you book a package tour or charter flight, you should have trip cancellation insurance to guarantee full reimbursement or refund should you, a traveling companion, or a member of your immediate family get sick, forcing you to cancel your trip or *return home early.*

The key here is *not* to buy just enough insurance to guarantee full reimbursement for the cost of the package or charter in case of cancellation. The proper amount of coverage should be sufficient to reimburse you for the cost of having to catch up with a tour after its departure or having to travel home at the full economy airfare (from the farthest destination on your itinerary) if you have to forgo your return flight of your charter. There is usually quite a discrepancy between a charter fare and the amount necessary to travel the same distance on a regularly scheduled flight at full economy fare. Before you decide on a policy, also be sure to check the fine print for stipulations concerning "family members" and "pre-existing medical conditions," as well as allowances for living expenses if you must delay your return due to bodily injury or illness.

Trip cancellation insurance is available from travel agents and tour operators in two forms: as part of a short-term, all-purpose travel insurance package (sold by the travel agent); or as specific cancellation insurance designed by the tour operator for a specific charter tour. Generally, tour operators' policies are less expensive, but also less inclusive. Cancellation insurance also is available directly from insurance companies or their agents as part of a short-term, all-inclusive travel insurance policy.

Default and/or Bankruptcy Insurance – Although trip cancellation insurance usually protects you if *you* are unable to complete — or begin — your trip, a fairly recent innovation is coverage in the event of default and/or bankruptcy on the part of the tour operator, airline, or other travel supplier. In some travel insurance packages, this contingency is included in the trip cancellation portion of the coverage; in others, it is a separate feature. Either way, it is becoming increasingly important. While default/bankruptcy insurance will not ordinarily result in reimbursement in time to pay for new arrangements, it can ensure that you will get your money back, and even independent travelers buying no more than an airplane ticket may want to consider it.

Flight Insurance – Airlines have carefully established limits of liability for injury to or the death of passengers for international flights. For international flights to, from, or with a stopover in the US, all carriers are liable for up to $75,000 per passenger. For all other international flights, the liability is based on where you purchase the ticket: If booked in advance in the US, the maximum liability is $75,000; if arrangements are made abroad, the liability is $10,000. But remember, these liabilities are not the same thing as insurance policies; every penny that an airline eventually pays in the case of injury or death will likely be subject to a legal battle.

But before you buy last-minute flight insurance from an airport vending machine, consider the purchase in light of your total existing insurance coverage. A careful review of your current policies may reveal that you already are amply covered for accidental death, sometimes up to three times the amount provided for by the flight insurance you're buying at the airport.

Be aware that airport insurance, the kind typically bought at a counter or from a vending machine, is among the most expensive forms of life insurance coverage, and that even within a single airport, rates for approximately the same coverage vary widely. Often policies sold in vending machines are more expensive than those sold over the counter, even when they are with the same national company.

If you buy your plane ticket with a major credit card, you generally receive automatic insurance coverage at no extra cost. Additional coverage usually can be obtained at extremely reasonable prices, but a cardholder must sign up for it in advance. (Note that rates vary slightly for residents of some states.) As we went to press, the travel accident and life insurance policies of these major credit cards were as follows:

American Express: Automatically provides $100,000 in insurance to its *Green, Gold,* and *Optima* cardholders, and $500,000 to *Platinum* cardholders. With *American Express,* $4 per ticket buys an additional $250,000 worth of flight insurance; $6.50 buys $500,000 worth; and $13 provides an added $1 million worth of coverage.

Carte Blanche: Automatically provides $150,000 flight insurance. An additional $250,000 worth of insurance is available for $4; $500,000 costs $6.50.

Diners Club: Provides $350,000 free flight insurance. An additional $250,000 worth of insurance is available for $4; $500,000 costs $6.50.

Discover Card: Provides $500,000 free flight insurance. An additional $250,000 worth of insurance is available for $4; $500,000 costs $6.50.

MasterCard and Visa: Insurance coverage for each is set by the issuing institution.

Automobile Insurance – When you rent a car, the rental company is required to offer you insurance. In your car rental contract, you'll see that for about $11 to $13 a day, you may buy optional collision damage waiver (CDW) coverage, which relieves you of all responsibility for damage to the rental car. If you do not accept this coverage, you may be liable for the full retail cost of the car.

Before agreeing to this coverage, however, ask your insurance agent if your personal automobile insurance policy covers rented vehicles — it very well may cover your entire liability exposure without any additional cost. Be aware, too, that increasing numbers of credit cards automatically provide CDW coverage if the car rental is charged to the appropriate credit card. As the specific terms of such coverage differ sharply among individual credit card companies, contact the issuing institution for information on the nature and amount of coverage provided. (Business travelers should be aware that, at the time of this writing, *American Express* had withdrawn its automatic CDW coverage from some corporate *Green* card accounts — watch for similar cutbacks by other companies.)

You also should know that an increasing number of the major international car rental companies are including the cost of the CDW in their quoted prices. This does not mean that they are absorbing this cost and you are receiving free coverage — total car rental prices have increased to include this coverage. The disadvantage of this inclusion is that you may not have the option to refuse this coverage, and will end up paying the added charge — even if you already are adequately covered by your own insurance policy or through a credit card company.

Combination Policies – Short-term insurance policies, which may include any combination of any or all of the types of insurance discussed above, are available through retail insurance agencies, automobile clubs, and many travel agents. These combination policies are designed to cover you for the duration of a single trip.

Companies offering policies of this type include the following:

Access America (600 Third Ave., PO Box 807, New York, NY 10163; phone: 800-284-8300 or 212-490-5345).

Carefree Travel Insurance (Arm Coverage, PO Box 310, Mineola, NY 11501; phone: 800-645-2424 or 516-294-0220).

Near (1900 N. MacArthur Blvd., Suite 210, Oklahoma City, OK 73127; phone: 800-654-6700 or 405-949-2500).

Tele-Trip (PO Box 31685, 3201 Farnam St., Omaha, NE 68131; phone: 402-345-2400 in Nebraska; 800-228-9792 elsewhere in the US).

Travel Assistance International (1133 15th St. NW, Suite 400, Washington, DC 20005; phone: 202-347-2025 in Washington, DC; 800-821-2828 elsewhere in the US).

The Travelers Company (Ticket and Travel Plans, One Tower Sq., Hartford, CT 06183-5040; phone: 203-277-2319 in Connecticut; 800-243-3174 elsewhere in the US).

Travel Guard International (1145 Clark St., Stevens Point, WI 54481; phone: 715-345-0505 in Wisconsin; 800-826-1300 elsewhere in the US).

WorldCare Travel Assistance Association (605 Market St., Suite 1300, San Francisco, CA 94105; phone: 800-666-4993 or 415-541-4991).

Hints for Handicapped Travelers

From 40 to 50 million people in the US alone have some sort of disability, and over half this number are physically handicapped. Like everyone else today, they — and the uncounted disabled millions around the world — are on the move. More than ever before, they are demanding facilities they can use comfortably, and they are being heard.

Those who have chosen to visit Mexico are in luck, because more and more disabled travelers are returning from this most luscious of destinations bearing tales of ramped sidewalks, a style of warm-weather architecture that erects fewer barriers between the indoors and the outdoors, and sightseeing tours designed especially for them. Also, in recent years, a series of imaginative, pan-American programs aimed at improving facilities and services for the handicapped in Mexico and Latin America have been initiated. Chief among these is *Partners of the Americas,* with chapters based in 45 states, which coordinates joint projects with these states in various Mexican and Latin American areas. *Partners of the Americas* also maintains an extensive library with information on programs for the handicapped throughout Mexico, as well as Central and South America, and they often can put disabled travelers in touch with self-help organizations of disabled persons in these locations. For more information, contact the central office of *Partners of the Americas,* 1424 K St., NW, Suite 700, Washington, DC 20005 (phone: 800-322-7844 or 202-628-3300).

Despite this effort to develop special facilities for the disabled, however, handicapped travelers face pretty much the same problems in Mexico as in most other parts of the world. Rural areas have no facilities. Cities have some, but there is no consistency.

PLANNING: Collect as much information as you can about your specific disability and facilities for the disabled in Mexico; make your travel arrangements well in advance, and specify to all services involved the exact nature of your condition or restricted mobility to ensure accommodations and facilities to suit your needs. The best way to find out if your intended destination can accommodate a handicapped traveler is to write or call the local tourist authority or hotel and ask specific questions. If you require a corridor of a certain width to maneuver a wheelchair or if you need handles on the bathroom wall for support, ask the hotel manager (some large hotels have rooms designed for the handicapped). A travel agent or an organization that deals with your particular disability — for example, the *American Foundation for the Blind* — will supply the most up-to-date information on the subject. The following organizations offer general information on access:

ACCENT on Living (PO Box 700, Bloomington, IL 61702; phone: 309-378-2961). This information service for persons with disabilities provides a free list of travel agencies specializing in trips for the disabled, as well as a wide range of publications, including a quarterly magazine ($8 per year; $14 for 2 years).

Information Center for Individuals with Disabilities (Fort Point Pl., 1st Floor, 27-43 Wormwood St., Boston, MA 02210; phone: 800-462-5015 in Massachusetts; 617-727-5540/1 elsewhere in the US; both numbers provide voice and TDD — telecommunications device for the deaf). The center offers information and referral services on disability-related issues, publishes fact sheets on travel resources, and can help you research your trip.

Mobility International USA (*MIUSA;* PO Box 3551, Eugene, OR 97403; phone: 503-343-1284; both voice and TDD). This US branch of *Mobility International,* a nonprofit British organization with affiliates worldwide, offers members advice and assistance, information on travel services, and various publications, including a comprehensive sourcebook, *A World of Options for the 90s: A Guide to International Education Exchange, Community Service and Travel for Persons with Disabilities* ($14 for members; $16 for non-members) and a quarterly newsletter (included in the $20 yearly membership fee; $10 a year for non-members).

National Rehabilitation Information Center (8455 Colesville Rd., Suite 935, Silver Spring, MD 20910; phone: 301-588-9284). A general information, resource, research, and referral service.

Paralyzed Veterans of America (*PVA;* PVA/ATTS Program, 801 18th St. NW, Washington, DC 20006; phone: 202-416-7708 in Washington, DC; 800-424-8200 elsewhere in the US). The members of this national service organization all are veterans who have suffered spinal cord injuries, but it offers advocacy services and information to all disabled persons. *PVA* also sponsors *Access to the Skies,* a program that coordinates the efforts of the air travel industry to increase accessibility. Members receive several helpful publications and notification of conferences of interest to disabled travelers.

Royal Association for Disability and Rehabilitation (*RADAR;* 25 Mortimer St., London W1N 8AB, England; phone: 44-71-637-5400). Offers a number of useful publications, including a comprehensive guide to international travel, *Holidays and Travel Abroad 1991/1992 — A Guide for Disabled People* (just over £6 as we went to press; payment must be sent in British pounds).

Society for the Advancement of Travel for the Handicapped (*SATH;* 26 Court St., Penthouse, Brooklyn, NY 11242; phone: 718-858-5483). Members of this nonprofit organization include consumers and travel service professionals. For an annual fee of $45 ($25 for students and travelers 65 and older), members receive a quarterly newsletter and have access to information and referral services. Also offers two useful publications: *Travel Tips for the Handicapped* (a series of informative fact sheets) and *The United States Welcomes Handicapped Visitors* (a 48-page guide that includes hints for disabled travelers abroad).

Travel Information Service (Moss Rehabilitation Hospital, 1200 W. Tabor Rd., Philadelphia, PA 19141-3099; phone: 215-456-9600 for voice; 215-456-9602 for TDD). This service assists physically handicapped people in planning trips and supplies detailed information on accessibility for a nominal fee.

Blind travelers should contact the *American Foundation for the Blind* (15 W. 16th St., New York, NY 10011; phone: 212-620-2147 in New York State; 800-232-5463 elsewhere in the US) and *The Seeing Eye* (Box 375, Morristown, NJ 07963-0375;

phone: 201-539-4425); both provide useful information on resources for the visually impaired. *Note:* Seeing Eye dogs arriving in Mexico must be accompanied by a certificate of inoculation against rabies, hepatitis, and distemper, as well as a certificate of health, issued within the previous 3 months. Both must be authorized by a Mexican consul (for a fee of $20 at press time). *The American Society for the Prevention of Cruelty to Animals* (*ASPCA,* Education Dept., 441 E. 92 St., New York, NY 10128; phone: 212-876-7700) offers a useful booklet, *Traveling With Your Pet* ($5, postpaid), which lists inoculation and other requirements by country.

In addition, there are a number of publications — from travel guides to magazines — of interest to handicapped travelers. Among these are the following:

Access to the World, by Louise Weiss, offers sound tips for the disabled traveler ($16.95; Facts on File, 460 Park Ave. S., New York, NY 10016; phone: 212-683-2244 in New York State; 800-322-8755 elsewhere in the US; 800-443-8323 in Canada).

The Diabetic Traveler is a useful quarterly newsletter that focuses on resources and hints for diabetic travelers. To subscribe, send $15 ($4 per back issue) to PO Box 8223 RW, Stamford, CT 06905 (phone: 203-327-5832).

Guide to Traveling with Arthritis, a free brochure available by writing to the Upjohn Company (PO Box 307-B, Coventry, CT 06238), provides common-sense tips on trip planning and comfort while traveling.

Handicapped Travel Newsletter is a bimonthly publication edited by wheelchair-bound Vietnam veteran and world traveler Michael Quigley. To subscribe, send $10 to PO Box 269, Athens, TX 75751 (phone: 214-677-1260).

Handi-Travel: A Resource Book for Disabled and Elderly Travellers, by Cinnie Noble, is full of practical tips for those with disabilities affecting mobility, hearing, or sight. To order, send $12.95, plus postage, to the *Canadian Rehabilitation Council for the Disabled,* 45 Sheppard Ave. E., Suite 801, Toronto, Ontario M2N 5W9, Canada (phone: 416-250-7490; both voice and TDD).

The Itinerary, a bimonthly travel magazine for people with disabilities, includes information on accessibility, tours, adaptive devices and aids, special services, and travel hints. To subscribe, send $10 to PO Box 2012, Bayonne, NJ 07002-2012 (phone: 201-858-3400).

The Physically Disabled Traveler's Guide, by Rod W. Durgin and Norene Lindsay, rates accessibility and includes a list of organizations specializing in travel for the disabled. It is available for $9.95, plus shipping and handling, from *Resource Directories,* 3361 Executive Pkwy., Suite 302, Toledo, OH 43606 (phone: 419-536-5353 in the Toledo area; 800-274-8515 elsewhere in the US).

Ticket to Safe Travel offers useful information for diabetic travelers. This reprint of an article is available from the *American Diabetes Association;* for the nearest local chapter, contact the central office at 505 Eighth Ave., 21st Floor, New York, NY 10018 (phone: 212-947-9707 in New York State; 800-232-3472 elsewhere in the US).

Travel for the Patient with Chronic Obstructive Pulmonary Disease, a publication of the George Washington University Medical Center, provides practical suggestions for those with asthma, bronchitis, or other lung ailments. To order, send $2 to Dr. Harold Silver, 1601 18th St. NW, Washington, DC 20009 (phone: 202-667-0134).

Traveling Like Everybody Else: A Practical Guide for Disabled Travelers, by Jacqueline Freedman and Susan Gersten, offers travel tips and resources, including lists of accessible accommodations and tour operators specializing in tours for disabled travelers. To order, send $11.95, plus postage, to Modan Publishing, PO Box 1202, Bellmore, NY 11710 (phone: 516-679-1380).

Travel Tips for Hearing-Impaired People, a free pamphlet for deaf and hearing-impaired travelers, is available by sending a self-addressed, stamped, business-size envelope to the *American Academy of Otolaryngology,* One Prince St., Alexandria, VA 22314 (phone: 703-836-4444).

Travel Tips for People with Arthritis, a free 31-page booklet, provides helpful information regarding transportation, trip planning, medical considerations, and conserving your energy while traveling. It also includes listings of helpful resources for disabled travelers. For a copy, contact your local *Arthritis Foundation* chapter, or write to the national office, PO Box 19000, Atlanta, GA 30326 (phone: 404-872-7100).

The Wheelchair Traveler lists accessible accommodations in Mexico, including Ixtapa. To order a copy, and for current pricing, contact the author, Douglass R. Annand, 123 Ball Hill Rd., Milford, NH 03055 (phone: 603-673-4539).

A few more basic resources to look for are *Travel for the Disabled* ($9.95) and *Directory of Travel Agencies for the Disabled* ($19.95), both by Helen Hecker, and *Wheelchair Vagabond* (hardcover, $14.95; paperback, $9.95), by John G. Nelson. All three are published by Twin Peaks Press, PO Box 129, Vancouver, WA 98666 (phone: 800-637-CALM or 206-694-2462).

PLANE: Disabled passengers always should make reservations well in advance. Provide the airline with all relevant details of your condition, including information on mobility and equipment that you will need the airline to supply — such as a wheelchair for boarding or portable oxygen for in-flight use. Be sure that the person to whom you speak fully understands your needs, and on the day before the flight call back to make sure that all arrangements have been prepared. Arrive early for your flight so that you can board before the rest of the passengers.

Because most airports have jetways (corridors connecting the terminal with the door of the plane), a disabled passenger usually can be taken as far as the plane, and sometimes right onto it, in a wheelchair. If not, a narrow boarding chair may be used to take you to your seat. Your own wheelchair, which will be folded and put in the baggage compartment, should be tagged as escort luggage to assure that it's available at planeside upon landing rather than in the baggage claim area. (If your wheelchair is battery-operated, it might not be accepted on board unless it has non-spillable batteries, or is specially packaged for the flight; check with the airline ahead of time.) Usually people in wheelchairs are asked to wait until other passengers have disembarked. If you are making a tight connection, be sure to tell the attendant.

Passengers who use oxygen may not use their personal supply in the cabin, though it may be carried on the plane as cargo when properly packed and labeled. If you will need oxygen during the flight, the airline will supply it to you (there is a charge) provided you have given advance notice — 24 hours to a few days, depending on the carrier.

Among the airlines flying to Ixtapa and Zihuatanejo, TDD toll-free lines for the hearing-impaired are provided by *American* (phone: 800-582-1573 in Ohio; 800-543-1586 elsewhere in the US), *Continental* (phone: 800-343-9195), *Delta* (phone: 800-831-4488), *Pan American* (phone: 800-722-3323), and *United* (phone: 800-942-8819 in Illinois; 800-323-0170 elsewhere in the US).

Useful information on every stage of air travel, from planning to arrival, is provided in the booklet *Incapacitated Passengers Air Travel Guide.* To receive a free copy, write to the International Air Transport Association (Publications Sales Department, 2000 Peel St., Montreal, Quebec H3A 2R4, Canada; phone: 514-844-6311). Another helpful publication is *Air Transportation of Handicapped Persons,* which explains the general guidelines that govern air carrier policies. For a copy of this free booklet, write to the US Department of Transportation (Distribution Unit, Publications Section, M-443-2, Washington, DC 20590) and ask for "Free Advisory Circular #AC-120-32."

SHIP: Check with your travel agent or cruise line when making reservations, as some cruise ships cannot accommodate handicapped travelers because of their many sets of narrow steps, which are less convenient than wide ramps.

For those in wheelchairs or with limited mobility, one of the best sources for evaluating a ship's accessibility is the free chart issued by the *Cruise Lines International Association* (500 Fifth Ave., Suite 1407, New York, NY 10110; phone: 212-921-0066). The chart lists accessible ships and indicates whether they accommodate standard-size or only narrow wheelchairs, have ramps, wide doors, low or no doorsills, handrails in the rooms, and so on. (For information on ships cruising Mexican waters, see *Traveling by Ship,* in this section.)

GROUND TRANSPORTATION: Perhaps the simplest solution to getting around is to travel with an able-bodied companion who can drive. Another alternative in Mexico is to hire a driver/translator with a car — be sure to get a recommendation from a reputable source. The organizations listed above may be able to help you make arrangements — another source is your hotel concierge.

If you are accustomed to driving your own hand-controlled car and determined to rent one in Mexico, you may have to do some extensive research. If agencies do provide hand-controlled cars, they are apt to be offered only on a limited basis and usually are in high demand. The best course is to contact the major car rental companies listed in *Traveling by Car,* in this section, well before your departure.

The *American Automobile Association (AAA)* publishes a helpful booklet, *The Handicapped Driver's Mobility Guide.* Contact the central office of your local *AAA* club for availability and pricing, which may vary in different branch offices.

TOURS: Programs designed for the physically impaired are run by specialists who have researched hotels, restaurants, and sites to be sure they present no insurmountable obstacles. The following travel agencies or tour operators specialize in making group or individual arrangements for travelers with physical or other disabilities:

Access: The Foundation for Accessibility by the Disabled (PO Box 356, Malverne, NY 11565; phone: 516-887-5798). A travelers' referral service that acts as an intermediary with tour operators and agents worldwide, and provides information on accessibility.

Accessible Journeys (412 S. 45th St., Philadelphia, PA 19104; phone: 215-747-0171). This company offers cruises and tours for people with special needs and can arrange for medical professional traveling companions.

Accessible Tours/Directions Unlimited (720 N. Bedford Rd., Bedford Hills, NY 10507; phone: 914-241-1700 in Westchester County, NY; 800-533-5343 elsewhere in the continental US). Arranges group or individual tours for disabled persons traveling in the company of able-bodied friends or family members. Accepts the unaccompanied traveler if completely self-sufficient.

Dialysis at Sea Cruises (611 Barry Place, Indian Rocks Beach, FL 34635; phone: 813-596-7604 or 800-544-7604 throughout the US and Canada). Offers cruises for dialysis patients that include full medical services, including a nephrologist (a specialist in kidney disease) and dialysis nurses. Although family and companions are welcome, the number of patients usually is limited to roughly ten travelers per trip.

Evergreen Travel Service (4114-198th St. SW, Suite 13, Lynnwood, WA 98036-6742; phone: 206-776-1184 or 800-435-2288 throughout the continental US and Canada). Offers tours and cruises for the disabled (Wings on Wheels Tours), sight-impaired/blind (White Cane Tours), and hearing-impaired/deaf (Flying Fingers Tours). Most programs are first class and escorted.

Flying Wheels Travel (143 W. Bridge St., Box 382, Owatonna, MN 55060; phone: 507-451-5005; 800-535-6790 throughout the US and Canada). Handles both tours and individual arrangements.

The Guided Tour (555 Ashbourne Rd., Elkins Park, PA 19117; phone: 215-782-

1370). Arranges tours for people with developmental and learning disabilities, and those who are physically disabled or who need a slower pace.

Handi-Travel (First National Travel Limited, Thornhill Sq., 300 John St., Suite 405, Thornhill, Ontario L3T 5W4, Canada; phone: 416-731-4714). Handles tours and individual arrangements.

USTS Travel Horizons (11 E. 44th St., New York, NY 10017; phone: 800-487-8787 or 212-687-5121). Travel agent and registered nurse Mary Ann Hamm makes all arrangements for travelers requiring kidney dialysis.

Whole Person Tours (PO Box 1084, Bayonne, NJ 07002-1084; phone: 201-858-3400). Owner Bob Zywicki travels the world with his wheelchair and offers a lineup of escorted tours (many conducted by himself) for the disabled. *Whole Person Tours* also publishes *The Itinerary* (see above).

Travelers who would benefit from being accompanied by a nurse or physical therapist also can hire a companion through *Traveling Nurses' Network,* a service provided by Twin Peaks Press (PO Box 129, Vancouver, WA 98666; phone: 800-637-CALM or 206-694-2462). For $10, the client receives the names of three nurses, whom he or she can then contact directly; for $125, the agency will do the screening and hiring. Travel arrangements also may be made in some cases.

A similar service is offered by *MedEscort International* (ABE International Airport, PO Box 8766, Allentown, PA 18105; phone: 800-255-7182 in the continental US; elsewhere call 215-791-3111). The potential companions include nurses, paramedics, respiratory therapists, and physicians. Fees are based on the disabled traveler's needs, and *MedEscort* also can assist in making travel arrangements.

Hints for Single Travelers

Just about the last trip in human history on which the participants were neatly paired was the voyage of Noah's Ark. Ever since, passenger lists and tour groups have reflected the same kind of asymmetry that occurs in real life, as countless individuals set forth to see the world unaccompanied (or unencumbered, depending on your outlook) by spouse, lover, friend, or relative. Unfortunately, traveling alone also can turn a traveler into a second class citizen.

The truth is that the travel industry is not very fair to people who vacation by themselves. People traveling alone almost invariably end up paying more than individuals traveling in pairs. Most travel bargains, including package tours, accommodations, resort packages, and cruises, are based on *double occupancy* rates. This means that the per-person price is offered on the basis of two people traveling together and sharing a double room (which means they each will spend a good deal more on meals and extras). The single traveler will have to pay a surcharge, called a single supplement, for exactly the same package. In extreme cases, this can add as much as 30% to 55% to the basic per-person rate.

Don't despair, however. Throughout Mexico, there are scores of smaller hotels and other hostelries where, in addition to a cozier atmosphere, prices still are quite reasonable for the single traveler. And some ship lines have begun to offer special cruises for singles.

The obvious, most effective alternative is to find a traveling companion. Even special "singles' tours" that promise no supplements are based on people sharing double rooms. Perhaps the most recent innovation along these lines is the creation of organizations that "introduce" the single traveler to other single travelers (somewhat like a dating service) in order to match compatible travel mates. Among these organizations are the following:

Jane's International (2603 Bath Ave., Brooklyn, NY 11214; phone: 718-266-2045). This service puts potential traveling companions in touch with one another. No age limit, no fee.

Partners-in-Travel (PO Box 491145, Los Angeles, CA 90049; phone: 213-476-4869). Members receive a list of singles seeking traveling companions; prospective companions make contact through the agency. The membership fee is $40 per year and includes a chatty newsletter (6 issues per year).

Singleworld (401 Theodore Fremd Ave., Rye, NY 10580; phone: 914-967-3334 or 800-223-6490 in the continental US). For a yearly fee of $25, this club books members on tours and cruises, and arranges shared accommodations, allowing individual travelers to avoid the single supplement charge; members also receive a quarterly newsletter. *Singleworld* also offers its own package tours for singles, with departures categorized by age group.

Travel Companion Exchange (PO Box 833, Amityville, NY 11701; phone: 516-454-0880). This group publishes a newsletter for singles and a directory of individuals looking for travel companions. On joining, members fill out a lengthy questionnaire and write a small listing (much like an ad in a personal column). Based on these listings, members can request copies of profiles and contact prospective traveling companions. It is wise to join well in advance of your planned vacation so that there's enough time to determine compatibility and plan a joint trip. Membership fees, including the newsletter, are $36 for 6 months or $60 a year for a single-sex listing; $66 and $120, respectively, for a complete listing. Subscription to the newsletter alone costs $24 for 6 months or $36 per year.

In addition, a number of tour packagers cater to single travelers. These companies offer packages designed for individuals interested in vacationing with a group of single travelers or in being matched with a traveling companion. Among the better established of these agencies are the following:

Grand Circle Travel (347 Congress St., Boston, MA 02210; phone: 800-221-2610 or 617-350-7500). Arranges extended vacations, escorted tours and cruises for the over-50 traveler, including singles. Membership, which is automatic when you book a trip through *Grand Circle,* includes travel discounts and other extras, such as a Pen Pals service for singles seeking traveling companions.

Saga International Holidays (120 Boylston St., Boston MA 02116; phone: 617-451-6808 or 800-343-0273). A subsidiary of a British company specializing in older travelers, many of them single, *Saga* offers a broad selection of packages for people age 60 and over, or those 50 to 59 traveling with someone 60 or older.

Singles in Motion (545 W. 236th St., Suite 1D, Riverdale, NY 10463; phone: 212-884-4464). Offers a number of packages for single travelers, including tours, cruises, and excursions focusing on outdoor activities such as hiking and biking.

Marion Smith Singles (611 Prescott Place, North Woodmere, NY 11581; phone: 516-791-4852, 516-791-4865, or 212-944-2112). Specializes in tours for singles ages 20 to 50, who can choose to share accommodations to avoid paying single supplement charges.

Solo Flights (127 S. Compo Rd., Westport, CT 06880; phone: 203-226-9993). Represents a number of packagers and cruise lines and books singles on individual and group tours.

STI (8619 Reseda Blvd., Suite 103, Northridge, CA 91324; phone: 800-525-0525 throughout the US). Specializes in travel for 18- to 30-year-olds. Offers escorted tours ranging from 2 weeks to 2 months.

Travel in Two's (239 N. Broadway, Suite 3, N. Tarrytown, NY 10591; phone: 914-631-8409). This company books solo travelers on packages offered by a number of companies (at no extra cost to clients), offers its own tours, and matches singles with traveling companions. Many offerings are listed in their quarterly *Singles Vacation Newsletter,* which costs $7.50 per issue or $20 per year.

A good book for single travelers is *Traveling On Your Own,* by Eleanor Berman, which offers tips on traveling solo and includes information on trips for singles, ranging from outdoor adventures to educational programs. Available in bookstores, it also can be ordered by sending $12.95, plus postage and handling, to Random House, Order Dept., 400 Hahn Rd., Westminster, MD 21157 (phone: 800-733-3000).

Single travelers also may want to subscribe to *Going Solo,* a newsletter that offers helpful information on going on your own. Issued eight times a year, a subscription costs $36. Contact Doerfer Communications, PO Box 1035, Cambridge, MA 02238 (phone: 617-876-2764).

An attractive alternative for the single traveler is *Club Med,* which operates scores of resorts in more than 37 countries worldwide and caters to the single traveler, as well as couples and families. Though the clientele often is under 30, there is a considerable age mix; the average age is 37. *Club Med* has five Mexican resorts — including one in Ixtapa — and offers single travelers package vacations that include airfare, food, wine, lodging, entertainment, and athletic facilities. The atmosphere is relaxed, the dress is informal, and the price reasonable. For information, contact *Club Med* (3 E. 54th St., New York, NY 10022; phone: 800-CLUB-MED). For further information on accommodations options suitable for singles, see our discussions in *On the Road,* in this section.

Hints for Older Travelers

Special discounts and more free time are just two factors that have given Americans over age 65 a chance to see the world at affordable prices. Senior citizens make up an ever-growing segment of the travel population, and the trend among them is to travel more frequently and for longer periods of time.

PLANNING: When planning a vacation, prepare your itinerary with one eye on your own physical condition and the other on a topographical map. Keep in mind variations in climate, terrain, and altitudes, which may pose some danger for anyone with heart or breathing problems.

Older travelers may find the following publications of interest:

The Discount Guide for Travelers Over 55, by Caroline and Walter Weintz, is an excellent book for budget-conscious older travelers. It is available by sending $7.95, plus shipping and handling, to Penguin USA (Att. Cash Sales, 120 Woodbine St., Bergenfield, NJ 07621); when ordering specify the ISBN number: 0-525-48358-6.

The International Health Guide for Senior Citizen Travelers, by Dr. W. Robert Lange, covers a variety of topics. It also includes a list of resource organizations that provide medical assistance for travelers. It is available for $4.95 postpaid from Pilot Books, 103 Cooper St., Babylon, NY 11702 (phone: 516-422-2225).

The Mature Traveler is a monthly newsletter that provides information on travel discounts, places of interest, and useful tips for travelers 49 and up. To subscribe, send $21.95 to GEM Publishing Group, PO Box 50820, Reno, NV 89513 (phone: 702-786-7419).

Travel Easy: The Practical Guide for People Over 50, by Rosalind Massow, discusses a wide range of travel-related subjects. It's available for $6.50 (plus postage) to members of the *American Association of Retired Persons (AARP),* and for $8.95 (plus postage) to non-members. Order from AARP Books, c/o Customer Service, Scott, Foresman & Company, 1900 E. Lake Ave., Glenview, IL 60025 (phone: 708-729-3000).

Travel Tips for Older Americans is a useful booklet with general advice. To order send a check or money order for $1 to the Superintendent of Documents (US Government Printing Office, Washington, DC 20402) or call 202-783-3238 for credit card orders; request stock number 044-000-02270-2.

Unbelievably Good Deals & Great Adventures That You Absolutely Can't Get Unless You're Over 50, by Joan Rattner Heilman, offers travel tips for older travelers, including discounts on accommodations and transportation, as well as a list of organizations for seniors. It is available for $7.95, plus shipping and handling, from Contemporary Books, 180 N. Michigan Ave., Chicago, IL 60601 (phone: 312-782-9181).

HEALTH: Health facilities in Mexico generally are good; however, an inability to speak the language can pose a problem. For information on organizations that help travelers avoid or deal with medical emergencies abroad, see *Medical and Legal Aid and Consular Services,* in this section.

Pre-trip medical and dental checkups are strongly recommended for older travelers. Prepare a personal medical kit to take abroad, which should include vital medical information, enough of any medication you need to last for the duration of your trip, and some basic first-aid ingredients (for further information, see *Staying Healthy,* in this section).

DISCOUNTS AND PACKAGES: Although guidelines change from place to place, many hotel and motel chains, airlines, car rental companies, and other travel suppliers offer discounts to older travelers. In order to take advantage of these discounts, you should carry proof of your age (or eligibility). A driver's license, membership card in a recognized senior citizens' organization, or a Medicare card should be adequate.

Some of these discounts, however, are extended only to bona fide members of certain senior citizens organizations. Because the same organizations frequently offer package tours, the benefits of membership are twofold: Those who join can take advantage of discounts as individual travelers and also reap the savings that group travel affords. In addition, because the age requirements for some of these organizations are quite low (or nonexistent), the benefits can begin to accrue early. Among the organizations dedicated to helping older travelers see the world are the following:

American Association of Retired Persons (*AARP;* 1909 K St. NW, Washington, DC 20049; phone: 202-872-4700). The largest and best known of these organizations. Membership is open to anyone 50 or over, whether retired or not; dues are $5 a year, $12.50 for 3 years, or $35 for 10 years, and include spouse. The *AARP* Travel Experience program, available through *American Express Travel Related Services,* offers members tours, cruises, and other travel programs designed exclusively for older travelers that cover the globe. Members can book these services by calling *American Express* at 800-927-0111 for land and air travel, or 800-745-4567 for cruises.

Mature Outlook (Customer Service Center, 6001 N. Clark St., Chicago, IL 60660; phone: 800-336-6330). Through its *TravelAlert,* tours, cruises, and other vacation packages are available to members at special savings. Hotel and car rental discounts and travel accident insurance also are available. Membership is open to anyone 50 years of age or older, costs $9.95 a year, and includes a bimonthly newsletter and magazine.

National Council of Senior Citizens (925 15th St. NW, Washington, DC 20005; phone: 202-347-8800). Here, too, the emphasis is on keeping costs low. This nonprofit organization offers members a different roster of package tours each year, as well as individual arrangements through its affiliated travel service *(Vantage Travel Service).* Although most members are over 50, membership is open to anyone (regardless of age) for an annual fee of $12 per person or couple. Lifetime membership costs $150.

Certain travel agencies and tour operators offer special trips geared to older travelers. Among them are the following:

Evergreen Travel Service (4114-198th St. SW, Suite 13, Lynnwood, WA 98036-6742; phone: 206-776-1184 or 800-435-2288 throughout the continental US and Canada). This specialist in trips for persons with disabilities recently introduced Lazybones Tours, a program offering leisurely tours for older travelers.

Gadabout Tours (700 E. Tahquitz, Palm Springs, CA 92262; phone: 619-325-5556 or 800-521-7309 in California; 800-952-5068 elsewhere in the US). Offers a variety of escorted tours and cruises.

Grand Circle Travel (347 Congress St., Boston, MA 02210; phone: 800-221-2610 or 617-350-7500). Caters exclusively to the over-50 traveler and packages a large variety of escorted tours, cruises, and extended vacations. Membership, which is automatic when you book a trip through *Grand Circle,* includes discount certificates on future trips and other extras, including a helpful free booklet, *Going Abroad: 101 Tips for Mature Travelers.*

Saga International Holidays (120 Boylston St., Boston MA 02116; phone: 617-451-6808 or 800-343-0273). Offers a broad selection of packages for people age 60 and over or those 50 to 59 traveling with someone 60 or older. Although anyone can book a *Saga* trip, a $15 club membership includes a subscription to their newsletter, as well as other publications and travel services.

Many travel agencies, particularly the larger ones, are delighted to make presentations to help a group of senior citizens select destinations. A local chamber of commerce should be able to provide the names of such agencies. Once a time and place are determined, an organization member or travel agent can obtain group quotations for transportation, accommodations, meal plans, and sightseeing. Larger groups usually get the best breaks.

Hints for Traveling with Children

What better way to encounter the world's variety than in the company of the young, wide-eyed members of your family? Their presence does not have to be a burden or an excessive expense. The current generation of discounts for children and family package deals can make a trip together quite reasonable.

A family trip will be an investment in your children's future, making geography and history come alive to them, and leaving a sure memory that will be among the fondest you will share with them someday. Their insights will be refreshing to you; their impulses may take you to unexpected places with unexpected dividends. The experience will be invaluable to them at any age.

PLANNING: Here are several hints for making a trip with children easy and fun:

1. Children, like everyone else, will derive more pleasure from a trip if they know something about their destination before they arrive. Begin their education about a month before you leave. Using maps, travel magazines, and books gives children a clear idea of where you are going and how far away it is.

2. Children should help to plan the itinerary, and where you go and what you do should reflect some of their ideas. If they already know something about the sites they'll visit, they will have the excitement of recognition when they arrive.
3. Children also will enjoy learning some Spanish phrases — a few basics like "*hola!*" (hello), "*adiós*" (good-bye), and "*gracias*" (thanks).
4. Familiarize the children with *pesos.* Give them an allowance for the trip, and be sure they understand just how far it will or won't go.
5. Give children specific responsibilities: The job of carrying their own flight bags and looking after their personal things, along with some other light travel chores, will give them a stake in the journey.
6. Give each child a travel diary or scrapbook to take along.

One useful resource to which you may want to refer is the *Berlitz Jr. Spanish* instructional series for children. The series combines an illustrated storybook with a lively 60-minute audiocassette; the set is available for $19.95, plus shipping and handling, from Macmillan Publishing Company, Front and Brown Sts., Riverside, NJ 08075 (phone: 800-257-5755).

For parents, *Travel With Your Children* (*TWYCH;* 80 Eighth Ave., New York, NY 10011; phone: 212-206-0688) publishes a newsletter, *Family Travel Times,* that focuses on families with young travelers and offers helpful hints. An annual subscription (10 issues) is $35 and includes a copy of the "Airline Guide" issue (updated every other year), which focuses on the subject of flying with children. This special issue is available separately for $10.

Another newsletter devoted to family travel is *Getaways.* This quarterly publication provides reviews of family-oriented literature, activities, and useful travel tips. To subscribe, send $25 to *Getaways,* att. Ms. Brooke Kane, PO Box 11511, Washington, DC 20008 (phone: 703-534-8747).

Also of interest to parents traveling with their children is *How to Take Great Trips With Your Kids,* by psychologist Sanford Portnoy and his wife, Joan Flynn Portnoy. The book includes helpful tips from fellow family travelers, a chapter on child development relating to travel, tips on economical accommodations and touring by car, as well as over 50 games to play with your children en route. It is available for $8.95, plus shipping and handling, from Harvard Common Press, 535 Albany St., Boston, MA 02118 (phone: 617-423-5803).

Another book on family travel, *Travel with Children* by Maureen Wheeler, offers a wide range of practical tips on traveling with children. It is available for $10.95, plus shipping and handling, from Lonely Planet Publications, Embarcadero West, 112 Linden St., Oakland, CA 94607 (phone: 415-893-8555).

Parents arranging a trip with their children may want to deal with an agency specializing in family travel, such as *Let's Take the Kids* (1268 Devon Ave., Los Angeles, CA 90064; phone: 800-726-4349 or 213-274-7088). In addition to arranging and booking trips for individual families, this group occasionally organizes trips for single-parent families traveling together. They also offer a "parent travel network," whereby parents who have been to a particular destination can evaluate it for others.

GETTING THERE AND GETTING AROUND: Begin early to investigate all available family discount and charter flights, as well as any package deals and special rates offered by the major airlines.

Plane – When you make your reservations, tell the airline that you are traveling with a child. Children ages 2 through 12 generally travel at about half to two-thirds of an adult economy fare on international flights (although excursion and other discount fares may be even less expensive). Depending on the airline, children under 2 may travel free or at 10% of the adult fare if they sit on an adult's lap. The fare for a second infant without a second adult would be the same as the fare applicable to children ages 2 through 11.

Although some airlines will, on request, supply bassinets for infants, most carriers encourage parents to bring their own safety seat on board, which then is strapped into the airline seat with a regular seat belt. This is much safer — and certainly more comfortable — than holding the child in your lap. If you do not purchase a seat for your baby, you have the option of bringing the infant restraint along on the off-chance that there might be an empty seat next to yours — in which case some airlines will let you use that seat at no charge for your baby and infant seat. However, if there is no empty seat available, the infant seat no doubt will have to be checked as baggage (and you may have to pay an additional charge), since it generally does not fit under the seat or in the overhead racks. The safest bet is to pay for a seat.

Be forewarned: Some safety seats designed primarily for use in cars do not fit into plane seats properly. Most seats carry labels indicating whether they meet federal standards for use aboard planes, but actual seat sizes may vary from carrier to carrier. At the time of this writing, the FAA was in the process of reviewing and revising the federal regulations regarding infant travel and safety devices — it was still to be determined if children should be *required* to sit in safety seats and whether the airlines will have to provide them.

If using one of these infant restraints, you should try to get bulkhead seats, which will provide extra room to care for your child during the flight. You also should request a bulkhead seat when using a bassinet — again, this is not as safe as strapping the child in. On some planes bassinets hook into a bulkhead wall; on others it is placed on the floor in front of you. (Note that bulkhead seats often are reserved for families traveling with children.) As a general rule, babies should be held during takeoff and landing.

Request seats on the aisle if you have a toddler or if you think you will need to use the bathroom frequently. Carry onto the plane all you will need to care for and occupy your children during the flight. Dress your baby simply, because the only place you may have to change a diaper is at your seat or in a small lavatory.

You also can ask for a hot dog or hamburger instead of the airline's regular dinner if you give at least 24 hours' notice. Some, but not all, airlines have baby food aboard. While you should bring along toys from home, also ask about children's diversions. Some carriers have terrific free packages of games, coloring books, and puzzles.

When the plane takes off and lands, make sure your baby is nursing or has a bottle, pacifier, or thumb in its mouth. This sucking will make the child swallow and help to clear stopped ears. A piece of hard candy will do the same thing for an older child.

Parents traveling by plane with toddlers, children, or teenagers may want to consult *When Kids Fly,* a free booklet published by Massport (Public Affairs Dept., 10 Park Plaza, Boston, MA 02116-3971; phone: 617-973-5600), which includes helpful information on airfares for children, infant seats, what to do in the event of overbooked or canceled flights, and so on.

■ **Note:** Newborn babies, whose lungs may not be able to adjust to the altitude, should not be taken aboard an airplane. And some airlines may refuse to allow a pregnant woman in her 8th or 9th month aboard, for fear that something could go wrong with an in-flight birth. Check with the airline ahead of time and carry a letter from your doctor stating that you are fit to travel — and indicating the estimated date of birth.

Ship – Some shipping lines offer cruises that feature special activities for children, particularly during periods that coincide with major school holidays like *Christmas, Easter,* and the summer months. On such cruises, children may be charged special cut-rate fares. Occasionally, a shipping line even offers free passage during the summer months for children under the age of 16 occupying a stateroom with two (full-fare) adult passengers. Your travel agent should know which cruise lines offer such programs.

Car – Traveling by car allows greater flexibility in traveling and packing. You may want to stock the car with a variety of favorite snacks, and if you pack an ice chest and a grill, you can stop for picnics (most beaches are public and free in Mexico). You may want to bring dry ice, since ice isn't so easy to come by in rural areas. Near the larger cities, ice cubes are sold at gasoline service stations and ice blocks are available from the local beer distributors. However, use this ice only for keeping food chilled in coolers — *never* put it in drinks, as you can't count on the quality of the water from which it was made.

ACCOMMODATIONS AND MEALS: Often a cot will be placed in a hotel room at little or no extra charge. If you wish to sleep in separate rooms, special rates sometimes are available for families; some places do not charge for children under a certain age. Cabins, bungalows, condominiums, and other rental options offer families privacy, flexibility, some kitchen facilities, and often low costs.

It is difficult to find adequate baby-sitting services in most Mexican cities, but most better hotels will try to arrange for a sitter. Whether the sitter is hired directly or through an agency, ask for and check references and keep in mind that the candidates may not speak much, if any, English.

At mealtime, don't deny yourself or your children the delights of a new style of cooking. Children like to know what kind of food to expect, so it will be interesting to look up Mexican dishes before leaving. Encourage your children to try new things; however, even though simple tacos, burritos, and cheese-filled tortillas are similar to hamburgers and grilled cheese sandwiches, they may not fill the bill for some children. In resort areas such as Ixtapa and Zihuatanejo, you should be able to find American-style food.

Things to Remember

1. If you are spending your vacation touring, pace the days with children in mind. Break the trip into half-day segments, with running around or "doing" time built in.
2. Don't forget that a child's attention span is far shorter than an adult's. Children don't have to see every sight or all of any sight to learn something from their trip; watching, playing with, and talking to other children can be equally enlightening.
3. Let your children lead the way sometimes; their perspective is different from yours, and they may lead you to things you would never have noticed on your own.
4. Remember the places that children love to visit: aquariums, zoos, beaches, nature trails, and so on. Among activities that may pique their interest are bicycling, snorkeling, boat trips, exploring ruins, and viewing natural habitat exhibits.

Staying Healthy

The surest way to return home in good health is to be prepared for medical problems that might occur on vacation. Below we've outlined some things you need to think about before you go.

Typically, tourists suffer two kinds of health problems in Mexico, but neither is inevitable. The first is the stomach upset known the world over as the scourge of travelers: Cairo Crud, Delhi Belly, *la turista,* and in Mexico, Montezuma's Revenge. The second is even more familiar: sunburn. And as a number of diseases are contracted through bug bites (see below), some precaution against biting insects is strongly advised.

Older travelers or anyone suffering from a chronic medical condition, such as diabetes, high blood pressure, cardiopulmonary disease, asthma, or ear, eye, or sinus trouble, should consult a physician before leaving home. Those with conditions requiring special consideration when traveling should consider seeing, in addition to their regular physician, a specialist in travel medicine. For a referral in a particular community, contact the nearest medical school or ask a local doctor to recommend such a specialist. Dr. Leonard Marcus, a member of the *American Committee on Clinical Tropical Medicine and Travelers' Health,* provides a directory of more than 100 travel doctors across the US. For a copy, send a 9-by-12-inch self-addressed, stamped envelope, plus postage, to Dr. Marcus at 148 Highland Ave., Newton, MA 02165 (phone: 617-527-4003).

FIRST AID: Put together a compact, personal medical kit including Band-Aids, first-aid cream, antiseptic, nose drops, insect repellent, aspirin or non-aspirin tablets, an extra pair of prescription glasses or contact lenses (and a copy of your prescription for glasses or contact lenses), sunglasses, over-the-counter remedies for diarrhea, indigestion, and motion sickness, a thermometer, and a supply of those prescription medicines you take regularly.

In a corner of your kit, keep a list of all the drugs you have brought and their purpose, as well as duplicate copies of your doctor's prescriptions (or a note from your doctor). As brand names may vary in different countries, it's a good idea to ask your doctor for the generic name of any drugs you use so that you can ask for their equivalent should you need a refill. Unless it is an emergency, however, some prescriptions may require the signature of a Mexican physician. (In recent years the Mexican Health Ministry has developed a list of restricted drugs and medicines, which includes certain seasickness tablets, that require a written prescription from a local doctor.)

It also is a good idea to ask your doctor to prepare a medical identification card that includes such information as your blood type, any allergies or chronic health problems you have, and any special information that may aid diagnosis of an emergency condition — for instance, if you have heart problems, a copy of your most recent electrocardiogram. This kit also should include your doctor's name, address, and telephone number, as well as your social security number and information on your medical insurance. Considering the essential contents of this kit, keep it with you, rather than in your checked luggage.

■ **Note:** A word of warning is necessary about injections (given by doctors or by pharmacists): The needles may be used more than once, and sterilization is not as dependable as it is in the US. Improperly disinfected needles can be a source of AIDS (Acquired Immune Deficiency Syndrome), hepatitis, and other infectious diseases, so insist that the doctor or pharmacist use disposable syringes. (If you have a condition that may require occasional injections, bring your own supply; disposable syringes also are available in Mexico.) Also be aware that some over-the-counter remedies sold in Mexico contain antibiotics sold only by prescription in the US, which may cause allergic reactions or other side effects.

DIARRHEA AND STOMACH UPSETS: Without a doubt, a traveler's most serious complaint traveling in Mexico is dysentery or diarrhea, accompanied by severe intestinal pain and a foul taste in the mouth.

It is very important to take the first few days easy, especially if you land in Mexico City, where the high altitude will be tiring and exacerbate the effect of any alcohol on your system; so drink and eat lightly on arrival.

Fortunately, the vast majority of intestinal disorders encountered during travel represent only a temporary inconvenience, which will go away with rest and time. Serious intestinal trouble almost invariably is the product of drinking water contaminated by a particular strain of *E. coli* bacteria. These bacteria inhabit the human intestinal tract and are transmitted through fecal matter, and from there into plumbing and any unpurified water system. The result most often is called Montezuma's Revenge.

There is a very simple way to avoid it: Don't drink the water. Brush your teeth with bottled water (be sure you're not getting a used bottle refilled with tap water). Wash fruit with purified water, and don't drink iced drinks where the ice has been made from tap water. If you are staying in a first class hotel in a major tourist area, you will be in no danger. Elsewhere, and as a matter of course, it is wise to stick to bottled water (ask for *agua purificada* or *agua mineral*) or substitute wine or beer at meals. You also might carry standard GI water purification tablets (tetraglycine hydroperiodide). Just drop one of these tablets in a carafe of water and let it stand for half an hour.

We also recommend that you eat only those fruits that have been peeled (oranges, bananas, and so on), and cooked vegetables. Garnishes of fresh vegetables (even a small amount of shredded lettuce and tomatoes) and salads (especially those with creamy or mayonnaise-based dressings that have been out on serving tables for any period of time) can wreak havoc with your gastrointestinal system the morning after. Stay away from unfamiliar dishes that are hard to identify, and those tempting-looking alcoholic concoctions served in coconuts or pineapples, as well as fruit juices — even in the better hotels, these may be diluted with tap water. Do not drink or eat raw milk, unpasteurized or uncooked dairy products, and, above all, stay away from food vendors on streets and beaches.

Be sure to carry along an anti-diarrhea medication and recommended antibiotic in case you do develop symptoms. Before you go, pick up a mild over-the-counter preparation, such as Kaopectate, which if used according to directions should have you back on your feet within 12 to 14 hours (although this comes in a bulky bottle). Many find Pepto-Bismol equally effective, and it comes in a handier tablet form. You also may want to ask your doctor to recommend one of the stronger medications containing an antibiotic. If you are stricken with diarrhea and have no medication with you, have your hotel call a doctor or visit the nearest pharmacy.

INFECTIOUS HEPATITIS OR JAUNDICE: The most serious potential threat to a good vacation, hepatitis (nicknamed the Big H by gringos) frequently is caused by dirty hypodermic needles, a risk even in hospitals. If you are a diabetic or require regular injections for any other condition, carry disposable plastic hypodermic syringes (available in pharmacies). It also may be contracted from contaminated drinking water or food.

■ **Note:** Before you leave for Mexico, check specifically with your local county or state health department, or call the US State Department's *Citizens' Emergency Center* at 202-647-5225 for the most up-to-date information on health conditions and other vital information.

SUNBURN: The burning power of the sun can quickly cause severe sunburn or sunstroke. To protect yourself against these ills, wear sunglasses, take along a broad-brimmed hat and cover-up, and use a sunscreen lotion.

INSECTS AND OTHER PESTS: Insects in parts of Mexico — including the Pacific Coast — can be not only a nuisance but also a real threat, carrying infectious diseases such as malaria. To avoid contact in areas of infestation, do not sleep on the ground and, if possible, sleep under mosquito netting.

It is a good idea to use some form of topical insect repellent — those containing DEET (N,N-diethyl-m-toluamide) are among the most common and effective. The US Environmental Protection Agency (EPA) stresses that you should not use any pesticide that has not been approved by the EPA (check the label) and that all such preparations should be used in moderation. If picnicking, burn mosquito coils or candles containing allethrin, pyrethrin, or citronella, or use a pyrethrum-containing flying insect spray. For further information about active ingredients in repellents, call the National Pesticide Telecommunications Network's 24-hour hotline number: 800-858-7378.

If you do get bitten — by mosquitoes or other bugs — the itching can be relieved with baking soda, topical first-aid creams, or antihistamine tablets. Should a bite become infected, treat it with a disinfectant or antibiotic cream.

Though rarer, bites from scorpions, snakes, or spiders can be serious. If possible, always try to catch the villain for identification purposes. If bitten, the best course of action may be to head directly to the nearest emergency ward or outpatient clinic of a hospital. Cockroaches and termites thrive in warm climates, but pose no serious health threat.

PREVENTION AND IMMUNIZATION: Specific information on the health status of any area in Mexico can be secured from its consular services in the US. The Centers for Disease Control publishes a comprehensive booklet, *Health Information for International Travel,* which lists vaccination requirements and other health information for Mexico. To order, send a check or money order for $5 to the Superintendent of Documents (US Government Printing Office, Washington, DC 20402), or charge it to your credit card by calling 202-783-3238. For information on vaccination requirements, disease outbreaks, and other health information pertaining to traveling abroad, you also can call the Centers for Disease Control's 24-hour International Health Requirements and Recommendations Information Hotline: 404-332-4559.

Another useful publication, *Health Hints for the Tropics,* offers tips on immunization and other preventive measures. It is available by sending $4 to Dr. Karl A. Western, *American Society of Tropical Medicine and Hygiene,* 6436 31st St. NW, Washington, DC 20015-2342.

If you live in or near New York City, you can take advantage of the *International Health Care Service* (New York Hospital–Cornell Medical Center, 525 E. 68th St., Box 210, New York, NY 10021; phone: 212-746-1601), which provides a variety of travel-related health services, including pre- and post-travel screenings and various inoculations at per-shot rates. Appointments are required for all services. Their *International Health Care Traveler's Guide,* a compendium of facts and advice on health care and diseases around the world, can be obtained by sending $4.50 and a self-addressed, stamped envelope to the service.

WATER SAFETY: Mexico's beaches are so beautiful, with sands so caressing and waters so crystalline, that it's hard to remember that the waters also can be treacherous. A few precautions are necessary. Beware of the undertow, that current of water running back down the beach after a wave has washed ashore; it can knock you off your feet and into the surf. Even more dangerous is the riptide, a strong current of water running against the tide, which can pull you out toward the sea. If you get caught offshore, don't panic or try to fight the current, because it will only exhaust you; instead, ride it out while waiting for it to subside, which usually happens not too far from shore, or try swimming away parallel to the beach.

Sharks are sometimes sighted, but they usually don't come in close to shore, and they are well fed on fish. Should you meet up with one, just swim away as quietly and smoothly as you can, without shouting or splashing.

The tentacled Portuguese man-of-war and other jellyfish drift in quiet salt waters and often wash up onto the beach; the long tentacles of these creatures sting whatever they touch. Specialists recommend carrying a small bottle of household vinegar and a container of unseasoned meat tenderizer in your beach bag. If stung, pour vinegar over the irritation to neutralize the effect of the sting and then apply a paste made of vinegar and meat tenderizer to break down the residual venom.

Mexico's coral reefs are extensive and razor sharp. Treat all coral cuts with an antiseptic, and then watch for any signs of infection, since coral is a living organism with bacteria on its surface. If you step on a sea urchin, you'll find that the spines are very sharp, pierce the skin, and break off easily. Like splinters, the tips left embedded in the skin are difficult to remove, but they will dissolve in a week or two; rinsing with vinegar may help to dissolve them more quickly. To avoid these hazards, keep your feet covered whenever possible.

Following all these precautions will not guarantee an illness-free trip, but should minimize the risk. As a final hedge against economic if not physical problems, make sure your health insurance will cover all eventualities while you are away. If not, there are policies designed specifically for travel. Many are worth investigating. As with all insurance, they seem like a waste of money until you need them. For more information, also see *Insurance* and *Medical and Legal Aid and Consular Services,* both in this section.

HELPFUL PUBLICATIONS: Practically every phase of health care — before, during, and after a trip — is covered in *The New Traveler's Health Guide,* by Drs. Patrick J. Doyle and James E. Banta. It is available for $4.95, plus postage and handling, from Acropolis Books Ltd., 13950 Park Center Rd., Herndon, VA 22071 (phone: 800-451-7771 or 703-709-0006).

The *Traveling Healthy Newsletter,* which is published six times a year, also is brimming with health-related travel tips. For an annual subscription, which costs $24, contact Dr. Karl Neumann (108-48 70th Rd., Forest Hills, NY 11375; phone: 718-268-7290). Dr. Neumann also is the editor of the useful free booklet *Traveling Healthy,* which is available by writing to the Travel Healthy Program (PO Box 10208, New Brunswick, NJ 08906-9910; phone: 215-732-4100).

For more information regarding preventive health care for travelers, contact the *International Association for Medical Assistance to Travelers* (*IAMAT;* 417 Center St., Lewiston, NY 14092; phone: 716-754-4883).

On the Road

Credit and Currency

It may seem hard to believe, but one of the greatest (and least understood) costs of travel is money itself. So your one single objective in relation to the care and retention of your travel funds is to make them stretch as far as possible. This requires more than merely ferreting out the best airfare or the most charming budget hotel. It means being canny about the management of money itself. Herewith, a primer on making money go as far as possible while traveling.

CURRENCY: The basic medium of exchange in Mexico is the peso, which, like the dollar, is based on a decimal system and subdivides into 100 units, called centavos. Used only as a basis for translating dollars into pesos, the centavo has been taken out of circulation. Paper bills *(billetes)* are found in denominations of 1,000, 2,000, 5,000, 10,000, 20,000 and 50,000 pesos. Coins *(monedas)* are found in 1-peso, 5-peso, 10-peso, 20-peso, 50-peso, 100-peso, 200-peso, 500-peso, 1,000-peso, and 5,000-peso denominations.

Although US dollars may be accepted in Mexico (particularly at points of entry), you certainly will lose a percentage of your dollar's buying power if you do not take the time to convert it into the local legal tender. By paying for goods and services in the local currency, you save money by not negotiating invariably unfavorable exchange rates for every small purchase, and avoid difficulty where US currency is not readily — or happily — accepted. *Throughout this book, unless specifically stated otherwise, prices are given in US dollars.*

There is no limit to the amount of US currency that can be brought into Mexico. To avoid problems anywhere along the line, it's advisable to fill out any customs forms provided when leaving the US on which you can declare all money you are taking with you — cash, traveler's checks, and so on. If taking over $10,000 out of the US, you must report this to US Customs *before* leaving the US, and if returning with such an amount you should include this information on your customs declaration when you return. Although travelers usually are not questioned by customs officials about currency when they enter or leave, the sensible course is to observe all regulations just to be on the safe side.

FOREIGN EXCHANGE: Because of the volatility of exchange rates, be sure to check the current value of the peso before finalizing any travel budget. And before you actually depart on your trip, shop around carefully for the most advantageous exchange rate offered by various financial institutions — US banks, currency exchange firms (at home or abroad), or foreign banks.

For the best sense of current trends, follow the rates posted in the financial section of your local newspaper or in such international newspapers as the *International Herald Tribune.* It also is possible to check with your own bank. *Harold Reuter and Company,* a currency exchange service in New York City (200 Park Ave., Suite 332 E., New York, NY 10166; phone: 212-661-0826), also is particularly helpful in determining current trends in exchange rates; or check with *Thomas Cook Foreign Exchange* (for the nearest location, call 800-972-2192 in Illinois; 800-621-0666 elsewhere in the US). *Ruesch International* also offers up-to-date foreign-currency information and currency-related services (such as converting foreign-currency checks into US dollars). *Ruesch* also offers a pocket-size *Foreign Currency Guide* (good for estimating general equivalents while planning) and a helpful brochure, *6 Foreign Exchange Tips for the Traveler.* Contact *Ruesch International* at one of the following addresses: 3 First National Plaza, Suite 2020, Chicago, IL 60602 (phone: 312-332-5900); 1925 Century Park E., Suite 240, Los Angeles, CA 90067 (phone: 213-277-7800); 608 Fifth Ave., "Swiss Center," New York, NY 10020 (phone: 212-977-2700); or 1350 Eye St. NW, 10th Floor and street level, Washington, DC 20005 (phone: 800-424-2923 or 202-408-1200).

In Mexico, you will find the official rate of exchange posted in banks, airports, money exchange houses, hotels, and some shops. As a general rule, expect to get more pesos for your US dollar at banks than at any other commercial establishment. Exchange rates do change from day to day, and most banks offer the same (or very similar) exchange rates. (In a pinch, the convenience of cashing money in your hotel — sometimes on a 24-hour basis — may make up for the difference in the exchange rate.) Don't try to bargain in banks (or hotels) — no one will alter the rates for you.

If banks are closed, you may want to try the money exchanges *(casas de cambio)* located throughout Mexico, including Ixtapa and Zihuatanejo. Money exchanges are financial institutions that charge a fee for the service of exchanging dollars into pesos. Note that the rates of exchange offered by these establishments usually are less favorable than the terms offered at nearby banks — don't be surprised if you get fewer pesos for your dollar than the rate published in the papers.

That said, however, the following rules of thumb are worth remembering:

Rule number one: Never (repeat: *never*) voluntarily exchange dollars for foreign currency at hotels, restaurants, or retail shops. If you do, you are sure to lose a significant amount of your dollar's buying power. If you do come across a storefront exchange counter offering what appears to be an incredible bargain, there's too much counterfeit specie in circulation to take the chance (see Rule number three, below).

Rule number two: Estimate your needs carefully; if you overbuy, you lose twice — buying and selling back. Every time you exchange money, someone is making a profit, and rest assured it isn't you. Use up foreign notes before leaving, saving just enough for airport departure taxes (which often must be paid in local currency), other last-minute incidentals, and tips.

Rule number three: Don't buy money on the black market. The exchange rate may be better, but it is a common practice to pass off counterfeit bills to unsuspecting foreigners who aren't familiar with the local currency. It's usually a sucker's game, and you almost always are the sucker; it also can land you in jail.

Rule number four: Learn the local currency quickly and keep abreast of daily fluctuations in the exchange rate. Rates change to some degree every day. For rough calculations, it is quick and safe to use round figures, but for purchases and actual currency exchanges, carry a small pocket calculator to help you compute the exact rate. Inexpensive calculators specifically designed to convert currency amounts quickly for travelers are widely available.

When changing money, don't be afraid to ask how much commission you're being charged, and the exact amount of the prevailing exchange rate. In fact, in any exchange of money for goods or services, you should work out the rate before making any payment.

TIP PACKS: It's not a bad idea to buy a *small* amount of foreign coins and banknotes before your departure. The advantage of tip packs are threefold:

1. You become familiar with the currency (really the only way to guard against making mistakes or being cheated during your first few hours in a new country).

2. You are guaranteed some money should you arrive when a bank or exchange counter isn't open or available.
3. You don't have to depend on hotel desks, porters, or taxi drivers to change your money.

TRAVELER'S CHECKS: It's wise to carry traveler's checks on the road instead of (or in addition to) cash, since it's possible to replace traveler's checks if they are stolen or lost; you usually can receive partial or full replacement funds the same day if you have your purchase receipt and proper identification. With adequate proof of identification (credit cards, driver's license, passport), traveler's checks are as good as cash in most hotels, restaurants, stores, and banks. Traveler's checks are issued in both US and Mexican currencies. However, the exchange rates offered by banks generally are better than those offered by the issuing companies, so plan on carrying the bulk of your funds abroad in US dollar denomination traveler's checks.

You will be able to cash traveler's checks fairly easily in major resort areas like Ixtapa and Zihuatanejo, but don't expect to meander into a one-burro town and be able to get instant cash. Also note that more and more establishments are beginning to restrict the amount of traveler's checks they will accept or cash, so it is wise to purchase at least some of your checks in small denominations — say, $10 and $20.

Every type of traveler's check is legal tender in banks around the world, and each company guarantees full replacement if checks are lost or stolen. After that the similarity ends. Some charge a fee for purchase, others are free; you can buy traveler's checks at almost any bank, and some are available by mail. Most important, each traveler's check issuer differs slightly in its refund policy — the amount refunded immediately, the accessibility of refund locations, the availability of a 24-hour toll-free emergency hotline and refund service, and the time it will take for you to receive replacement checks. For instance, *American Express* guarantees replacement of lost or stolen traveler's checks in under 3 hours at any *American Express* office — other companies may not be as prompt. (Note that *American Express*'s 3-hour policy is based on a traveler's being able to provide the serial numbers of the lost checks — without these numbers, refunds can take much longer.)

We cannot overemphasize the importance of knowing how to replace lost or stolen checks. Be sure to make a photocopy of the refund instructions that will be given to you by the issuing institution at the time of purchase. To avoid complications should you need to redeem lost checks (and to speed up the replacement process), keep the purchase receipt and an accurate list, by serial number, of the checks that have been spent or cashed. You may want to incorporate this information in an "emergency packet," also including the numbers of the credit cards you are carrying and any other bits of information you shouldn't be without. Always keep these records separate from the checks and the original records themselves (you may want to give them to a traveling companion to hold).

Although most people understand the necessity of carrying funds in the form of traveler's checks as protection against loss or theft, an equally good reason is that traveler's checks may get a better rate of exchange than cash does — usually by at least 1%. The reasons for this are technical, and less prevalent in Mexico than elsewhere — the official rate of exchange posted by Mexican banks usually is the rate used to exchange *any* form of US currency — but potential savings still exist, and it's a fact of travel life that should not be ignored.

That 1% bonus won't do you much good, however, if you have already have spent it *buying* your traveler's checks. Several of the major traveler's check companies charge 1% for the acquisition of their checks; others don't. To receive fee-free traveler's checks, you may have to meet certain qualifications — for instance, *Thomas Cook* checks issued in US currency are free if you make your travel arrangements through its travel agency; *American Express* traveler's checks are available without charge to members of the *American Automobile Association (AAA).* Holders of some credit cards (such as the *American Express Platinum* card) also may be entitled to free traveler's checks. The issuing institution (e.g., the particular bank at which you purchase them) may itself charge a fee. If you purchase traveler's checks at a bank in which you or your company maintains significant accounts (especially commercial accounts of some size), the bank may absorb the 1% fee as a courtesy.

American Express, Bank of America, Citicorp, MasterCard, Thomas Cook, and *Visa* all offer traveler's checks. Here is a list of the major companies issuing traveler's checks and the numbers to call in the event that loss or theft makes replacement necessary:

American Express: To report lost or stolen checks in the US and Canada, call 800-221-7282; in Mexico, call the nearest *American Express* office, or the Mexican regional center at 905-661-3266 during business hours; 905-598-8133, collect, after 6 PM (eastern standard time).

Bank of America: To report lost or stolen checks throughout the US, call 800-227-3460; in Mexico, call 415-624-5400, collect.

Citicorp: To report lost or stolen checks throughout the US, call 800-645-6556; in Mexico, call 813-623-1709, collect.

MasterCard: To report lost or stolen checks throughout the US, call 800-223-9920; in Mexico, call 212-974-5696, collect.

Thomas Cook MasterCard: To report lost or stolen checks throughout the US, call 800-223-9920; in Mexico, call 609-987-7300, collect.

Visa: To report lost or stolen checks throughout the US, call 800-227-6811; in Mexico, call 415-574-7111, collect.

CREDIT CARDS: Some establishments you may encounter during the course of your travels may not honor any credit cards and some may not honor all cards, so there is a practical reason to carry more than one. The following is a list of credit cards that enjoy wide domestic and international acceptance:

American Express: Cardholders can cash personal checks for traveler's checks and cash at *American Express* or representatives offices in the US up to the following limits (within any 21-day period): up to $1,000 for *Green* and *Optima* cardholders; $5,000 for *Gold* cardholders; and $10,000 for *Platinum* cardholders. Check cashing also is available to cardholders who are guests at participating hotels in the US and Canada (up to $250) and at participating hotels abroad (up to $100), and for holders of airline tickets, at participating airlines (up to $50). Free travel accident, baggage, and car rental insurance if ticket or rental is charged to card; additional insurance also is available for additional cost. For further information or to report a lost or stolen *American Express* card, call 800-528-4800 throughout the continental US; elsewhere in the US and in Mexico, call 212-477-5700, collect.

Carte Blanche: Free travel accident, baggage, and car rental insurance if ticket or rental is charged to card; additional insurance also is available at additional cost. For medical, legal, and travel assistance available worldwide call 800-356-3448 throughout the US; elsewhere, call 214-680-6480, collect. For further information or to report a lost or stolen *Carte Blanche* card, call 800-525-9135 throughout the US; in Mexico, call 303-790-2433, collect.

Diners Club: Emergency personal check cashing for cardholders staying at participating hotels and motels in the US and abroad (up to $250 per stay). Free travel accident, baggage, and car rental insurance if ticket or rental is charged to card;

additional insurance also is available for an additional fee. For medical, legal, and travel assistance available worldwide, call 800-356-3448 throughout the US; elsewhere, call 214-680-6480, collect. For further information or to report a lost or stolen *Diners Club* card, call 800-525-9135 throughout the US; 303-790-2433, collect, in Mexico.

Discover Card: Offered by a subsidiary of Sears, Roebuck & Co., it provides cardholders with cash advances at numerous automatic teller machines and *Sears* stores throughout the US. Please note that *Discover* is *not* accepted in Mexico. For further information or to report a lost or stolen *Discover* card, call 800-DISCOVER.

MasterCard: Cash advances are available at participating banks worldwide. Check with your issuing bank for information. *MasterCard* also offers a 24-hour emergency lost card service; call 800-826-2181 throughout the US; in Mexico, call 314-275-6690, collect.

Visa: Cash advances are available at participating banks worldwide. Check with your issuing bank for information. *Visa* also offers a 24-hour emergency lost card service; call 800-336-8472 throughout the US; elsewhere, call 415-574-7700, collect.

One of the thorniest problems relating to the use of credit cards abroad concerns the rate of exchange at which a purchase is charged. Be aware that the exchange rate in effect on the date that you make a foreign purchase or pay for a foreign service has nothing at all to do with the rate of exchange at which your purchase is billed to you when you get the invoice (sometimes months later) in the US. The amount that the credit card company charges is either a function of the exchange rate at which the establishment's bank processed it or the rate in effect on the day your charge is received at the credit service center. (There is 1-year limit on the time a business can take to forward its charge slips.) If the dollar gets stronger in the time between purchase and billing, your purchase actually costs you less than you anticipated. If the dollar drops in value during the interim, you pay more than you thought you would. There isn't much you can do about these vagaries except to follow one very broad, very clumsy rule of thumb: If the dollar is doing well at the time of purchase, its value increasing against the local currency, use your credit card on the assumption that it still will be doing well when billing takes place. If the dollar is doing badly, assume it will continue to do badly and pay with traveler's checks or cash. If you get too badly stuck, the best recourse is to complain, loudly. Be aware, too, that most credit card companies charge an unannounced, un-itemized 1% fee for converting foreign currency charges to US dollars.

SENDING MONEY TO MEXICO: If you have used up your traveler's checks, cashed as many emergency personal checks as your credit card allows, drawn on your cash advance line to the fullest, and still need money, it is possible to have it sent to you via the following services:

American Express (phone: 800-543-4080). Offers a service called "Moneygram," completing money transfers in anywhere from 15 minutes to 5 days. The sender can go to any *American Express* office in the US and can transfer money by presenting cash, a personal check, money order, or credit card — *Discover, MasterCard, Visa,* or *American Express Optima* (no other *American Express* or other credit cards are accepted). *American Express Optima* cardholders also can arrange for this transfer over the phone. The minimum transfer charge is $25, which rises with the amount of the transaction; the sender can forward funds of up to $10,000 (credit card users are limited to the amount of pre-established credit line). To collect at the other end, the receiver must go to a branch office of *American Express* or an affiliated Mexican bank and show identification (passport, driver's license, or other picture ID).

Western Union Telegraph Company (phone: 800-325-4176). A friend or relative can go, cash in hand, to any *Western Union* office in the US, where, for a *minimum* charge of $14 (it rises with the amount of the transaction), the funds will be transferred to a centralized *Western Union* account. When the transaction is fully processed — in the case of Ixtapa and Zihuatanejo after 2 business days — you can go to any *Western Union* branch office or correspondent bank to pick up the transferred funds. For a higher fee, the US party to this transaction may call *Western Union* with a *MasterCard* or *Visa* number to send up to $2,000, although larger transfers will be sent to a predesignated location.

If you are literally down to your last cent and have no other way to obtain cash, in Ixtapa-Zihuatanejo your best bet is to contact the nearest US consular agent (in Acapulco; phone: 74-857207) who can advise you on how to set these matters in motion. (For further information, see *Medical and Legal Aid and Consular Services,* in this section).

CASH MACHINES: Automatic teller machines (ATMs) are increasingly common worldwide. Some banks provide ATM service only for their own customers at bank branches. If, however, your bank participates in one of the international ATM networks (most do), you can use the "cash card" and your personal identification code or number (also called a PIC or PIN) provided by the bank at any ATM in the same electronic network for financial transactions, including withdrawing cash.

At the time of this writing, ATMs that *are* connected generally belong to either the *Cirrus* (phone: 800-4-CIRRUS) or *Plus System* (phone: 800-THE-PLUS) network. Both networks maintain thousands of ATM locations worldwide, including hundreds of locations throughout Mexico. *MasterCard* holders may use their cards to draw cash against their credit lines on either system, and *Visa* cardholders can use their cards to draw cash from *Plus System* machines. (Note that as we went to press, there was an agreement pending between these two companies to join their networks.)

As we went to press, there was only one *Cirrus* machine in Zihuatanejo (4 Cuauhtémoc Centro). There are, however, a number of both *Cirrus* and *Plus System* machines in nearby Acapulco and other major resort and metropolitan areas, and other locations may be added in Ixtapa-Zihuatanejo by the time you are visiting.

Accommodations

The best Mexican hotels combine the modern, standardized style of American chains with the continental elegance of European service and a lush, tropical charm unique to Mexico. The enormous growth of tourism in Mexico in recent years has been marked by a corresponding growth in accommodations of all kinds and styles. The popular beach resort areas, such as Ixtapa and Zihuatanejo, offer some of the world's most luxurious hotels and resorts in splendid settings.

A number of properties in Ixtapa and Zihuatanejo are part of well-known international hotel chains. The most elegant of these offer a broad range of facilities and amenities, as well as competent, attentive service. These hotels are modern and comfortable, often include fine restaurants, and the prices, as you would expect, are relatively high. Comparable independent establishments in this area often are even more elegant than the chains. Medium-size hotels can be equally modern, or at least modernized, but are more likely to offer local ambience and charm; in general, they're also more reasonably priced. Some establishments offer the added allure of stunning views, snow white beaches, various sports facilities, and spas. In many hotels, you can splurge and enjoy a life of luxury and leisure, sipping exotic drinks beneath a bougainvillea on your own terrace, at a relatively low cost compared to that of the equivalent degree of decadence in the US.

At the other end of the spectrum are hotels that offer moderate to inexpensive accommodations. These include numerous clean and inexpensive hostelries of every type — modern or colonial, secluded, centrally located, or on the road — that offer basic amenities, which may or may not include a private bath, air conditioning, TV sets, in-room telephones, bar and/or meal service, and swimming pools. Here the charm consists of a genuine welcome, personal hospitality, often striking scenery, and privacy.

Since room prices in all Mexican hotels are controlled and regulated by the Mexican Ministry of Tourism, they remain stable within basic categories — reflected in this book in the categories expensive, moderate, and inexpensive. For information on specific properties, see THE CITIES, DIRECTIONS, and DIVERSIONS.

RENTAL OPTIONS: An attractive accommodations alternative for the visitor content to stay in one spot for a week or more is to rent one of the numerous properties available in Ixtapa and Zihuatanejo. These offer a wide range of luxury and convenience, depending on the price you want to pay. One of the charms of staying in a house, apartment, condominium, cottage, villa or other rented vacation home is that you will feel much more like a visitor than a tourist.

A vacation in a furnished rental has both the advantages and disadvantages of living "at home" abroad. It can be less expensive than staying in a first class hotel, although very luxurious and expensive rentals are available, too. It has the comforts of home, including a kitchen, which means saving on food. On the other hand, a certain amount of housework is involved because if you don't eat out, you have to cook, and though some rentals, especially the luxury ones, come with maid service, most don't. (If the rental doesn't include domestic help, arrangements often can be made with a nearby service for far less than in the US.)

For a family, two or more couples, or a group of friends, the per-person cost — even for a more luxurious rental — can be quite reasonable. Weekly and monthly rates are available to reduce costs still more. But best of all is the amount of space, which no conventional hotel room can equal. As with hotels, the rates for properties in some areas are seasonal, rising during the peak travel season, while for others they remain the same year-round. To have your pick of the properties available, you should begin to make arrangements for a rental at least 6 months in advance.

Rental Property Agents and Discounts – There are several ways of finding a suitable rental property. They are listed along with other accommodations in publications of local tourist boards, and it also is possible to find them through a travel agent. Many tour operators regularly include rental packages among their more conventional offerings. In addition, a number of companies specialize in rental vacation packages that typically include rental of the property (or several properties, but usually for a minimum 2- or 3-day stay per location), a rental car, and airfare.

A number of companies rent properties throughout Mexico. They handle the booking and confirmation paperwork, and can be expected to provide more information about the properties they handle than that which might ordinarily be gleaned from a listing in an accommodations guide. Following is a list of such agencies and their offerings in Ixtapa and Zihuatanejo:

La Cure Villas (11661 San Vicente Blvd., Suite 1010, Los Angeles, CA 90049; phone: 800-387-2726 or 416-968-2374). Rents private villas in Zihuatanejo.

Rent a Home International (7200 34th Ave. NW, Seattle, WA 98117; phone: 206-789-9377). Rents private villas in Ixtapa and Zihuatanejo.

Rent a Vacation Everywhere (*RAVE;* 328 Main St. E., Suite 526, Rochester, NY 14604; phone: 716-454-6440). Rents moderate to luxury condominiums and villas in Ixtapa and Zihuatanejo.

Travel Resources (PO Box 935, Coconut Grove, FL 33133; phone: 305-444-8583 or 800-327-5039 throughout the US). Rents condominiums in Ixtapa.

Villas International (71 W. 23rd St., New York, NY 10010; phone: 212-929-7585 in New York State; 800-221-2260 elsewhere in the US). Rents condominiums and villas in Ixtapa and Zihuatanejo.

In addition, a useful publication, the *Worldwide Home Rental Guide,* lists private villages and cottages throughout Mexico, as well as the managing agencies. Issued twice annually, single copies may be available at newsstands for $10 an issue. For a year's subscription (two issues), send $18 to *Worldwide Home Rental Guide,* PO Box 2842, Sante Fe, NM 87504 (phone: 505-988-5188).

When considering a particular vacation rental property, look for answers to the following questions:

- How do you get from the airport to the condominium?
- If the property is on the shore, how far is the nearest beach? Is it sandy or rocky, and is it safe for swimming?
- What size and number of beds are provided?
- How far is the property from whatever else is important to you, such as a golf course or nightlife?
- If there is no grocery store on the premises (which may be comparatively expensive, anyway), how far is the nearest market?
- Are baby-sitters, cribs, bicycles, or anything else you may need for your children available?
- Is maid service provided daily?
- Is air conditioning and/or a phone provided?
- Is a car rental part of the package? Is a car necessary?

Before deciding which rental is for you, make sure you have satisfactory answers to all your questions. Ask your travel agent to find out, or call the company involved directly.

Accommodation Discounts – Several organizations provide a substantial savings on rental (and some hotel) accommodations in Mexico. Reservations are handled by the central office of the organization, or members may deal directly with the rental agencies or individual property owners. To take advantage of the full selection of properties, these organizations often require that reservations be made as much as 6 months in advance — particularly for stays during the holidays or peak travel periods. Companies that provide discounts on accommodations in Ixtapa and Zihuatanejo include the following:

Entry Unlimited (6404 Nancy Ridge Rd., San Diego, CA 92121; phone: 800-843-0265 or 619-558-5838). Up to 50% discounts offered on rentals. Annual membership fee is $39.95 per family.

Hotel Express (3052 El Cajon Blvd., San Diego, CA 92104; phone: 800-634-6526 or 619-284-1135). Offers up to 50% off on rentals. Annual membership fee of $49.95 per family provides discounts on other travel services, but membership is not required for bargains on rental accommodations.

IntlTravel Card (6001 N. Clark St., Chicago, IL 60660; phone: 800-342-0558 or 312-465-8891). Provides discounts on rental and hotel accommodations. The $36 annual membership fee covers a spouse as well.

Time Zones, Business Hours, and Bank Holidays

TIME ZONES: Mexico's west coast operates on central standard time. In winter, if it is 9 AM in Ixtapa and Zihuatanejo (central standard time), it is 7 AM in Los Angeles (Pacific standard time), 8 AM in Denver (mountain standard time), and 10 AM in New York (eastern standard time). As Mexico does not observe daylight saving time, during the summer when this time change is in effect in the US, add 1 hour to each of the equivalent US times.

Mexican timetables use a 24-hour clock to denote arrival and departure times, which means that hours are expressed sequentially from 1 AM. By this method, 9 AM is recorded as 0900, noon as 1200, 1 PM as 1300, 6 PM as 1800, midnight as 2400, and so on. For example, the departure of a tour at 7 AM will be announced as "0700"; one leaving at 7 PM will be noted as "1900."

One further confusion may arise when you're keeping an appointment with a Mexican acquaintance. Although you may be certain that you have already adjusted your watch and that it is working correctly, your companion may not show up until an hour or more after the agreed time. This is neither unusual nor considered impolite. It is simply a different regard for time than is common in the US. And your trip to Mexico may be even more delightful if you relax and adopt this south-of-the-border attitude.

BUSINESS HOURS: While working hours number about the same as those in the US, the times differ considerably. Executives usually begin working at 10 AM and stop for a leisurely, 2-hour lunch around 2 or 3 PM. The afternoon shift runs from about 4 to 7 PM. Mexican stores are generally open from 10 AM to 7 PM.

Most banks are open from 9 AM to 1:30 PM Mondays through Fridays. Key branches of some major banks also may offer additional hours, opening from 4 to 6 PM on weekdays. A few banks may keep even longer hours — staying open from 8:30 AM through 5 PM. Some even may have weekend hours — staying open from 10 AM to 1:30 PM and from 4 to 6 PM on Saturdays, and 10 AM to 1:30 PM on Sundays.

If you are unable to get to the bank, you usually can cash your traveler's checks at money exchanges. Some are open Mondays through Fridays until 5 PM; others close for a midday siesta and stay open until 9 PM. Some also may be open Saturday mornings. (For further information, see *Credit and Currency,* in this section.)

BANK HOLIDAYS: Government offices, banks, and stores are closed on national holidays and often on the days just before and after as well. Many offices (but not banks) close between *Christmas* and *New Year's.* Following are Mexican national holidays and the dates they will be observed this year:

January 1: *New Year's Day (Año Nuevo).*
February 5: *Constitution Day* marks the signing of the constitutions of 1857 and 1915.
March 21: *Birthday of Benito Juárez* honors the man often called the "Abraham Lincoln of Mexico."
April 16: *Holy Thursday.*
April 17: *Good Friday.*
May 1: *Labor Day,* celebrated with parades.
May 5: Anniversary of Mexico's victory over the French at Puebla in 1862.
September 1: The president's state of the union report *(Informe)* and the opening of Congress.
September 16: *Independence Day.*
October 12: *Columbus Day (Día de la Raza).*

November 2: *All Souls' Day* (known in Mexico as the *Day of the Dead*).
November 20: Anniversary of the Mexican Revolution of 1910.
December 12: *Feast of Our Lady of Guadalupe.*
December 25: *Christmas.*
December 31: Banks closed for annual balance.

Mail, Telephone, and Electricity

MAIL: Almost every town throughout the country has a post office, and while there are not many street mailboxes *(buzónes)* on street corners, there are drops in most large hotels, office buildings, and in front of or in every post office.

All foreign postal service is now airmail. The real problem is how long it takes your letter to get from the post office to the plane: Service in Mexico is known as "Burro Express," and can take up several weeks. The good news, however, is that due to the efforts of the Mexican postal authorities, this system is gradually improving.

If you are planning to send packages to destinations either within or outside the country, be sure to have them registered. The procedure is the same as in the US. If your correspondence is important, you may want to send it via one of the special courier services; *Federal Express, DHL,* and other international services are widely available in Mexico. The cost is considerably higher than sending something via the postal service — but the assurance of its timely arrival is worth it.

Several places will receive and hold mail for travelers in Mexico. Mail sent to you at a hotel and clearly marked "Guest Mail, Hold for Arrival" is a safe approach. If you do not know what your address will be, have your mail addressed to the nearest post office in care of the local equivalent of General Delivery: *a/c Lista de Correos.* Note that you are expected to specify the branch, district, zip code *(codigo postal),* and city — and, under the best of conditions, this is very risky. To claim this mail, you must go in person to the post office, ask for General Delivery, and present identification (driver's license, credit card, birth certificate, or passport).

In sending mail to Mexico, avoid using middle names. Mexicans use the paternal and maternal surnames — the paternal is in the middle — and using a middle name could lead to confusion. When inquiring about mail addressed to you, should there be nothing under the first letter of your last name, ask the post office clerk to look for it under the first letter of your first or middle name. If you plan to remain in one place for more than a month, consider renting a post office box *(apartado postal)* in the central post office to eliminate the chance of mail getting lost in local delivery.

If you are an *American Express* customer (a cardholder, a carrier of *American Express* traveler's checks, or on an *American Express Travel Related Services* tour), you can have mail sent to the *American Express* branch office in Ixtapa (in the lobby of the *Camino Real Hotel,* hotel zone; phone: 753-30853). Letters are held free of charge — registered mail and packages are not accepted. You must be able to show an *American Express* card, traveler's checks, or a voucher proving you are on one of the company's tours to avoid paying for mail privileges. Those who aren't clients must pay a nominal charge each time they inquire if they have received mail, whether or not they actually have a letter. There also is a forwarding fee, for clients and non-clients alike. Mail should be addressed to you, care of *American Express,* and should be marked "Client Mail Service." Additional information on this mail service is listed in the pamphlet *Services and Offices,* available from any US branch of *American Express.*

TELEPHONE: Most large Mexican cities and resort areas — including Ixtapa and

Zihuatanejo — have direct dialing to the US. Telephones from which this is not possible require the assistance of the international operator, who can connect you. If you are staying in a small town or in a hotel with no phone, use the phones in local stores or larger hotels. And here again, the operator can tell you the charges.

The procedure for calling Mexico from the US is as follows: dial 011 (the international access code) + 52 (the country code) + the city code + the local number. (The city code for the Ixtapa-Zihuatanejo area is 753; for city codes of other areas, check the front of a telephone book or ask an international operator.) For example, to place a call from anywhere in the US to Ixtapa, dial 011 + 52 + 753 + the local number.

To call the US from anywhere in Mexico, dial 95 + the US area code + the local number. For instance, to call a number in New York City, dial 95 + 212 + the local number.

To make a call from one city in Mexico to another, dial 91 + the city code + the local number. To call a number within the same city code, just dial the local number.

Note that the number of digits in phone numbers is not standardized throughout Mexico and may vary. As making connections in Mexico for either local or international calls sometimes can be hit-or-miss, those who have to make an important call — to make a hotel reservation in another city, for instance — should start to do so as far in advance as possible.

Some important phone numbers throughout Mexico include the following:

Emergency assistance: 915-250-0123 and 915-250-0151 (within Mexico City, do not dial 915)
Long-distance operator: 02 (within Mexico)
International operator: 09 (English-speaking)
Local information: 04
Countrywide information: 01

Hotel Surcharges – Avoiding operator-assisted calls can cut international calling costs considerably and bring rates into a somewhat more reasonable range — except for calls made through hotel switchboards. One of the most unpleasant surprises travelers encounter in many foreign countries is the amount they find tacked onto their hotel bill for telephone calls, because foreign hotels routinely add on astronomical surcharges. (It's not at all uncommon to find 300% to 400% added to the actual telephone charges.)

Until recently, the only recourse against this unconscionable overcharging was to call collect when phoning from abroad or to use a telephone credit card — available through a simple procedure from any local US phone company. Now *American Telephone and Telegraph (AT&T)* offers *USA Direct,* a service that connects users, via a toll-free number, with an *AT&T* operator in the US, who then will put a call through at the standard international rate. A new feature of this service is that travelers abroad can reach US toll-free (800) numbers by calling a *USA Direct* operator, who will connect them. Charges for all calls made through *USA Direct* appear on the caller's regular US phone bill. Note that as we went to press, this service was offered only in a few areas of Mexico, including Ixtapa. For a brochure and wallet card listing toll-free numbers by country, contact International Information Service, *AT&T Communications,* 635 Grand St., Pittsburgh, PA 15219 (phone: 800-874-4000).

Until such services become universal, it's wise to ask about surcharges *before* calling from a hotel. If the rate is high, it's best to use a telephone credit card (although some hotels still may charge a fee for line usage); make a collect call; or place the call and ask the party to call right back. If none of these choices is possible, make international calls from the local post office or special telephone center to avoid surcharges. Another way to keep down the cost of telephoning from Mexico is to leave a copy of your itinerary and telephone numbers with people in the US so that they can call you instead.

■ **Note:** An excellent resource for planning your trip is *AT&T's Toll-Free 800 Directory,* which lists thousands of companies with 800 numbers, both alphabetically (white pages) and by category (yellow pages), including a wide range of travel services — from travel agents to transportation and accommodations. Issued in a consumer edition for $9.95 and a business edition for $14.95, both are available from *AT&T* Phone Centers or by calling 800-426-8686. Other useful directories include the *Toll-Free Travel & Vacation Information Directory* ($4.95 postpaid from Pilot Books, 103 Cooper St., Babylon, NY 11702; phone: 516-422-2225) and *The Phone Booklet* (send $2 to *Scott American Corporation,* Box 88, West Redding, CT 06896).

ELECTRICITY: Mexico's electrical current is the same as that used in the US, so American tourists can bring their own electrical appliances from home. If you want to be fully prepared, bring along an extension cord (the electrical outlet may be farther from the sink than the cord on your razor or hair dryer can reach), and a wall socket adapter with a full selection of plugs to ensure that you'll be able to plug in anywhere. In some areas and establishments, the current may be weak; your electrical equipment still should work, but not up to maximum capacity. So if you use an electric razor, it is wise to pack a manual safety razor, too, just in case.

One good source for sets of plugs and adapters for use worldwide is the *Franzus Company* (PO Box 142, Beacon Falls, CT 06403; phone: 203-723-6664). *Franzus* also publishes a useful brochure, *Foreign Electricity is No Deep Dark Secret,* which provides information about converters and adapter plugs for electrical appliances to be used abroad but manufactured for use in the US. To obtain a free copy, send a self-addressed, stamped envelope to *Franzus;* a catalogue of other travel accessories is available on request.

Medical and Legal Aid and Consular Services

MEDICAL AID: Nothing ruins a vacation or business trip more effectively than sudden injury or illness. As always is the case with both diseases and accidents, prevention is the best cure. And in Mexico this adage applies not only to diarrhea or dysentery, but to more serious diseases like hepatitis and typhoid fever.

Before you go, be sure to check with your insurance company about the applicability of your hospitalization and major medical policies while you're away (see *Insurance,* in this section). Also make sure you get the most up-to-date information available about health conditions in Mexico. Consult your personal physician or contact your county or state health departments, which generally also can administer necessary or recommended inoculations. (For information on specific health problems, recommended immunizations, and other precautions, see *Staying Healthy,* in this section.)

If you fall victim to any accident or malady that seems serious, do not hesitate to go to a doctor. The medical care available in Mexico is not very different from that offered in the US. There are private doctors, every kind of specialist, clinics, both private and government hospitals, dentists, optometrists, pharmacies, drugstores, and most medications found in the US. The quality of health care and the sophistication of medical facilities are less certain in rural and remote areas, and for specialized treatment it often is best to arrange for transportation to the nearest metropolitan center.

If a bona fide emergency occurs, the fastest way to get attention may be to take a taxi to the emergency room of the nearest hospital. An alternative is to dial one of the following numbers for emergency assistance: to summon the police, fire trucks, and ambulances: 915-250-0123 or 915-250-0151 (within Mexico City, do not dial 915). When calling these numbers, state immediately that you are a foreign tourist and then the nature of your problem and your location. Note that ambulance dispatchers may not be bilingual, so travelers with little or no Spanish language ability should try to get someone else to make the call. You also can dial for the operator and ask for someone who speaks English, although you may need an international operator to place a call to the local emergency service and stay on the line as an interpreter. Most emergency services send out well-equipped and well-staffed ambulances, although ambulances in some areas of Mexico may not be equipped with the advanced EMS technology found in the US and may provide only basic medical attention and be used mainly for transportation.

If a doctor is needed for something less than an emergency, there are several ways to find one. If you are staying in a hotel or resort, ask for help in reaching a doctor or other emergency services, or for the house physician, who may visit you in your room or ask you to visit an office. Travelers staying at a hotel of any size probably will find that the doctor on call speaks at least a modicum of English — if not, request one who does. When you register at a hotel, it's not a bad idea to include your home address and telephone number; this will facilitate the process of notifying friends, relatives, or your own doctor in case of an emergency.

Any US consul also can provide a list of English-speaking doctors and dentists in the area the consulate serves. (For a list of US consuls in Mexico, see "Legal Aid and Consular Services," below.) Dialing the emergency numbers (listed below) may also be of help.

Pharmacies *(farmacias)* are a slight variation on the theme to which you are accustomed. While they're owned and operated by licensed pharmacists, diagnoses, prescription filling, and even drug administration often also are done by pharmacists or their assistants. In some areas, pharmacies may take turns staying open for 24 hours. If none is open after normal business hours, you may be able to have one open in an emergency situation — such as for a diabetic needing insulin — for a fee. Contact a local hospital or medical clinic for information about on-call pharmacists. If your complaint is not serious and you wish to avoid the hassle or expense of consulting a physician, the local *farmacia* will be happy to recommend a drug, administer it either in bulk or in single doses, and even give or recommend a doctor to give injections.

Emergency assistance also is available from the various medical programs designed for travelers who have chronic ailments or whose illness requires them to return home:

International Association of Medical Assistance to Travelers (*IAMAT;* 417 Center St., Lewiston, NY 14092; phone: 716-754-4883). Entitles members to the services of participating English-speaking doctors around the world, as well as clinics and hospitals in various locations. Participating physicians agree to adhere to a basic charge of around $40 to see a patient referred by *IAMAT.* To join, simply write to *IAMAT;* in about 3 weeks you will receive a membership card, the booklet of members, and an inoculation chart. A nonprofit organization, *IAMAT* appreciates donations; with a donation of $25 or more, you will receive a set of worldwide climate charts detailing weather and sanitary conditions. (Delivery can take up to 5 weeks, so plan ahead.)

International SOS Assistance (PO Box 11568, Philadelphia, PA 19116; phone: 800-523-8930 or 215-244-1500). Subscribers are provided with telephone access — 24 hours a day, 365 days a year — to a worldwide, monitored, multilingual network of medical centers. A phone call brings assistance ranging from a telephone consultation to transportation home by ambulance or aircraft, or, in some cases, transportation of a family member to wherever you are hospitalized. Individual rates are $35 for 2 weeks of coverage ($3.50 for each additional day), $70 for 1 month, or $240 for 1 year; couple and family rates also are available.

Medic Alert Foundation (2323 N. Colorado, Turlock, CA 95380; phone: 800-ID-ALERT or 209-668-3333). If you have a health condition that may not be readily available to the casual observer — one that might result in a tragic error in an emergency situation — this organization offers identification emblems specifying such conditions. The foundation also maintains a computerized central file from which your complete medical history is available 24 hours a day by phone (the telephone number is clearly inscribed on the emblem). The onetime membership fee, between $25 and $45, is based on the type of metal from which the emblem is made — the choices ranging from stainless steel to 10K gold-filled.

TravMed (PO Box 10623, Baltimore, MD 21204; phone: 800-732-5309 or 301-296-5225). For $3 per day, subscribers receive comprehensive medical assistance while abroad. Major medical expenses are covered up to $100,000, and special transportation home or of a family member to wherever you are hospitalized is provided at no additional cost.

■ **Note:** Those who are unable to take a reserved flight due to personal illness or must fly home unexpectedly due to a family emergency should be aware that airlines may offer a discounted airfare (or arrange a partial refund) if the traveler can demonstrate that his or her situation is indeed a legitimate emergency. Your inability to fly or the illness or death of an immediate family member usually must be substantiated by a doctor's note or the name, relationship, and funeral home where the deceased will be buried. In such cases, airlines often will waive certain advance purchase restrictions, or you may receive a refund check or voucher for future travel at a later date. Be aware, however, that this bereavement fare may not necessarily be the least expensive fare available and, if possible, it is best to have a travel agent check all possible flights through a computer reservations system (CRS).

LEGAL AID AND CONSULAR SERVICES: There is one crucial place to keep in mind when outside the US, namely, the American Services section of the United States Consulate. If you are injured or become seriously ill, the consulate will direct you to medical assistance and notify your relatives. If, while abroad, you become involved in a dispute that could lead to legal action, or if you are stranded abroad without funds, the consulate, once again, is the place to turn. And in the case of natural disasters or civil unrest, consulates around the world handle the evacuation of US citizens if it becomes necessary.

It usually is far more alarming to be arrested abroad than at home. Not only are you alone among strangers, but the punishment can be worse. Granted, the US Consulate can advise you of your rights and provide a list of English-speaking lawyers, but it cannot interfere with the local legal process.

The best advice is to be honest and law-abiding. If you get a traffic ticket, pay it. If you are approached by drug hawkers, ignore them. The penalties for possession of hashish, marijuana, cocaine, and other narcotics are even more severe abroad than in the US. (If you are picked up for any drug-related offense, do not expect US Foreign Service officials to be sympathetic. Chances are they will notify a lawyer and your family and that's about all. See "Drugs," below.)

In the case of minor traffic accidents, it often is most expedient to settle the matter before the police get involved. If the police do get involved in minor accidents or violations, try to establish a fine on the spot and pay it quickly. If you speak the language and feel competent, try to bargain the fine, but wisdom decrees that you do what is necessary to get the matter settled on the spot.

If, however, you are involved in a serious accident, where an injury or fatality results, the first step is to contact the nearest US Consulate and ask the consul to locate a lawyer to assist you. The US Department of State in Washington, DC, insists that any US citizen who is arrested abroad has the right to contact the US embassy or consulate "immediately," but it may be a while before you are given permission to use a phone. Do not labor under the illusion, however, that in a scrape with foreign officialdom, the consulate can act as an arbitrator or ombudsman on an American citizen's behalf. Nothing could be farther from the truth. Consuls have no power, authorized or otherwise, to subvert, alter, or contravene the legal processes, however unfair, of the foreign country in which they serve. Nor can a consul oil the machinery of a foreign bureaucracy or provide legal advice. The consul's responsibilities do encompass "welfare duties" including providing a list of lawyers and information on local sources of legal aid, informing relatives in the US, and organizing and administrating any defense monies sent from home. If a case is tried unfairly or the punishment seems unusually severe, the consul can make a formal complaint to the authorities.

The consulate is not occupied solely with emergencies and is certainly not there to aid in trivial situations, such as canceled reservations or lost baggage, no matter how important these matters may seem to the victimized tourist. The main duties of any consulate are administering statutory services, such as the issuance of passports and visas; providing notarial services; distributing VA, social security, and civil service benefits to resident Americans; taking depositions; handling extradition cases; and reporting to Washington the births, deaths, and marriages of US citizens living within the consulate's domain.

We hope that none of the information in this section will be necessary during your stay in Mexico. If you can avoid legal hassles altogether, you will have a much more pleasant trip. If you run into a confrontation that might lead to legal complications developing with a citizen or with local authorities, the best tactic is to apologize and try to leave as gracefully as possible. In a foreign country where machismo is part of the national character, some things are best left unsettled.

The US Embassy is located in Mexico City (305 Paseo de la Reforma, México, DF 06500; phone: 5-211-0042). The US government also maintains consulates general in nine other cities of Mexico; consular agents operate in ten additional cities. When in Ixtapa-Zihuatanejo, the nearest consular agent is in Acapulco (*Club del Sol* hotel, Local 8, Costera Miguel Alemán, Acapulco, Guerrero; phone: 74-857207).

You also can obtain a booklet with addresses of most US embassies and consulates around the world by writing to the Superintendent of Documents (US Government Printing Office, Washington, DC 20402) and asking for publication #78-77, *Key Offices of Foreign Service Posts.*

The US State Department operates a *Citizens' Emergency Center,* which offers a number of services to US citizens traveling abroad and their families at home. In addition to giving callers up-to-date information on trouble spots, the center will contact authorities abroad in an attempt to locate a traveler or deliver an urgent message. In case of illness, death, arrest, destitution, or repatriation of an American citizen on foreign soil, it will relay information to relatives at home if the consulate is unable to do so. Travel advisory information is available 24 hours a day to people with Touch-Tone phones (phone: 202-647-5225). Callers with rotary phones can get information at this number from 8:15 AM to 10 PM (eastern standard time) on weekdays, 9 AM to 3 PM Saturdays. In the event of an emergency, this number also may be called during these hours. For emergency calls only, at all other times, call 202-634-3600 and ask for the duty officer.

Drinking and Drugs

DRINKING: There are no laws restricting drinking in Mexico — there is not even a minimum drinking age. In fact, the manufacture of alcoholic beverages is one of Mexico's most important industries. Mexican beer is so good that much of it is now being exported to the US, where in some areas it holds its own with American beers — depite its higher imported price. While you're in Mexico, try native brews like Bohemia, Carta Blanca, Corona, Dos Equis, Indio, Negro Modelo, Superior, and Tecate at the source.

Tequila, the national drink, is distilled from the juice of the agave plant, and is the beverage US visitors are most eager to sample. Take it straight, with salt and lime, or in a margarita cocktail, with lime juice and ice, but take it easy. Popular brands include Herradura, Hornitos, José Cuervo, Sauza, Viuda de Romero, and Xalisco.

Mescal is another hard liquor made from the agave cactus, although the taste is quite different from that of tequila; try Gusano de Oro, Gusano Rojo, or Monte Albán. Brandy also is one of Mexico's most popular drinks, and, strangely enough, it often is mixed with Coca-Cola, 7-Up, or mineral water. (Some institutional receptions only serve a choice of brandy and Coke or brandy and soda.) Rum, enjoyed straight, in a daiquiri, or with cola, remains a favorite of tourists and residents alike; Bacardi, Castillo, and Potosí all are well regarded.

If you're a wine buff, don't neglect Mexico's wines — they're continually improving. There is a big price difference between Mexican and imported wines in most restaurants. Among the better-known Mexican vintages are Calafia, La Cetto, Domecq, Don Angel, Hammerhaus, Hildago, Padre Kino, Pinson, Los Reyes, San Lorenzo, San Marcos, Santo Tomás, and Urbiñon.

As in the US, national taxes on alcohol affect the prices of liquor in Mexico, and as a general rule, mixed drinks made from imported liquors (such as whiskey and gin) are more expensive than at home. If you like a toddy before dinner, a good way to save money is to buy a bottle of your favorite brand at the airport before leaving the US and enjoy it in your hotel before setting forth. Or stick to locally produced beverages. If you are buying any quantity of alcohol (such as a case of tequila) in Mexico, be aware that whether you are bringing it with you or having it shipped, you will have to pay US import duties on any quantity over the allowed 1 liter (see *Customs and Returning to the US,* in this section.)

DRUGS: Another way to avoid legal trouble in Mexico is to avoid the drug scene — completely. Illegal narcotics are as prevalent in Mexico as in the US, but the moderate legal penalties and vague social acceptance that marijuana has gained in the US have no equivalents in Mexico. Due to the international war on drugs, enforcement of drug laws is becoming increasingly strict throughout the world. Local Mexican narcotics officers and customs officials are renowned for their absence of understanding and lack of a sense of humor — especially where Americans are involved.

Despite the government's campaign against it, marijuana still is grown in abundance throughout Mexico and is widely available. It is, however, just as illegal in Mexico as it is in the US, and penalties for selling, growing, and smoking it are just as severe. Opiates and barbiturates and other increasingly popular drugs — "white powder" substances like heroin and cocaine, and "crack" (the cocaine derivative) — also are a problem in Mexico, as elsewhere.

The concerted effort by Mexican and other foreign authorities to stamp out drug traffic, with the support and encouragement of the United States, has now become a real war on buyers and sellers in the country — a war that has been — and continues to be — deadly.

It is important to bear in mind that the quantity of drugs involved is of very minor importance. Persons arrested are subject to the laws of the country they are visiting, and in Mexico these laws and their procedures often are very harsh. Once you are in jail, the best lawyers in the country won't be able to get you out — and neither will the US government. Eventually, at the whim of the authorities, you will be tried and, upon conviction, given a stiff sentence. The best advice we can offer is: Don't carry, use, buy, or sell illegal drugs.

Those who carry medicines that contain a controlled drug should be sure to have a current doctor's prescription with them. Ironically, travelers can get into almost as much trouble coming through US customs with over-the-counter drugs picked up abroad that contain substances that are controlled in the US. Cold medicines, pain relievers, and the like often have codeine or codeine derivatives that are illegal, except by prescription, in the US. Throw them out before leaving for home.

- **Be forewarned:** US narcotics agents warn travelers of the increasingly common ploy of drug dealers asking travelers to transport a "gift" or other package back to the US. Don't be fooled into thinking that the protection of US law applies abroad — if accused of illegal drug trafficking, you will be considered guilty until you prove your innocence. In other words, do not, under any circumstances, agree to take anything across the border for a stranger.

Tipping

TIPPING: Many waiters, waitresses, porters, and bellhops in Mexico depend upon tips for their livelihood. The salaries they receive, if they do receive salaries, are far below the equivalent paid in the US (even with the lower Mexican standards of living taken into consideration). There also are situations in which you wouldn't tip in the US but should in Mexico.

In restaurants, tip between 10% and 20% of the bill. For average service in an average restaurant, a 15% tip to the waiter is reasonable, although one should never hesitate to penalize poor service or reward excellent and efficient attention by leaving less or more. (If you notice a 6% or 15% addition to your bill, this usually is a standard tax, called IVA, not a service charge, and a tip still is in order — if you suspect that a gratuity might already be included, ask.)

Although it's not necessary to tip the maître d' of most restaurants — unless he or she has been especially helpful in arranging a special party or providing a table (a few extra dollars *may,* however, get you seated sooner or procure a preferred table) — when tipping is desirable or appropriate, the least amount should be the local equivalent of $5. In the finest restaurants, where a multiplicity of servers are present, plan to tip 5% to the captain. The sommelier (wine waiter) is entitled to a gratuity of approximately 10% of the price of the bottle of wine.

In allocating gratuities at a restaurant, pay particular attention to what has become the standard credit card charge form, which now includes separate places for gratuities for waiters and/or captains. If these separate boxes are not on the charge slip, simply ask the waiter or captain how these separate tips should be indicated. In some establishments, tips indicated on credit card receipts may not be given to the help, so you may want to leave tips in cash.

If you arrive by air, you probably will find a porter with a cart ready to roll your baggage from customs to the cabstand. He should be paid the current equivalent of about $1 to $2 in pesos, depending on how much luggage you have. If you are traveling by train, porters *expect* a tip of about 25¢ to 35¢ per bag — you might want to go higher. Bellhops, doormen, and porters at hotels generally are tipped at the rate of 50¢ to $1 per piece of luggage, along with a small additional amount if a doorman helps with a cab. If you arrive without the right denominations in pesos, tip in US money. (When in doubt, it is preferable to tip — in any denomination or currency — than not to tip.)

In a large hotel or resort, where it is difficult to determine just who out of a horde of attendants actually performed particular services, it is perfectly proper for guests to ask to have an extra 10% to 15% added to their bill. If you prefer to distribute tips yourself, leave the hotel maid at least $1 per day. Tip the concierge and hall porter for specific services only, with the amount of such gratuities dependent on the level of service provided. For any special service you receive in a hotel, a tip is expected — $1 being the minimum for a small service.

Authorized taxi rates are set either by kilometers traveled or by zone, depending on the city or town; in metered cabs current fares are often posted (especially if there has been an increase in fares and the meter has not yet been adjusted). Many cab drivers set their own unofficial fares, and it is a good idea to ask what it will cost to get to a destination before entering the cab and letting the driver take over. Like so many fees in Mexico, this fare is likely to be negotiable. Cab drivers do not expect tips unless they perform some special service. Cabs that you call by phone are slightly more expensive than those that have meters and you hail in the streets.

In Mexico, you may be offered services by young children such as watching your car while you shop and sightsee or cleaning your windshield while you stop at a light. You must be firm with them immediately if you don't want their services; otherwise, when the service is complete give your helper a couple hundred pesos. Arriving and departing from airline terminals also can turn into a battle royal with youngsters over carrying your luggage.

You also may come across uniformed adult car watchers who earn their livelihoods this way. If you find one near your car, give him the current equivalent of $1 in pesos when you return — once you've unlocked the car and made sure everything is still there. If you park your car in a garage or lot, the parking attendant who returns it to you will expect a comparable tip. Unlike in the US, gas station attendants in Mexico expect a tip, even if they don't clean your windshield or check your oil (you should request these services if you want them); 500 to 1,000 pesos is adequate.

Miscellaneous tips: Ushers in theaters should be given about 50¢ after leading you to a seat and giving you a program. Sightseeing tour guides should be tipped. If you are traveling in a group, decide together what you want to give the guide and present it from the group at the end of the tour. If you have been individually escorted, 10% or more of the total tour price is appropriate. Museum and monument guides also are usually tipped a few dollars. Coat checks are worth about 50¢ to $1 a coat, and washroom attendants are tipped — there usually is a little plate with a coin already in it suggesting the expected amount. In barbershops and beauty parlors, tips also are expected, but the percentages vary according to the type of establishment — 10% in the most expensive salons; 15% to 20% in less expensive establishments. (As a general rule, the person who washes your hair should get a small additional tip.)

Tipping aboard ships: Although some cruise lines do have a no-tipping-required policy and you are not penalized by the crew for not tipping, naturally you aren't penalized for tipping either. Never, however, make the mistake of not tipping on the majority of ships, where it is a common, expected practice. Tips should be paid by and for each individual in a cabin, and the general rule of thumb (or palm) is to expect to pay from 10% to 20% of the total cost of the cruise for gratuities — the actual amount within this range is based on the length of the cruise and the extent of personalized services provided. Allow at least $2 to $5 a day for each cabin and dining room steward. Others who may merit tips are deck and wine stewards, porters, and any others who provide personal service. On some ships you can charge your bar tab to your cabin; throw in the tip when you pay it at the end of the cruise. Smart travelers tip twice during a cruise: about midway through the cruise and at the end; even wiser travelers tip a bit at the start of the trip to ensure better service throughout.

Tipping always is a matter of personal preference. In the situations covered above, as well as in any others that arise where you feel a tip is expected or due, feel free to express your pleasure or displeasure. Again, never hesitate to reward excellent and efficient attention and to penalize poor service. Give an extra gratuity and a word of thanks when someone has gone out of his or her way for you. Either way, the more personal the act of tipping, the more appropriate it seems. And if you didn't like the service — or the attitude — don't tip.

Duty-Free Shopping

Duty-free shops are located in all the major international airports throughout Mexico, including Ixtapa and Zihuatanejo. If common sense says that it is always less expensive to buy goods in an airport duty-free shop than to buy them at home or in the streets of a foreign city, travelers should best be aware of some basic facts. Duty-free, first of all, does not mean that the goods travelers buy will be free of duty when they return to the US. Rather, it means that the shop has paid no import tax acquiring goods of foreign make because the goods are not to be used in the country where the shop is located. This is why duty-free goods are available only in the restricted, passengers-only area of international airports or are delivered to departing passengers on the plane. In a duty-free store, travelers save money only on goods of foreign make because they are the only items on which an import tax would be charged in any other store.

There is little reason to delay buying locally made merchandise and/or souvenirs until reaching the airport. In fact, because airport duty-free shops usually pay high rents, the locally made goods sold in them may well be more expensive than they would be in downtown stores. The real bargains are foreign goods, but — let the buyer beware — not all foreign goods are automatically less expensive in an airport duty-free shop. You can get a good deal on even small amounts of perfume, costing less than the usually required minimum purchase, tax-free. Other fairly standard bargains include spirits, smoking materials, cameras, clothing, watches, chocolates, and other food and luxury items — but first be sure to know what these items cost elsewhere. Terrific savings do exist (they are the reason for such shops, after all), but so do overpriced items that an unwary shopper might find equally tempting. In addition, if you wait to do your shopping at airport duty-free shops, you will be taking the chance that the desired item is out of stock or unavailable.

Customs and Returning to the US

Whether you return to the United States by air or land, you must declare to the US Customs official before departing everything you have bought or acquired while in Mexico. The customs check can go smoothly, lasting only a few minutes, or can take hours, depending on the officer's instinct. To speed up the process, keep all your receipts handy and try to pack your purchases together in an accessible part of your suitcase. It might save you from unpacking all your belongings.

DUTY-FREE ARTICLES: In general the duty-free allowance for US citizens returning from abroad is $400. This limit includes items used or worn while abroad, souvenirs for friends, and gifts received during the trip. A flat 10% duty based on the "fair retail value in country of acquisition" is assessed on the next $1,000 worth of merchandise brought in for personal use or gifts. Amounts over $1,400 are dutiable at a variety of rates. The average rate for typical tourist purchases is about 12%, but you can find out rates on specific items by consulting *Tariff Schedules of the United States* in a library or at any US Customs Service office.

Families traveling together may make a joint declaration to US Customs, which permits one member to exceed his or her duty-free exemption to the extent that another falls short. Families also may pool purchases dutiable under the flat rate. A family of three, for example, would be eligible for up to a total of $3,000 at the 10% flat duty rate (after each member had used up his or her $400 duty-free exemption) rather than three separate $1,000 allowances.

There are certain articles, however, that are duty-free only up to certain limits. Individuals are allowed 1 carton of cigarettes (200), 100 cigars, and 1 liter of liquor or wine if over 21. Alcohol above this allowance is liable for both duty and an Internal Revenue tax. Antiques, if they are 100 or more years old and you have proof from the seller of that fact, are duty-free, as are paintings and drawings if done entirely by hand. Gold, gold medals, bullion, and up to $10,000 in currency or negotiable instruments may be brought into the US without being declared; sums over $10,000 must be declared in writing. And to avoid paying duty twice, register the serial numbers of computer, watches, and expensive electronic equipment with the nearest US Customs bureau.

Personal exemptions can be used once every 30 days; in order to be eligible, an individual must have been out of the country for more than 48 hours. If any portion of the exemption has been used once within any 30-day period or if your trip is less than 48 hours long, the duty-free allowance is cut to $25.

The allotment for individual "unsolicited" gifts mailed from abroad (no more than one per day per recipient) is $50 retail value per gift. These gifts do not have to be declared and are not included in your duty-free exemption (see below). The package should be clearly marked "Not for Sale," and you should include a receipt for purchases with each package. The US Customs examiner usually will accept this as indicative of the articles' fair retail value, but he or she is empowered to impose a duty if he or she feels the goods have been undervalued. The duty owed is collected by the US Postal Service when the package is delivered.

It is a good idea, if you have accumulated too much while abroad, to mail home any personal effects (made and bought in the US) that you no longer need rather than your foreign purchases. These personal effects pass through US Customs as "American goods returned" and are not subject to duty. More information on mailing packages home from abroad is contained in the US Customs Service pamphlet *Buyer Beware, International Mail Imports* (see below for where to write for this and other useful brochures).

DUTY-FREE CRAFT ITEMS: In January 1976, the United States approved a Generalized System of Preferences (GSP) to help developing nations improve their economies through exports. The GSP, which recognizes dozens of developing nations, including Mexico, allows Americans to bring certain kinds of goods into the US duty-free, and has designated some 2,800 items as eligible for duty-free treatment.

This system entitles you to exceed your $400 duty-free exemption as long as the purchases are eligible for GSP status. The extensive list of eligible goods includes a wide range of categories. A useful pamphlet, which identifies GSP beneficiary nations and goods included in the program, is *GSP and the Traveler;* order "US Customs Publication No. 515" from the US Customs Service (Customs Information, 6 World Trade Center, Rm. 201, New York, NY 10048; phone: 212-466-5550). When in Mexico, information about the GSP status of particular items is available from any US Customs office or at the nearest US consulate (see *Medical and Legal Aid and Consular Services*).

CLEARING CUSTOMS: This is a simple procedure. Forms are distributed by airline or ship personnel before arrival. (Note that a $5-per-person service charge — called a user fee — is collected by airline and cruise lines to help cover the cost of customs checks, but this is included in the ticket price.) If your purchases total no more than the duty-free $400 limit, you need only fill out the identification part of the form and make an oral declaration to the customs inspector. If entering the US with more than $400 worth of goods, you must submit a written declaration.

Customs agents are businesslike, efficient, and not unkind. During the peak season, clearance can take time, but this generally is because of the strain imposed by a number of jumbo jets simultaneously discharging their passengers, not because of unwarranted zeal on the part of the customs people.

Efforts to streamline procedures used to include the so-called Citizens' Bypass Program, which allowed US citizens whose purchases were within their duty-free allowance to go to the "green line," where they simply showed their passports to the customs inspector. Although at the time of this writing this procedure still is being followed at some international airports in the US, most airports have returned to an earlier system. Americans arriving from abroad now have to go through a passport check by the Immigration & Naturalization Service (INS) prior to recovering their baggage and proceeding to customs. (US citizens will not be on the same line as foreign visitors, however, though this additional wait does delay clearance on re-entry into the US.) Although all passengers have to go through this obligatory passport inspection, those entering with purchases within the duty-free limit may be spared a thorough customs inspection, although inspectors still retain the right to search any luggage they choose — so don't do anything foolish.

It is illegal not to declare dutiable items; not to do so, in fact, constitutes smuggling, and the penalty can be anything from stiff fines and seizure of the goods to prison sentences. It simply isn't worth doing. There is a basic rule to buying goods abroad, and it should never be broken: *If you can't afford the duty on something, don't buy it.*

FORBIDDEN IMPORTS: Narcotics, plants, and many types of food are not allowed into the US. Drugs are totally illegal, with the exception of medication prescribed by a physician. It's a good idea to travel with no more than you actually need of any medication and to have the prescription on hand in case any question arises either abroad or when re-entering the US.

Any authentic archaeological find, Spanish colonial art, and other original artifacts cannot be exported from Mexico. They will be confiscated upon departure, and the violator runs the risk of being fined or imprisoned. Mexico also restricts export of gold and silver coins; people interested in such items should check with Mexican Customs. For further information, contact the *Instituto Nacional de Antropología e Historia* (National Institute of History and Anthropology), 45 Cordova, Col. Roma, México, DF 06700 (phone: 5-533-4976).

Tourists have long been forbidden to bring into the United States foreign-made, US-trademarked articles purchased abroad (if the trademark is recorded with US Customs) without written permission. It is now possible to enter with one such item in your possession as long as it's for personal use.

The US Customs Service implements the rigorous Department of Agriculture regulations concerning the importation of vegetable matter, seeds, bulbs, and the like. Living vegetable matter may not be imported without a permit, and everything must be inspected, permit or not. Approved items (which do not require a permit) include dried bamboo; beads made of most seeds (but not jequirity beans — the poisonous scarlet and black seed of the rosary pea), Mexican jumping beans, and some viable seeds; coconut shells (unhusked and empty); cones of pine and other trees; roasted coffee beans; most flower bulbs; flowers (without roots); dried or canned fruits, jellies, or jams; polished rice, dried beans, and teas; herb plants (not witchweed); nuts (but not acorns, chestnuts, or nuts with outer husks); dried lichens, mushrooms, and seaweed; most dried spices; and woven items made of straw.

Other processed foods and baked goods usually are okay. Regulations on meat products generally depend on the country of origin and manner of processing. As a rule, commercially canned meat, hermetically sealed and cooked in the can so that it can be stored without refrigeration, is permitted, but not all canned meat fulfills this requirement. Be careful in buying canned chili, for instance. Chili made with peppers, beans, and meat in itself is acceptable, but the pork fat that often is part of it may not be. (The imported brands you see in US stores have been prepared and packaged according to US regulations.) So before stocking up on a newfound favorite, it pays to check in advance — otherwise you might have to leave it behind.

The US Customs Service also enforces federal laws that prohibit the entry of articles made from the furs or hides of animals on the endangered species list. Don't be tempted by sweaters and other garments made from the fine hair of the vicuña (a relative of the domestic llama and alpaca), which is an endangered species. Also beware of shoes, bags, and belts made of crocodile or certain kinds of lizard, and anything made from tortoiseshell; this also applies to preserved crocodiles, lizards, and turtles sometimes sold in gift shops. Some protected species of coral — particularly large chunks of fresh coral and black coral in any form — are restricted (although most jewelry and other items made of coral usually are permitted). And if you're shopping for big-ticket items, beware of fur coats made from the skins of spotted cats. They are sold abroad, but they will be confiscated upon your return to the US, and there will be no refund. For information about other animals on the endangered species list, contact the Department of the Interior, US Fish and Wildlife Service (Publications Unit, 4401 N. Fairfax Dr., Rm. 130, Arlington, VA 22203; phone: 703-358-1711), and ask for the free publication *Facts About Federal Wildlife Laws.*

Also note that some foreign governments prohibit the export of items made from certain species of wildlife, and the US honors any such restrictions. Before you go shopping in any foreign country, check with the US Department of Agriculture (G110 Federal Bldg., Hyattsville, MD 20782; phone: 301-436-8413) and find out what items are prohibited from the country you will be visiting.

The US Customs Service publishes a series of free pamphlets with customs information. It includes *Know Before You Go,* a basic discussion of customs requirements pertaining to all travelers; *Buyer Beware, International Mail Imports; Travelers' Tips on Bringing Food, Plant, and Animal Products into the United States; Importing a Car; GSP and the Traveler; Pocket Hints; Currency Reporting; Pets, Wildlife, US Customs; Customs Hints for Visitors (Nonresidents);* and *Trademark Information for Travelers.* For the entire series or individual pamphlets, write to the US Customs Service (PO Box 7407, Washington, DC 20044) or contact any of the seven regional offices — in Boston, Chicago, Houston, Long Beach (California), Miami, New Orleans, and New York. The US Customs Service has a taped message whereby callers using Touch-Tone phones can get more information on various topics; the number is 202-566-8195. These pamphlets provide great briefing material, but if you still have questions when you're in Mexico you can contact the US Customs representative at the nearest US consulate.

Sources and Resources

Mexican Consulates and Tourist Offices in the US

The Mexican government tourist offices and consulates in the US all are sources of general travel information and provide free maps and useful travel literature. You can request information on specific areas, as well as publications relating to your particular areas of interest: accommodations, restaurants, special events, guided tours, and facilities for specific sports. There is no need to send a self-addressed stamped envelope with your request, unless specified.

Where required, the consulates also issue tourist cards and are empowered to sign other official documents — such as commercial and residence visas — and to notarize copies or translations of American documents, which often is necessary for those papers to be considered legal in Mexico.

The Mexican Embassy is located in Washington, DC (1019 19th St. NW, Suite 810, Washington, DC 20036; phone: 202-293-1710). In most cases, however, visitors to Mexico should direct their inquiries and requests to one of the consulates or tourist offices listed below. Below is a complete list of Mexican consulates general, consulates, and Mexican government tourist offices in the US:

Consulates and Consulates General

Albuquerque: Consulate General, Western Bank Bldg., 401 Fifth St. NW, Albuquerque, NM 87102 (phone: 505-247-2139).

Atlanta: Consulate General, 410 S. Tower, CNN Center, Atlanta, GA 30303-2705 (phone: 404-688-3258).

Austin: Consulate General, 200 E. Sixth St., Suite 200, Austin, TX 78701 (phone: 512-478-2866).

Boston: Consulate General, Statler Bldg., 20 Park Plaza, Suite 1212, Boston, MA 02116 (phone: 617-426-4942).

Brownsville: Consulate General, 724 E. Elizabeth St., PO Box 1711, Brownsville, TX 78520 (phone: 512-542-4431).

Buffalo: Consulate, 1875 Harlem Rd., Buffalo, NY 14212 (phone: 716-895-9800).

Calexico: Consulate, 231 W. 2nd St., Calexico, CA 92231 (phone: 619-357-3863).

Chicago: Consulate General, 300 N. Michigan Ave., 2nd Floor, Chicago, IL 60601 (phone: 312-855-1380).

Corpus Christi: Consulate General, 800 N. Shoreline Blvd., N. Tower, 4th Floor, Corpus Christi, TX 78410 (phone: 512-882-3375).

Dallas: Consulate General, 1349 Empire Center, Suite 100, Dallas, TX 75347 (phone: 214-630-7341).

Del Rio: Consulate General, 1010 S. Main St., Del Rio, TX 78840 (phone: 512-774-5031).

Denver: Consulate General, 707 Washington St., Suite A, Denver, CO 80203 (phone: 303-830-0523).

Detroit: Consulate General, 1515 Book Bldg., Washington Blvd., Detroit, MI 48226 (phone: 313-965-1868).

Eagle Pass: Consulate General, 140 Adams St., Eagle Pass, TX 78852 (phone: 512-773-9255).

El Paso: Consulate General, 910 E. San Antonio St., PO Box 812, El Paso, TX 79901 (phone: 915-533-3645).

Fresno: Consulate General, 905 N. Fulton St., Fresno, CA 93728 (phone: 209-233-3065).

Green Bay: Consulate, 901 Howard St., Green Bay, WI 54303 (phone: 414-435-0710).

Honolulu: Consulate, Control Data Bldg., 2828 Paa St., Suite 2115, Honolulu, HI 96819 (phone: 808-833-6331).

Houston: Consulate General, 3015 Richmond Ave., Suite 100, Houston, TX 77098 (phone: 713-524-2300).

Laredo: Consulate General, 1612 Farragut St., PO Box 659, Laredo, TX 78040 (phone: 512-723-6360).

Los Angeles: Consulate General, 2401 W. Sixth St., Los Angeles, CA 90057 (phone: 213-351-6800).

Madison: Consulate, 312 Newcastle Way, Madison, WI 53704 (phone: 608-249-5201).

McAllen: Consulate General, 1418 Beech St., Suite 102, McAllen, TX 78501 (phone: 512-686-0243).

Miami: Consulate General, 780 W. 42nd Ave., Suite 525, Miami, FL 33126 (phone: 305-441-8780).

Nashville: Consulate, 226 Capitol Blvd., Suite 212, Nashville, TN 37219 (phone: 615-244-7430).

New Orleans: Consulate General, World Trade Center, 2 Canal St., Suite 1140, New Orleans, LA 70130 (phone: 504-522-3596).

New York: Consulate General, 8 E. 41st St., New York, NY 10017 (phone: 212-689-0456).

Nogales: Consulate General, 137 Terrace Ave., Nogales, AZ 85621 (phone: 602-287-4850).

Norfolk: Consulate, 5121 E. Virginia Beach Blvd., Suite EZ, Norfolk, VA 23502 (phone: 804-461-4553).

Philadelphia: Consulate General, Bourse Bldg., 215 Fifth St., Suite 575, Philadelphia, PA 19106 (phone: 215-922-4262).

Phoenix: Consulate General, 1190 W. Camelback, Suite 110, Phoenix, AZ 85015 (phone: 602-242-7398).

Portland: Consulate, 545 NE 47th Ave., Portland, OR 97213 (phone: 503-233-5662).

Richmond: Consulate, 2420 Pemberton Rd., Richmond, VA 23233 (phone: 804-747-1961).

Rochester: Consulate, World Travel Bureau, 3 First Ave. SW, Rochester, MN 55901 (phone: 507-288-3130).

Sacramento: Consulate, 9845 Horn Rd., Sacramento, CA 95827 (phone: 916-363-3885).

St. Louis: Consulate General, 1015 Locust St., St. Louis, MO 63101 (phone: 314-436-3233).

Salt Lake City: Consulate General, 182 S. 600 East, Suite 202, Salt Lake City, UT 84102 (phone: 801-521-8502).

San Antonio: Consulate General, 127 Navarro St., San Antonio, TX 78205 (phone: 512-227-9145).

San Bernardino: Consulate General, 588 W. 6th St., San Bernardino, CA 92401 (phone: 714-889-9836).

San Diego: Consulate General, 610 A St., Suite 200, San Diego, CA 92101 (phone: 619-231-8414).

San Francisco: Consulate General, 870 Market St., Suite 528, San Francisco, CA 94102 (phone: 415-392-5554).

San Jose: Consulate General, 380 N. First St., Suite 100, San Jose, CA 95112 (phone: 408-294-3413).

Seattle: Consulate General, 2132 Third Ave., Seattle, WA 98121 (phone: 206-448-3526).

Spokane: Consulate, 12005 E. Sprague Ave., Spokane, WA 99214 (phone: 509-926-9531).

Tampa: Consulate, General Shipping Co., 315 Madison St., Tampa, FL 33602 (phone: 813-223-1481).

Tucson: Consulate General, 553 South Stone Ave., Tucson, AZ 85701 (phone: 602-882-5595).

Ministry of Tourism Offices

Chicago: 70 E. Lake St., Suite 1413, Chicago, IL 60601 (phone: 312-565-2786).

Houston: 2707 N. Loop W, Suite 450, Houston, TX 77008 (phone: 713-880-5153).

Los Angeles: 10100 Santa Monica Blvd., Suite 224, Los Angeles, CA 90067 (phone: 213-203-8191).

New York: 405 Park Ave., Suite 1002, New York, NY 10022 (phone: 212-838-2949).

Washington, DC: 1615 L St. NW, Suite 430, Washington, DC 20036 (phone: 202-293-1710).

Cameras and Equipment

Vacations are everybody's favorite time for taking pictures and home movies. After all, most of us want to remember the places we visit — and show them off to others. Here are a few suggestions to help you get the best results from your travel photography or videography.

BEFORE THE TRIP

If you're taking your camera or camcorder out after a long period in mothballs — or have just bought a new one — check it thoroughly before you leave to prevent unexpected breakdowns or disappointing pictures.

1. Still cameras should be cleaned carefully and thoroughly, inside and out. If using a camcorder, run a head cleaner through it. Always use filters to protect your lenses while traveling.
2. Check the batteries for your camera's light meter and flash, and take along extras just in case yours wear out during the trip. For camcorders, bring along extra Nickel-Cadmium (Ni-Cad) batteries; if you use rechargeable batteries, a recharger will cut down on the extras.
3. Using all the settings and features, shoot at least one test roll of film or one videocassette, using the type you plan to take along with you.

EQUIPMENT TO TAKE ALONG

Keep your gear light and compact. Items that are too heavy or bulky to be carried comfortably on a full-day excursion will likely stay in your hotel room, so leave them at home.

1. Invest in a broad camera or camcorder strap if you now have a thin one. It will make carrying the equipment much more comfortable.
2. A sturdy canvas, vinyl, or leather camera or camcorder bag, preferably with padded pockets (not an airline bag), will keep your equipment organized and easy to find. If you will be doing much shooting around the water, a waterproof case is best.
3. For cleaning, bring along a camel's hair brush that retracts into a rubber squeeze bulb. Also take plenty of lens tissue, soft cloths, and plastic bags to protect equipment from dust and moisture.

FILM AND TAPES: If you are concerned about airport security X-rays damaging rolls of undeveloped still film (X-rays do not affect processed film) or tapes, store them in one of the lead-lined bags sold in camera shops. This possibility is not as much of a threat as it used to be, however. In the US, incidents of X-ray damage to unprocessed film (exposed or unexposed) are few because low-dosage X-ray equipment is used virtually everywhere. While the international trend also is toward equipment that delivers less and less radiation, equipment in Mexico tends to be less up-to-date than in some other foreign countries, and is, therefore, less predictable.

If you're traveling without a protective bag, you may want to ask to have your photo equipment inspected by hand. One type of film that should never be subjected to X-rays is the new, very-high-speed ASA 1000 film. The walk-through metal detector devices at airports do not affect film, though the film cartridges may set them off.

You should have no problem finding film or tapes throughout Mexico, particularly in metropolitan and major resort areas. When buying film, tapes, or photo accessories abroad, the best rule of thumb is to stick to name brands with which you are familiar. The availability of film processing labs and equipment repair shops will vary from area to area.

■ **A note about courtesy and caution:** When photographing in Mexico (and anywhere else in the world), ask first. In many of the smaller towns, and even some of the cities, the Indians have superstitions or religious beliefs that photographing them is an insult at best, and at worst a violation. Furthermore, some governments have security regulations regarding the use of cameras and will not permit the photographing of certain subjects. When in doubt, look for an official who can tell you if your chosen subject is on the restricted list.

USEFUL WORDS AND PHRASES

Useful Words and Phrases

Unlike the French, who tend to be a bit brusque if you don't speak their language perfectly, the Mexicans do not expect you to speak Spanish — but are very flattered when you try. In many circumstances, you won't have to, because the staffs at most hotels, museums, and tourist attractions, as well as at a fair number of restaurants, speak serviceable English, or at least a version of it, which they are usually eager to try — and that means practicing with you. Particularly when you get off the beaten path, however, you will find at least a rudimentary knowledge of Spanish very helpful. Don't be afraid of misplaced accents or misconjugated verbs. Mexicans appreciate your efforts to speak their language and will do their best to understand you. They will also make an effort to be understood.

Mexican Spanish has a number of regional dialects, but the dialect of educated people in Mexico City is regarded as standard, is used on national television, and is understood by almost everybody, even though their local speech may be quite different. Most people can communicate in what is considered "standard" Spanish, and the spelling of standard Mexican Spanish is a very reliable guide to pronunciation.

The list below is a selection of commonly used words and phrases to speed you on your way. Note that in Spanish all nouns are either masculine or feminine, as well as singular and plural, and that the adjectives that modify them must agree in both gender and number. Most nouns ending in *o* are masculine (the corresponding articles are *el* and *uno* or *un*); most nouns ending in *a* are feminine (the feminine articles are *la* and *una*). Plurals are formed by adding *s* (the articles are *los, unos, las,* and *unas*). Adjectives almost always follow nouns in Spanish. Otherwise, word order is very much as in English.

The following pronunciation rules may also be helpful:

The vowel before the last consonant in a word (except *n* or *s*) is accented, unless there is an accent mark on another vowel. When the last consonant is *n* or *s,* the vowel before the preceding consonant is accented. In addition:

a is pronounced as in *father*
e is pronounced as in *red*
i is pronounced as in *machine*
o is pronounced as in *note*
u is pronounced as in *rude*
ei/ey are pronounced as in *vein*
oi/oy are pronounced as in *joy*
ai/ay are pronounced like *y* in *by*
au is pronounced like *ou* in *house*

In general, in vowel letter sequences (*ae, ie, ue, ia,* and so on), each letter is pronounced.

Mexican Spanish consonants are pronounced as in English, with these exceptions:

The consonants *b, d,* and *g* are pronounced with the air passage slightly open, producing a softer sound. The consonants *p, t,* and *c/k* are pronounced without the aspiration (the strong puff of breath) that characterizes them in English.

b within words is pronounced like the English *v*
d within words is pronounced like *th* in *other*
g before *e* or *i* is pronounced like a strongly aspirated English *h* or German *ch;* otherwise, as above
h is silent
j is pronounced like a strongly aspirated *h*
ll is pronounced like *y* in *youth*
ñ is pronounced like *ny* in *canyon*
qu is pronounced *k* before *e* or *i: quilo* is pronounced as the English *kilo*
r is pronounced like the casual English *d* in *pedal*
rr is trilled, as in the Scottish *farm*
s and *z* are pronounced *z* within words preceding a voiced consonant (*b, d, g, m, n, r, l*); otherwise they are pronounced as the English *s*

Greetings and Everyday Expressions

Good morning (also, Good day)	*Buenos días*
Good afternoon/evening	*Buenas tardes*
Good night	*Buenas noches*
Hello	*Hola!*
How are you?	*Cómo está usted?*
Pleased to meet you	*Mucho gusto en conocerle*
Good-bye!	*Adiós!*
So long!	*Hasta luego!*
Yes	*Sí*
No	*No*
Please	*Por favor*
Thank you	*Gracias*
You're welcome	*De nada*
I beg your pardon	
(Excuse me)	*Perdón*
(I'm sorry)	*Lo siento*
It doesn't matter	*No importa*
I don't speak Spanish.	*No hablo Español.*
Do you speak English?	*Habla usted inglés?*
I don't understand.	*No comprendo.*
Do you understand?	*Comprende?/Entiende?*
My name is . . .	*Me llamo . . .*
What is your name?	*Cómo se llama?*
miss (younger unmarried woman)	*señorita*
madame (mature married woman)	*señora*
(mature unmarried woman)	*doña*
mister	*señor*

open	*abierto/a*
closed	*cerrado/a*
entrance	*entrada*
exit	*salida*
push	*empujar*
pull	*tirar*
today	*hoy*
tomorrow	*mañana*
yesterday	*ayer*

Checking In

I have a reservation.	*He hecho una reserva.*
I would like . . .	*Quisiera . . .*
a single room	*una habitación sencilla*
a double room	*una habitación doble*
a quiet room	*una habitación tranquila*
with bath	*con baño*
with shower	*con ducha*
with a sea view	*con vista asi el mar*
with air conditioning	*con aire acondicionado*
with balcony	*con balcón*
overnight only	*sólo una noche*
a few days	*unos cuantos días*
a week (at least)	*una semana (por los menos)*
with full board	*con pensión completa*
with half board	*con media pensión*
Does that price include . . .	*Esta incluído en el precio . . .*
breakfast?	*el desayuno?*
taxes?	*los impuestos?*
Do you accept traveler's checks?	*Acepta usted cheques de viajero?*
Do you accept credit cards?	*Acepta tarjetas de credito?*
It doesn't work.	*No funcióna.*

Eating Out

ashtray	*un cenicero*
(extra) chair	*una silla (adicional)*
table	*una mesa*
bottle	*una botella*
cup	*una taza*
plate	*un plato*
fork	*un tenedor*
knife	*un cuchillo*
spoon	*una cuchara*
napkin	*una servilleta*

hot chocolate (cocoa)	*un chocolate caliente*
black coffee	*un café negro*
coffee with milk	*café con leche*
cream	*crema*
milk	*leche*
tea	*un té*
fruit juice	*un jugo de fruta*
lemonade	*una limonada*
water	*agua*
mineral water	*agua mineral*
carbonated	*con gas*
noncarbonated	*sin gas*
orangeade	*una naranjada*
beer	*una cerveza*
port	*oporto*
sherry	*jerez*
red wine	*vino tinto*
white wine	*vino blanco*
cold	*frío/a*
hot	*caliente*
sweet	*dulce*
(very) dry	*(muy) seco/a*
bread	*pan*
butter	*mantequilla*
bacon	*tocino*
eggs	*huevos*
hard-boiled	*un huevo cocido*
fried	*huevos fritos*
omelette	*torta de huevos*
soft-boiled	*un huevo cocido pasado por agua*
scrambled	*huevos revueltos*
honey	*miel*
jam, marmalade	*mermelada*
orange juice	*jugo de naranja*
pepper	*pimienta*
salt	*sal*
sugar	*azúcar*
Waiter!	*Camarero!/Mesero!*
I would like	*Quisiera*
a glass of	*un vaso de*
a bottle of	*una botella de*
a half bottle of	*una media botella de*
a carafe of	*una garrafa de, una jarra de*
a liter of	*un litro de*
The check, please.	*La cuenta, por favor.*

Is a service charge included?	*Está el servicio incluído?*
I think there is a mistake in the bill.	*Creo que hay un error en la cuenta.*

Shopping

bakery	*la panadería*
bookstore	*la librería*
butcher shop	*la carnicería*
camera shop	*la tienda de fotografía*
delicatessen	*la tienda de comestibles preparados*
department store	*el almacén grande*
grocery	*la tienda de comestibles*
jewelry store	*la joyería*
newsstand	*el puesto de periódicos*
pastry shop	*la pastelería*
perfume (and cosmetics) store	*perfumería*
pharmacy/drugstore	*las farmacia*
shoestore	*la zapatería*
supermarket	*el supermercado*
tobacconist	*el estanquero*

inexpensive	*barato/a*
expensive	*caro/a*
large	*grande*
larger	*más grande*
too large	*demasiado grande*
small	*pequeño/a*
smaller	*más pequeño/a*
too small	*demasiado pequeño/a*
long	*largo/a*
short	*corto/a*
old	*viejo/a*
new	*nuevo/a*
used	*usado/a*
handmade	*hecho/a a mano*

Is it machine washable?	*Es lavable a máquina?*
How much does it cost?	*Cuánto cuesta esto?*
What is it made of?	*De qué está hecho?*
camel's hair	*pelo de camello*
cotton	*algodón*
corduroy	*pana*
filigree	*filigrana*
lace	*encaje*
leather	*cuero*
linen	*lino*
suede	*ante*
synthetic	*sintético/a*
tile	*baldosa*

wood	*madera*
wool	*lana*
brass	*latón*
copper	*cobre*
gold	*oro*
gold plated	*dorado*
silver	*plata*
silver plated	*plateado*
stainless steel	*acero inoxidable*

Colors

beige	*beige*
black	*negro/a*
blue	*azul*
brown	*café*
green	*verde*
gray	*gris*
orange	*naranjo/a*
pink	*rosa*
purple	*morado/a*
red	*rojo/a*
white	*blanco/a*
yellow	*amarillo/a*
dark	*obscuro/a*
light	*claro/a*

Getting Around

north	*norte*
south	*sur*
east	*este*
west	*oeste*
right	*derecho/a*
left	*izquierdo/a*
Go straight ahead	*Siga todo derecho*
far	*lejos*
near	*cerca*
gas station	*la gasolinería*
train station	*la estación de ferrocarril*
bus stop	*la parada de autobúses*
subway station	*estación de metro*
airport	*el aeropuerto*
tourist information	*información turística*
map	*el mapa*
one-way ticket	*un billete de ida*
round-trip ticket	*un billete de ida y vuelta*
track	*el andén*
first class	*primera clase*
second class	*segunda clase*

smoking	*fumar*
no smoking	*no fumar*

gasoline	*gasolina*
regular	*nova*
premium	*extra*
leaded	*con plomo*
unleaded	*sin plomo*
diesel	*diesel*
Fill it up, please	*Llénelo, por favor*
oil	*el aceite*
tires	*las llantas*
Where is . . . ?	*Dónde está . . . ?*
Where are . . . ?	*Dónde estan . . . ?*
How far is it from here to . . . ?	*Qué distancia hay desdeaquí hasta . . . ?*
Does this train go to . . . ?	*Va este ferrocarril a . . . ?*
Does this bus go to . . . ?	*Va este autobús a . . . ?*
What time does it leave?	*A qué hora sale?*

Danger	*Peligro*
Caution	*Precaución*
Detour	*Desvio*
Do Not Enter	*Paso Prohibido*
No Parking	*Estacionamiento Prohibido*
No Passing	*Prohibido Pasar*
One Way	*Dirección Unica*
Pay Toll	*Peaje*
Pedestrian Zone	*Zona Peatonal*
Reduce Speed	*Despacio*
Steep Incline	*Fuerte Declive*
Stop	*Alto*
Use Headlights	*Encender los faros*
Yield	*Ceda el Paso*

Personal Items and Services

aspirins	*aspirinas*
Band-Aids	*curitas*
barbershop	*la barbería*
beauty shop	*el salón de belleza*
condom	*condón*
dry cleaner	*la tintorería*
hairdresser's	*la peluquería*
laundromat	*la lavandería*
post office	*el correo*
postage stamps	*estampillas*

sanitary napkins	*unos paños higiénicos*
shampoo	*un champú*
shaving cream	*espuma de afeitar*
soap	*el jabón*
tampons	*unos tampones higiénicos*
tissues	*Kleenex*
toilet paper	*papel higiénico*
toothpaste	*pasta de dientes*
Where is the bathroom?	*Dónde está el baño?*
toilet?	*excusado?*
MEN	*Caballeros*
WOMEN	*Señoras*

Days of the Week

Monday	*Lunes*
Tuesday	*Martes*
Wednesday	*Miércoles*
Thursday	*Jueves*
Friday	*Viernes*
Saturday	*Sábado*
Sunday	*Domingo*

Months

January	*Enero*
February	*Febrero*
March	*Marzo*
April	*Abril*
May	*Mayo*
June	*Junio*
July	*Julio*
August	*Agosto*
September	*Septiembre*
October	*Octubre*
November	*Noviembre*
December	*Diciembre*

Numbers

zero	*cero*
one	*uno*
two	*dos*
three	*tres*
four	*cuatro*
five	*cinco*
six	*seis*
seven	*siete*
eight	*ocho*
nine	*nueve*
ten	*diez*
eleven	*once*
twelve	*doce*
thirteen	*trece*
fourteen	*catorce*
fifteen	*quince*

sixteen	*dieciséis*
seventeen	*diecisiete*
eighteen	*dieciocho*
nineteen	*diecinueve*
twenty	*veinte*
thirty	*treinta*
forty	*cuarenta*
fifty	*cincuenta*
sixty	*sesenta*
seventy	*setenta*
eighty	*ochenta*
ninety	*noventa*
one hundred	*cien*
one thousand	*mil*

THE CITIES

IXTAPA AND ZIHUATANEJO

(pronounced Eeks-*tah*-pa and Zee-whah-ta-*neh*-hoe)

Mexico's immensely long Pacific Coast is blessed with port towns, fishing villages, and resort cities for every taste. From Kino Bay, just west of Hermosillo, to Acapulco, they dot the coast like convenient commas in a long sentence, and no one spot provides a stopping place exactly like any of the others. Among the newest of these resort areas are the twin towns of Ixtapa and Zihuatanejo, 130 miles (208 km) northwest of Acapulco. Though Ixtapa is only 3 miles (5 km) from Zihuatanejo, what is most exciting is how little alike they are; side by side, they provide alternate moods of Pacific Mexico.

They are a prime example of the Mexican government's program of resort development (Cancún is another) beginning in the 1960s. Zihuatanejo is a beautiful town that at one time could be reached only by a wandering old road or by private plane, and where a dozen oysters and a cold beer is still the standard breakfast. In its early stages of development, some said Ixtapa was sired by a computer and incubated under the watchful eyes of urbanologists, sociologists, financial wizards, and tourist industry experts.

And therein lies a tale.

Back in the 1960s, some of the Harvard-trained whiz kids from Mexico's central bank hit on the idea that tourism, if it were increased, could help solve some of Mexico's economic problems. At the time, these fellows were looking for projects to reduce imports and increase exports, for decentralizing industry and increasing farm output, but every time they turned around, their figures showed that tourism was more rewarding.

The hospitality business directly generates a tremendous number of jobs, from customs inspectors and baggage handlers to taxi drivers, bellhops, room clerks, chambermaids, bartenders, and waiters. A number of jobs are also indirectly generated. These include the artisans who make handicrafts bought by tourists, store clerks who sell the handicrafts, and truck drivers who transport them across the country. Tourism even provides work for musicians who strum guitars to help gringo couples add a note of vacation romance.

Mexico's traditional resorts were pretty nearly saturated, and while some foreign vacationers came back year after year, most travelers wanted to try a new place. In the early 1960s, they didn't have too much choice in Mexico.

What was needed were new resorts. While the first inclination was to develop already existing facilities, the central bankers had a better idea. They would build new resorts where there was nothing, thus helping to settle Mexico's largely empty coastal areas. They had to find places where tourists would want to go, but building a successful new resort involves all the risks of trying to come out with a popular new automobile or a hit movie. The bankers busied themselves investigating the sun spots around the country and then fed their data into a computer.

High on the list (along with Cancún on the Caribbean) was Ixtapa, a town that was literally carved out of an immense, lush coconut plantation and included 24 miles of beachfront lining seven picturesque coves. Although the resort town is said to be named after nearby Ixtapa Island (once known as Parrot Island), the first complete map of "New Spain" drawn by Spanish conquerors in 1579 shows a village called "Istapa" (north of "Cauantanzejo") near the resort's present location.

No one in Mexico had ever heard of Ixtapa, but it could usually be located by its proximity to Zihuatanejo, which itself was far from a household word during the 1960s, but which did have its devotees. The name "Zihuatanejo" comes from the Nahuatl word *cihuatlan,* which means "place of women," indicating that a matriarchal society might have flourished here at one time. Although the Spaniards added the derogatory "nejo" to the end of the word, twisting the meaning to "place of women of little importance," many longtime residents assert that Zihuatanejo possesses a distinctive female energy that enhances the town's charm and allure.

FONATUR, the agency established to transform the central bank's dreams into reality, undertook a $50-million development program. A spiffy two-lane highway was put through from Acapulco; Zihuatanejo was given a sewage system, electrical and communications systems, and a general sprucing up, but its essential nature as a fishing village was untouched. Ixtapa, on the other hand, is something out of the 21st century. Shopping centers, a Robert Trent Jones, Jr. 18-hole golf course, luxurious hotels, manicured lawns — a sleek and elegant resort in high Mexican style.

Zihuatanejo's hotels are on the bay. Many of them are small, ranging from 13 to 50 rooms, and operate more like inns or what Europeans call *pensiones.*

The sea brings people to Ixtapa-Zihuatanejo, and activity centers around the water. Hotel guests usually are content to enjoy the stretch of sand on their doorstep, but those who enjoy exploring will find more than a dozen beaches in the area. There are boat trips to be taken and popular excursions to Ixtapa Island, a favorite snorkeling and scuba spot. Both light-tackle and deep-sea fishing are available.

On shore, golfers will want to try the Jones, Jr. course at the *Ixtapa Golf Club.* The club also has floodlit tennis courts, as do several hotels. There are lots of shops in Ixtapa — at the hotels and at the shopping centers.

Zihuatanejo is an enjoyable place just to poke around. The village is charming, with many nice handicraft shops, bars, and restaurants. Fishing is still an important industry here, and this is a good place to eat fresh lobster, snapper, oysters, and clams. After dark, there are a couple of discos in town, but most of the nightlife is centered around the big Ixtapa hotels, which make a point of keeping visitors active, with beach parties and special programs throughout the week.

Zihuatanejo has its share of resident and visiting celebrities who show up at local nightspots. Supermodel and actress Lauren Hutton, painter and jazz musician Larry Rivers, and writer Carlos Fuentes all blend in with the local community.

Ixtapa and Zihuatanejo have several attributes that have contributed to their success and separated them from other resorts along the Pacific Coast: The resort and town are clean and well kept; developers have — until now, at least — resisted the temptation to overbuild (Zihuatanejo residents have recently become concerned about several land development projects); all necessary services are in place; and both Ixtapa and Zihuatanejo remain uncrowded and uncongested. But perhaps the area's most impressive quality, aside from its great beauty and abundance of sun, sand, and sea, is the range of experiences possible — from elegant and sophisticated to primitive and rustic.

The only notable problems to beset the area are a dearth of flights to bring tourists in (an issue over which the tourist associations, government officials, and air carriers are constantly grappling) and the lack of the glamorous image necessary to catapult a resort destination to worldwide fame. Nevertheless, in 1990, Ixtapa and Zihuatanejo played host to nearly 280,000 tourists, including 173,000 from elsewhere in Mexico and 104,000 from the United States, Canada, and European countries.

Several major construction projects in both Ixtapa and Zihuatanejo are due to be completed within the next year. In Ixtapa, construction workers are transforming the great mangrove lagoon (north of the resort hotel zone and west of the urban center) into Marina Ixtapa. Under pressure from local ecology groups, developers have cut the mangroves rather than burn them, which has spared some wildlife but has still sacrificed an important breeding, nesting, and nutrient-producing coastal habitat. When completed, the FONATUR-supervised mega-project will include 6 hotels with nearly 2,000 rooms, 7 condominium hotels, 50 villas, a golf course and tennis club, a commercial center, recreational land, and a 500-slip marina. The development will create about 20,000 jobs and eventually accommodate 18,000 guests.

Zihuatanejo's two main development projects, Puerto Maris and Puerto Mío, are dominating discussion and the landscape these days. In town, the lagoon behind the boat pier has been dredged to construct Puerto Maris, a marina with boat slips, a hotel and condominium, a shopping center, and a yacht club. Again local conservationists intervened and have insisted on certain construction restrictions to protect the surrounding environment, which in this case is Zihuatanejo Bay.

Puerto Mío is an ambitious marina and villa development at the northern tip of Zihuatanejo Bay. A restaurant-bar called *El Morro Viejo,* several saltwater pools, and a handful of suites are already open at scenic Morro Viejo cove; the rest of the construction is proceeding in stages.

IXTAPA-ZIHUATANEJO AT-A-GLANCE

SEEING THE CITY: The drive in from the airport pretty much skips Zihuatanejo (unless that's where you're headed), but from the hills you get a nice view of Ixtapa. The best way to see them both is from the ocean, aboard a boat leaving the bay for Ixtapa Island. You can also admire the sweep of Ixtapa from the glass-enclosed elevator at the *Stouffer Presidente* hotel or from La Ropa, Zihuatanejo's loveliest beach; or watch fishing boats come in from your perch at the bar at the *Catalina-Sotavento.* During the winter season, the 36-foot catamaran *Tequila* takes up to 12 passengers on a cruise around the bay, with a stop for snorkeling at Isla Ixtapa. It leaves from Playa Quieta at 11 AM and returns at 2 PM (phone: 30007). The *Rainbow* (phone: 31066) offers a similar cruise that departs from the *Holiday Inn* at 10 AM and 3 PM; they also offer a sunset cruise.

SPECIAL PLACES: The two communities are about 3 miles (5 km) apart. Both have a number of interesting spots to visit, and the countryside around them is worth going out to and enjoying.

Ixtapa Golf Club – One of the nicest developments of its kind in Mexico, this Robert Trent Jones, Jr.–designed course offers natural water hazards from the former marshlands on which it sits. Open to the public and worth a visit even if you don't want to play on its 18-hole course; the pro shop has a wide variety of athletic equipment and the bar is a popular gathering place at sundown. Note that no reservations are accepted; golfers should show up early in order to get their preferred tee-off time. Carts or caddies are required (phone: 31062 or 31163).

Zihuatanejo – The village is charming, with many nice shops, bars, and restaurants. Stroll along the Paseo del Pescador by the waterfront and browse along Calles Alvarez and Pedro Ascencio, where you will find some excellent handicrafts shops. Fishing is an important industry here, and by 10 in the morning fishermen have already returned with their catch. Lobster, snapper, oysters, and clams top the local menus.

La Ropa – La Ropa means "clothes," and this beach is said to be so named because many years ago clothes, apparently the cargo of a wrecked ship, washed up here. This is the main beach for the Zihuatanejo hotels and is on the bay. Boats of all kinds are available for sailing, water skiing, or just roaming about, and there are several good seafood restaurants.

Playa Quieta – The name means "quiet beach," but with the *Club Med* next door it's actually pretty lively. Sailing and windsurfing are popular activities, and boats leave for nearby Ixtapa Island from here.

Las Gatas – Also a beach on the bay, but best reached by boat from Zihuatanejo (a little over a dollar round-trip), it was the royal watering place of the Tarascan kings before the conquistadores arrived. The conquerors found the Tarascan name a tongue-twister and came up with Las Gatas, which means "the cats." A great place to go for lunch and a swim or snorkel. Be sure to check when the last boat leaves.

Barra de Potosí – A small fishing village surrounded by grapefruit, coconut, papaya, mango, and tamarind orchards, it lies about 12½ miles (20 km) south of Ixtapa and features part of the long beach called Playa Blanca. There are several *palapa* (thatch-roofed) restaurants that serve *pescado a la talla* (whole fish char-broiled on spits). Farther southeast is the town of Petatlán, where there's a small archaeological museum that houses artifacts uncovered at La Chole, an archaeological site.

■ **EXTRA SPECIAL:** Ixtapa Island, also known as Isla Grande, is a favorite place for a boat journey, and good for a day's — or a half-day's — visit. The island is a wildlife preserve inhabited by deer, badgers, armadillos, rabbits, raccoons, and many species of birds. Two of the four nearly deserted beaches are swimmable: the one where the boats dock, and a more isolated one you reach by following the trail by *La Princesa* restaurant (always bearing right). Snorkeling and diving are excellent, and you can rent hammocks on the beach for less than a dollar. Ten open-air seafood shanties with bar service, including the *Marlin* and the red brick *Isla Ixtapa,* run by the Solís family, serve the day's catch.

LOCAL SOURCES AND RESOURCES

TOURIST INFORMATION: A helpful tourist office is located in the Municipal Palace in Zihuatanejo (phone: 42001 or 42355). The government tourist office is in Ixtapa, at *La Puerta Shopping Center* (phone: 31967). Hotel personnel are pretty well informed, too.

Local Coverage – *The News,* Mexico City's English-language newspaper, is available at most Ixtapa hotels and often features the area in its *Vistas* Sunday supplement. The newsstand at 23 Cuauhtémoc in Zihuatanejo carries a few American magazines, as well as *The News. Qué Hacer y a Donde Ir* (What to Do and Where to Go), a monthly, is available in English. The best locally originated English-language guide to the area is the *A to Z Guide* (about $5), written by longtime local resident Linda-Fox Sullivan and published in 1989. Although some of the information is dated and the hand-drawn maps are a bit difficult to use, it does provide useful facts, including names of local doctors, car repair, shopping, dining, and outdoor activities. Available at most newsstands.

For US sporting events or fast-breaking world news, Zihuatanejo locals and visitors congregate around the TV sets at *Nacho's Steakhouse* and *Splash* lobster house in town, at *Kon Tiki* above the bay, and at *La Perla* restaurant at Playa La Ropa. There are very few TV sets in Zihuatanejo hotels; in Ixtapa, most rooms have them.

GETTING AROUND: Bus – A bus runs from Ixtapa into Zihuatanejo about every half hour until 11 PM. Within Zihuatanejo, there is regular bus service from the hotel area downtown. Minibus service is available between Ixtapa and the airport (phone: 42785 and 42046); when two or more people are making the trip, however, it can be less expensive to take a taxi. When leaving, get to the airport early and reconfirm your return flight well in advance. Frequent, inexpensive first class buses bound for inland destinations and other towns along the Pacific Coast depart from the Estrella de Oro bus station, 20 Calle Ejido, Zihuatanejo (phone: 42175).

Taxis – Rates are standard, but you'd never know it from what some drivers ask; talk money in advance. The fare between Ixtapa and Zihuatanejo should be about $3; to the airport, about $12; and from Zihuatanejo to La Ropa Beach, about $1.50.

Car Rental – *Avis* (phone: 42248), *Budget* (phone: 42189), *Dollar* (phone: 32025 at the *Dorado Pacífico;* 30333 at the *Krystal*), *Hertz* (phone: 42255), and *National* (phone: 42618) have airport locations and offices in Ixtapa hotels and in Zihuatanejo. On weekends and during the peak season reserve a vehicle in advance. Beware of very expensive rental prices, and if you have an accident, all gringos get blamed.

Cycles – Scooters and small motorcycles can be rented by the hour or by the day in Ixtapa at *Hola Renta Motos* (no phone), in *La Puerta Shopping Center* across the street from the *Dorado Pacífico* hotel.

Tours – *Ixtamar Tour and Travel Service* (4 Calle Pedro Ascencio, Zihuatanejo; phone: 43590) books excursions and fishing and diving trips. *Paseos Ixtapa* has booths at the *Sheraton Ixtapa* and the *Westin Resort Ixtapa* hotels; also in Ixtapa, *Turismo Caleta* (at *La Puerta Shopping Center;* phone: 30444), *Eturesa Travel* (in *Ixpamar Mall;* phone: 31607 or 31667), and travel desks at hotels all offer a number of programs, including trips into the backcountry and 1-day excursions to Acapulco and to Mexico City.

SHOPPING: There are about 400 shops in Ixtapa's seven shopping malls, and the shops in the *Westin Resort Ixtapa* hotel are fine for crafts, leather goods, beachwear, and silver. Paseo del Pescador and Calles Agustín Ramírez, Cinco de Mayo, Cuauhtémoc, and Pedro Ascencio in Zihuatanejo are good shopping streets. For rugs, hammocks, and crafts from all over the states of Guerrero, Oaxaca, and Chiapas, visit *La Zapoteca* and *El Jumil,* both located at 9 Paseo del Pescador, Zihuatanejo.

The artisans and municipal markets of Zihuatanejo may not be as grand and colorful as the markets of Guadalajara or Oaxaca, but they still offer plenty to delight visitors. The main municipal market, which is located on the south side of Benito Juárez between Calles González and Nava, sells food, clothing, and household goods. Local crafts can be found at the market on Calle Catalina González and the flea market on Calle Ejido.

African – Safari-style cothing and accesories for men and women. 10 *Las Fuentes Plaza,* Ixtapa (phone: 32415).

Alberto's – Fine silver and gold jewelry and semi-precious gems. At two locations: *La Puerta Shopping Center,* Ixtapa (phone: 31332), and 15 Cuauhtémoc, Zihuatanejo (same phone).

Alexandra – Casual and dressy women's clothing from Mexican designers. 15 Nicolás Bravo, Zihuatanejo (no phone).

Byblos – Best bookshop in the area for bilingual books and maps, plus a small selection of recorded music. 5 Agustín Ramírez, Zihuatanejo (phone: 42281).

Cecilia's – Silver jewelry at good prices. 19 Nicolás Bravo, Zihuatanejo (phone: 43192).

Chiquita Banana – Unusual handicrafts from all over Mexico. *Los Patios Shopping Center,* Ixtapa (no phone).

Coco Cabaña – Absolutely tops for Mexican crafts, especially folk-art collectibles from Oaxaca. Same owners as *Coconuts* restaurant. Calle Vicente Guerrero, Zihuatanejo (phone: 42518).

Florence – Gold jewelry in pre-Hispanic designs from Oaxaca, original art, regional crafts, and hand-embroidered linen. *La Puerta Shopping Center,* Ixtapa (no phone).

Fon Audio – Zihuatanejo's best selection of Mexican tapes and CDs, including tropical tunes and salsa, at reasonable prices. The manager will let you listen to selections before you buy them. Calle Ejido, 1 block from the municipal market (no phone).

La Fuente – Hand-embroidered cotton clothing for women, including designs from Suceso, Opus I, and Girasol, plus costume jewelry by Donna Brown *Los Patios Shopping Center,* Ixtapa (phone: 30812).

Galería Maya – Folk art, leather goods, crafts, and other unique items, many from Oaxaca. 31 Nicolás Bravo, Zihuatanejo (phone: 44606).

Galería San Angel – Mexican arts and crafts, gold jewelry, and sculptures depicting fantasy and quasi-religious subjects — devils, unicorns, and lizard-like creatures — produced by some of Mexico's finest artisans. *Los Patios Shopping Center,* Ixtapa (phone: 30392).

El Huizteco – Collection of more than 300 masks — ceremonial, mystical, ritual — in all sizes. 19 *Plaza Ixpamar,* Ixtapa (no phone).

Laddi Gucci – Select Oaxacan woolen tapestries and craft items. *Los Patios Shopping Center,* Ixtapa (no phone).

Luisa Conti – A sophisticated line of jewelry made with interesting combinations of materials in unique designs. Also carries an exclusive line of hand-knit sweaters. *Los Patios Shopping Center,* Ixtapa (no phone).

María de Guadalajara – Easy-to-wear and easy-to-care-for crinkled cotton designs for women. *Los Patios Shopping Center,* Ixtapa (no phone).

Polo Ralph Lauren – The well-known line of clothing for men and women, manufactured in Mexico and available for considerably less than in the US. *Las Fuentes Plaza,* Ixtapa (no phone).

Roberto's – Silver jewelry and ornamental pieces from Taxco. 9 *Las Fuentes Plaza,* Ixtapa (no phone).

Scruples – Fashions from Christian Dior, Nina Ricci, Julio Sport, and Bill Blass. *La Puerta Shopping Center,* Ixtapa (phone: 31493).

Sergio Bustamante – Another in the growing chain of Bustamante resort galleries, featuring the artist's much-imitated fantasy animals. Vicente Guerrero, across from the *Captain's Table* restaurant, Zihuatanejo (phone: 44767).

Tane – The famed Mexico City silversmith's original jewelry plus his reproductions of pre-Columbian and other antique pieces. *Westin Resort Ixtapa* (phone: 32121).

La Tarraya – Women's fashions from this exclusive Mexican designer. *La Puerta Shopping Center,* Ixtapa (phone: 31559).

Taxco El Viejo – A varied selection of silver from Taxco, plus attractive leather bags. Fluent English spoken here. *Los Patios Shopping Center,* 2nd Floor, Ixtapa (no phone).

Wanda Ameiro – Colorful high-fashion clothing, all from Mexico. *Las Fuentes Plaza,* Ixtapa (phone: 43625).

Xochitl Bazar/Hyacinth – Art, handicrafts, and handmade dresses and jewelry — all in unique designs. *Plaza Bugambilias Shopping Center,* Zihuatanejo (no phone).

SPORTS: Deep-Sea Fishing – Before Ixtapa was a gleam in anyone's eye, sportsmen came to Zihuatanejo to fish for marlin and sailfish. To arrange an excursion, work with a tour agency, or obtain better prices (though slightly less reliable service) go to the *Sociedad Cooperativo* at the pier (phone: 42056), where boats for four people cost about $180 for 7 hours. Or ask workers at the local dive shops to recommend a good fisherman; Captain Maciel of the *Don Chana,* is one of the best. Beware of individuals who approach you on the street and offer deep-sea fishing deals that sound too good to be true — they usually are.

Small-Game Fishing – Another favorite sport in the area. Boats carry beer and soft drinks as well as tackle and bait. Arrangements can be made to put in at some isolated beach where the crew will cook the catch. Boats are available at the pier in downtown Zihuatanejo.

Golf – The 18-hole *Ixtapa Golf Club,* designed by Robert Trent Jones, Jr., is both beautiful and challenging (see *Special Places*). It is open to anyone willing to pay the greens fee. There's also a practice course behind *La Puerta Shopping Center* in Ixtapa.

Horseback Riding – Guided tours on horseback leave from Playa Linda and Playa Quieta in Ixtapa. The cost for a 3½-hour tour is about $30.

Parasailing – This is fun but risky: While wearing an open parachute, you are pulled by a speedboat racing across the bay at Ixtapa; at a certain speed, you become airborne, flying above the Pacific. Accidents are rare, but they do happen. Available at the beaches of the *Stouffer Presidente, Holiday Inn, Westin Resort Ixtapa,* and *Dorado Pacífico* hotels in Ixtapa. Also available on Playa La Ropa in Zihuatanejo.

Sailing – Catamarans and other boats are available with or without crew. Sailing and windsurfing are popular at La Quieta Beach, near *Club Med.*

Scuba and Snorkeling – Equipment and instruction are available at Las Gatas Beach in Zihuatanejo from *Carlos Scuba* (no phone) and the *Zihuatanejo Scuba Center* (phone: 42147).

Swimming and Sunning – Though the surf seldom gets very rough at Ixtapa, the red flag goes up once in a while — beware of a dangerous undertow. The water always is calmer at La Quieta, La Ropa, and Las Gatas beaches. Don't count on lifeguards anywhere. A triathlon (swimming, bicycling, and running), held every year in early December, has become very popular.

Tennis – The *Ixtapa Golf Club* has lighted courts open to the public. *Club Med, Dorado Pacífico, Holiday Inn, Krystal, Sheraton Ixtapa, Stouffer Presidente, Villa del Sol,* and *Westin Resort Ixtapa* hotels all have their own tennis courts.

NIGHTCLUBS AND NIGHTLIFE: The action after dark centers around the hotels, especially those in Ixtapa, which attempt to see that guests don't get bored. A highlight of the activities are fiestas — colorful stage shows featuring traditional Mexican music and dance — which take place at different hotels each night; the best is at the *Dorado Pacífico* on Fridays. All cost about $25 per person. On weekend evenings, *OK's Cantina* restaurant (see *Eating Out*) features live salsa and tropical music. The new *Euforia* disco, next to the *Lighthouse* restaurant (see *Eating Out*), is as popular as it is spectacular, and *Christine's* at the *Krystal* is an old favorite. Some of the Ixtapa hotels, such as the *Krystal* and *Sheraton Ixtapa,* have bars or restaurants with live music and dancing; during the season, reservations are recommended. A dance party held nightly on a raised platform over the beach at *Carlos 'n' Charlie's* always draws a crowd.

The nightlife in Zihuatanejo is minimal. The tropical bar at *Coconuts* remains the best spot to hear the latest gossip and see who's in town, and most nights you can hear live jazz until about 10 PM at the *Bay Club,* on the hill above Playa La Madera. Across the street is *Ibiza,* Zihuatanejo's only disco, where last season the featured act was a transvestite show reminiscent of less than high class entertainment offered at some Puerto Vallarta and Acapulco clubs — fun for some, a real drag for others. On the main road to Ixtapa is *El Coyote,* a former bordello and dance club, now a bar for locals — *not tourists. Note:* Zihuatanejo offers free music and dance performances every Sunday from 7 to 9 PM at the plaza on the waterfront. Performers range from schoolchildren dressed in traditional costumes to members of professional dance troups.

BEST IN TOWN

CHECKING IN: Ixtapa has elegant, luxury hotels, each with an English-speaking staff member and each nice in its own way. Zihuatanejo's hostelries are older, mostly mom-and-pop operations, cozy and homey. The only trouble with the area is that it's likely to be either crowded or empty, depending upon when you visit. The best chance of striking a happy medium is during midweek from December through March. On weekends or during other busy times, try to arrive before late afternoon. Expect to pay up to $200 per night for a double room at the very expensive hotels; $130 in the expensive category; $100, moderate; and $50, inexpensive. Rates are often 30% to 40% less during the summer. Most hotels listed below accept MasterCard and Visa; a few also accept American Express and Diners Club. All telephone numbers are in the 753 area code unless otherwise indicated.

IXTAPA

Club Med – The 21-acre secluded estate is one of this organization's best-run resorts. Geared toward families, with supervised *mini club* activities for children from 4 months to 12 years of age, it also offers boat trips to Ixtapa Island, 12 tennis courts, golf nearby, all water sports, and even a computer workshop. Rates include all meals and most sports. Playa Quieta (phone: 30944; 800-CLUB MED in the US; FAX: 30393). Very expensive.

Sheraton Ixtapa – One of Ixtapa's most luxurious properties, it has 343 rooms and 11 suites rimming an immense atrium, the fine *Casa Real* restaurant, and a lobby bar where mariachis play. There are 4 lighted tennis courts, too, and the pool is enormous. Across from *Ixtapa Golf Club* (phone: 31858). Very expensive.

Villa Ixtapa – Under the same ownership as *Villa del Sol* in Zihuatanejo, this is a 3-home complex with a Spanish-Moorish influence (the homes could use some renovation). Each villa has 3 bedrooms, 3½ baths, living room, terrace, air conditioning, fans, and maid service. Special services, such as private cooks and chauffeurs, are provided on request. The complex is set on a golf course. The rate is $400 per day during the winter ($300 in the summer) for a maximum of 6 people. No credit cards accepted. 229-231 Paseo de las Golondrinas (phone: 31619; FAX: 42758). Very expensive.

Westin Resort Ixtapa – Absolutely the best place to stay in Ixtapa, Westin Hotels' immense property is set cliffside on its own beach. Facilities include 428 rooms with hammock-slung balconies, 4 good restaurants, a lively lobby bar (though some find the lobby decor reminiscent of a "Moorish maximum security prison"), 4 tennis courts, 4 swimming pools, and some fine shops. Vista Hermosa, the hotel's nearly private beach, is one of the area's best (phone: 32121; 800-228-3000 in the US; FAX: 31091). Very expensive.

Dorado Pacífico – One of Ixtapa's nicest accommodations, its 285 balconied rooms are pleasant and spacious, its restaurants (see *Eating Out*) and bars appealing. There's also a large pool with swim-up bar, 2 lighted tennis courts, and parasailing (phone: 32025; FAX: 30126). Expensive.

Holiday Inn – It's not glamorous but it's extremely popular, with 230 pleasant rooms, lovely grounds, 2 restaurants, a coffee shop, 2 bars, pool, 2 tennis courts, and parasailing from the hotel's beach. The social program includes exercise classes (phone: 31066; 800-HOLIDAY in the US; FAX: 31991). Expensive.

Krystal Ixtapa – The most exciting beachfront in Ixtapa. Besides 256 rooms, there is *Bogart's*, a *Casablanca*-style, continental restaurant (see *Eating Out*), as well as *Rarotonga* (another restaurant), a cafeteria, tennis and racquetball courts (tennis classes available), and live music with dancing in the bar and at *Christine's* disco. The large pool has its own fountain, waterfall, and slide (phone: 30333; 800-231-9860 in the US; FAX: 30216). Expensive.

Omni Ixtapa – Inaugurated in August 1989, it has 281 rooms, 13 junior suites, 12 master suites, and a presidential suite with a private pool. Facilities include a gymnasium, huge pool, restaurants, coffee shop, lobby bar, and *palapa* bar (phone: 30003; 800-THE OMNI; FAX: 31555). Expensive.

Stouffer Presidente – One of the first properties in Ixtapa and now, with its tower, one of the largest; it has 401 rooms. The balconies drip with greenery, and the facilities include restaurants, 2 bars, 2 pools and 2 tennis courts (phone: 30018; FAX: 32312). Expensive.

ZIHUATANEJO

Villa del Sol – Right on the beach in Zihuatanejo, this delightful hostelry is just the right size with 22 pleasant rooms and 4 rather spectacular 2-bedroom suites — all air conditioned. The hotel is a spot that's hard to beat for self-sufficient beach lovers who enjoy just a little bit of sophistication with their casual, unstructured vacations. Facilities include a tennis court, lovely pools, water sports, and exceptional food (see *Eating Out*). Price in high season includes breakfast and dinner for two. Children under 14 are not accepted during the winter season. No credit cards accepted. La Ropa Beach (phone: 42239; 800-223-6510 in the US; FAX: 42758). Very expensive.

Catalina-Sotavento – Two old favorites, the *Catalina* and the *Sotavento,* are now under the same management. This complex offers 121 spacious rooms on 8 terraced levels, plus hammocks strung on the balconies. The bar hangs high above La Ropa Beach and is a peaceful place to find oneself at dusk. The steep meandering steps here may be a problem for some. Service is good. Request a room with a view. Winter rates include breakfast and dinner. La Ropa Beach (phone: 42137; FAX: 42975). Moderate.

Fiesta Mexicana – A fine beachfront location, with 58 rooms and a pool. The restaurant is poorly run. La Ropa Beach (phone: 43776 or 43636; FAX: 43738). Moderate.

Irma – A favorite with frequent visitors, this pleasant 80-room hostelry has a bar, restaurant, beach club, and 2 small pools; daily deep-sea fishing tours can be arranged. La Madera Beach (phone: 42025). Moderate.

Puerto Mío – These 9 nicely decorated suites are part of the first phase of a marina and villa development. Also open is a restaurant-bar with great views of the sunset. 5 Paseo del Morro (phone: 43624 or 42748). Moderate.

Avila – It has a superb location on the beach; some of its 27 rooms are air conditioned. 8 Juan Alvarez (phone: 42010). Inexpensive.

Calpulli – A pleasant inn with 44 rooms with fans, plus a pool and a restaurant-bar. On Ixtapa-Zihuatanejo's best beach. La Ropa Beach (phone: 42166). Inexpensive.

Real Tres Marías – Twenty-five comfortable rooms, all with fans and balconies that overlook the bay. One block from the pier. Calle Juan Alvarez (phone: 42191). Inexpensive.

Las Uracas – Guests drive through a stone entryway into gardens filled with trees, plants, and paths connecting 10 bungalows, each one unique, with a living room, bedroom, and kitchen, and each named for a different bird. The name of the hotel itself translates as "the blue jays." The management caters to longtime repeat guests. Minimum 3-day stay. No credit cards accepted. La Ropa Beach (phone: 42049). Inexpensive.

Villas Miramar – Eighteen attractive private villas with air conditioning, modern furnishings, and views of the beach and the bay. There are 2 swimming pools and a restaurant-bar. Short walk or taxi ride from downtown. Playa La Madera (phone: 42106; FAX: 42149). Inexpensive.

OTHER ZIHUATANEJO ACCOMMODATIONS

Casa de Las Piedras – This secluded *palapa*-style hut above Playa La Ropa offers great bay views and enough hammocks and beds to sleep six. The weekly rate of $450 includes a maid and a gardener. Five-minute walk from beach and restaurants (phone: 43797; 415-488-9207 in the US). Moderate.

Casa Loma – These attractive, secure, and secluded bungalows (three with full kitchen and terrace) are a 2-minute walk from Playa La Ropa. Rates range from

$40 to $45 per night in-season to $250 to $300 per month off-season, including maid service (phone: 42743). Inexpensive.

Lilya Martínez arranges home rentals in Zihuatanejo and Ixtapa (phone: 43797). Elizabeth Williams arranges daily, weekly, and monthly rental of the condominiums that surround Ixtapa's golf course. Rates range from $70 to $200 per day to $2,000 per month, including maid service (phone: 42606).

EATING OUT: There are some excellent dining choices in Ixtapa and Zihuatanejo, with new places popping up every day. Listed as expensive are restaurants where dinner for two costs $50 or more; moderate, where the bill may reach $35; and inexpensive, $15 or less. Drinks and tips are extra. Most restaurants listed below accept MasterCard and Visa; a few also accept American Express and Diners Club. Unless otherwise noted, all restaurants are open daily. All telephone numbers are in the 753 area code unless otherwise indicated.

IXTAPA

Bogart's – Choose from an international menu in an exotic Moroccan atmosphere; dinner only. Reservations advised. *Krystal Ixtapa,* Paseo del Palmar (phone: 30333). Expensive.

Las Brasserie – Longtime residents rave about the *Dorado Pacífico*'s mezzanine-level eatery, where the chef focuses on the specialties of a different country each night. A local favorite, pianist Esther Walter, provides the lovely background music. Reservations advised (phone: 32025). Expensive.

El Faro – Part of the *Club Pacífica* condominium complex, next to the funicular that connects the condos to the beach. Try the *medallones del chef* (three medallions of beef, each topped with a different sauce) or the "El Faro" (grilled fish served with an achiote-flavored sauce). Open for breakfast and dinner. Reservations advised (phone: 31027, ext. 124). Expensive.

Lighthouse – A replica of a 19th-century lighthouse, it features an international menu especially created by chef Erick Du Bael and includes US prime meats, chicken, seafood casseroles, and pasta. If you climb up the 54-foot tower and ring the bell, you get a drink on the house. Reservations advised. Blvd. Ixtapa next to *Euforia* disco (phone: 31190). Expensive.

Portofino – Romance is in the air at the *Westin Resort Ixtapa*'s intimate eatery. Two suggestions from the Italian menu are veal *piccata* in marsala wine sauce and lobster in basil sauce. Reservations advised (phone: 32121). Expensive.

Villa Sakura – This modern, spacious Japanese place spans two levels, and has a rock garden complete with a bridge and brook for wishing. The menu includes tempura, sashimi, *yakitori,* and seafood dishes. Open for lunch and dinner; closed Wednesdays in the off-season. Reservations advised. *Centro Comercial Ixtapa* (phone: 30272). Expensive.

Villa de la Selva – What was once the home of Luis Echeverría Alvarez, former President of Mexico, is now one of Ixtapa's most fashionable restaurants. It's wonderful for sunset cocktails and dinner, and special lighting after 7:30 PM makes a lovely view of the ocean possible even after sundown. Reservations advised. Beyond the *Westin Resort Ixtapa.* Paseo de la Roca (phone: 30362). Expensive.

Da Baffone – An Italian eatery that serves fine pasta. Lunch and dinner only. Reservations unnecessary. *La Puerta Shopping Center* (phone: 31122). Moderate.

Benji Pio – Excellent Mexican and continental choices, steaks, and seafood. Open for lunch and dinner. Reservations unnecessary. *El Portal Shopping Center* (no phone). Moderate.

Café Onyx – At midday, join Ixtapa's chic residents and visitors for tacos, pizza, seafood, and salads. Reservations unnecessary. Blvd. Ixtapa beside *Las Galerías Shopping Mall* (phone: 30346). Moderate.

Carlos 'n' Charlie's – It's part of the ribs 'n' beer chain, though more sophisticated than most. No reservations. Beachfront location next door to the *Posada Real Hotel* (phone: 30085). Moderate.

Los Mandiles – Good appetizers, *flautas, fajitas,* and spicy Mexican specialties like chicken *chipotle* (grilled chicken in a fiery red chile pepper sauce). Reservations unnecesary. Behind *Las Galerías Shopping Center* (phone: 30379). Moderate.

O.K. Cantina & Oyster Bar – Fast becoming one of Ixtapa's most popular spots, this is the latest venture of one of the partners of the *Villa de la Selva* in Ixtapa and the plush *Sumiya* restaurant in Cuernavaca. The menu is international, and the decor is strikingly modern with accents of carved wood; the dining area surrounds a huge bar. A salsa group plays nightly. Open daily from 6 PM to 2 AM. Reservations advised. *Los Patios Shopping Center* (phone: 30973). Moderate.

Raffaello's – Succesful Italian franchise serving straightforward beef, fish, and pasta dishes on an open-air terrace. Reservations unnecessary. *Galerías Shopping Center* (phone: 30092). Moderate.

El Sombrero – Even though the owner is an expatriate German, the emphasis here is on fine Mexican specialties, with meat, seafood, and some international dishes also on the menu. Open for dinner only. Closed Sundays. Reservations advised. *Los Patios Shopping Center* (phone: 30439). Moderate.

Mamma Norma's – Come in the morning for standard breakfast fare — scrambled eggs or beans and tortillas — or later in the day for pizza. Delivery service available. No reservations. 101 *La Puerta Shopping Center* (phone: 30274). Inexpensive.

Las Margaritas – The small, circular *palapa* bar in the center of the shopping mall serves refreshing tropical drinks and fruit *licuados,* or milk shakes; drinks without alcohol (*sin alcohol*) available upon request. *Las Fuentas Plaza* (no phone). Inexpensive.

El Toko Tucan – Shaded outdoor café serving natural foods and burgers and fresh fruit juices and shakes. Exotic Guatamalan toucans and other caged birds provide a tropical backdrop. Reservations unnecessary. *Los Patios Shopping Center* (phone: 33611). Inexpensive.

ZIHUATANEJO

Bay Club – Elegant continental dining indoors and a mesquite grill on the terrace. There's live jazz every evening during the high season. Open from 2 PM to 1 AM. Reservations advised. On the road to Playa La Ropa (phone: 44844). Expensive.

El Castillo – Mexican and international dining in an elegant (for Zihuatanejo) Spanish colonial–style setting with big wooden tables and high-back chairs. Reservations advised. 25 Calle Ejido (phone: 43850). Expensive.

Coconuts – This elegant terrace setting with hand-painted parasol lampshades is a favorite with the local café society for its good seafood, pâté, black bean soup, and salads. Closed September and October. Reservations advised. 1 Agustín Ramírez (phone: 42518). Expensive.

Villa del Sol – The perfect place for a candlelit alfresco dinner, complete with strains of Beethoven wafting through the palms. Reservations necessary. No credit cards accepted. In the hotel of the same name, on Playa La Ropa (phone: 42239 or 44066). Expensive.

Canaima – Popular shrimp and seafood spot on the embarcadero. Ceiling fans and artsy decor. Reservations unnecessary. Paseo del Pescador (phone: 42003). Moderate.

Chez Kim – Zihuatanejo's first and only outlet for lovers of Chinese food. Features a Szechuan menu by Canadian Kim Danielson. Nicolás Bravo and Galeana (no phone). Moderate.

La Gaviota – Try the *filete de pescado mexicano* (fish filet cooked with tomatoes, onions, and mild peppers) at this romantic dinner spot, just a few yards away from the surf. Off-season, have a taxi wait for you while you dine, or be prepared to walk close to a half mile to find a cab on a busier section of the beach. End of Playa La Ropa (phone: 43677). Moderate.

La Mesa del Capitán (The Captain's Table) – Steaks, lobster, and other seafood, topped off with Irish coffee, all prepared under the careful supervision of Luz María de la Garza. Open for lunch and dinner, and the place is usually packed. Reservations for large groups only. 18 Nicolás Bravo (phone: 42027). Moderate.

El Morro Viejo – This new dining spot, part of the Puerto Mío development project, was designed to make the most of the magnificent views at sunset. Specialties include tuna steaks cooked in beer. Reservations advised. 5 Paseo del Morro (phone: 42748). Moderate.

La Perla – Futuristic wooden mobiles by Gerald, an eccentric local artist, dangle from the immense *palapa* roof at this longtime favorite. Go for the shrimp *diablo,* the red snapper, or co-owner Doña Raquel's mouthwatering special filet: grouper baked in foil with pepper, tomato, and onion, and sprinkled with white cheese. Service can be slow, but no one seems to care. Open daily for breakfast, lunch, and dinner. Reservations unnecessary. Playa La Ropa (phone: 42700). Moderate.

Taboga – It's in a lovely Mexican-style home that was the first hotel in Zihuatanejo, now converted to an eatery. Shrimp Alberto baked with cheese and smothered in a mild chili sauce is a good choice. Closed Sundays. No reservations. Calle Juan N. Alvarez (phone: 42637). Moderate to inexpensive.

Andaluz Expresso – Go for bagels with smoked salmon for breakfast and big deli-style sandwiches at lunch and dinner. Sidewalk seating on the Cuauhtémoc pedestrian mall. Reservations unnecessary. 12 Cuauhtémoc (phone: 43127). Inexpensive.

La Bocana – One of Zihuatanejo's oldest establishments and a popular choice for breakfast on the embarcadero. Try the large fruit platters or *chilaquiles,* also known as "the poor man's dish" (a casserole made of day-old tortillas, shredded chicken, cheese, tomatoes, chilies, and cream). Frequented by mariachi musicians at dinner. Reservations unnecessary. Paseo del Pescador (phone: 43545). Inexpensive.

Las Brazas – Mexican food, well prepared and reasonably priced. No reservations. 13 Cuauhtémoc (phone: 42577). Inexpensive.

Café Marina – Come to this small, popular hangout for the best pizza in Zihuatanejo, as well as sandwiches, homemade yogurt, spaghetti on Wednesdays, lively music, local news, and a huge selection of used paperbacks. Opens at noon. 9 Paseo del Pescador (no phone). Inexpensive.

El Campesino y Sus Brazas – Prime people watching on the pedestrian mall, inexpensive barbecue and chicken mole, and a shrine to the Virgin of Guadalupe in the corner. Reservations unnecessary. 13 Cuauhtémoc (phone: 42577). Inexpensive.

Casa Elvira – Part of a small hotel, this recently renovated place is pleasant and unpretentious, and has served consistently good breakfasts, lunches, and dinners for the last 30 years. On the embarcadero (phone: 42061). Inexpensive.

Garrobos – Consistently good seafood, including octopus and squid, paella (which must be requested in advance), plus the best homemade flan around. Reservations advised. At *Real Tres Marías Hotel,* 52 Calle Juan Alvarez (phone: 42977). Inexpensive.

Kapi-Kofi – Popular for breakfast, this humble little coffee shop has become a downtown landmark. No reservations. No credit cards accepted. 12 Pedro Ascencio (no phone). Inexpensive.

Kon Tiki – "Designer" pizza — the "vegetarian" is topped with peanuts, avocado, and pineapple — and fine sunset views from the terrace. Reservations unnecessary. On the road to Playa La Ropa (phone: 42471). Inexpensive.

Nueva Zealandia – Popular coffeehouse for cappuccino, espresso, quick breakfast fare, fruit *licuados,* and attentive service. No reservations. *Plaza Bugambilias Shopping Center* (phone: 42340). Inexpensive.

100% Natural – A nice change of pace, this simple, wholesome spot offers fresh fruit drinks and salads, healthy breakfasts, sandwiches, and *tortas* (Mexican sandwiches made on a crusty roll with refried beans and avocado slices, plus a choice of tasty fillings). No reservations. Catalina González and Cuauhtémoc (no phone). Inexpensive.

Il Piccolo – A favorite for homemade pasta, crêpes, spaghetti — and its large video screen. Reservations unnecessary. Nicolás Bravo (phone: 42928). Inexpensive.

Puntarenas – It's a 20-second ride on a fishing boat (from the north edge of the boat pier downtown) across the lagoon to this Zihuatanejo eatery. Don't expect a waiter to take your order; instead, pick up one of the photocopied menus on the small table by the kitchen door, write your choice on a notepad, hand it in (there's someone waiting for it at the kitchen door), and find a seat at one of the big wooden tables. Basic breakfasts — egg dishes and *pan français* (French toast) — and dinners — seafood, pork chops, and chicken — served in a casual open-air setting. Arrive before 6:30 PM to avoid a long wait for dinner. Breakfast and dinner, October through April only. Across the mouth of the lagoon (no phone). Inexpensive.

Rubén's Hamburgers – Popular with locals and visitors (mostly Texans) craving a good burger. Reservations unnecessary. Above Playa La Madera (no phone). Inexpensive.

La Sirena Gorda – Located just off the pier, this casual open-air spot features tasty fish kebab tacos. Don't miss the whimsical mural of a rotund singing mermaid that hangs over the bar. Closed Wednesdays. 20-A Paseo del Pescador (phone: 42687). Inexpensive.

For a sampling of local fare, try the shady (and inexpensive) *enramada* (arbored) restaurants, known as *Los Arbolitos* (The Little Trees), that face the municipal beach at the center of town. Locals gather here, children skip by after school, and strolling musicians play on Friday afternoons. How to select the best one? Follow your nose to the most enticing aroma.

DIVERSIONS

For the Experience

QUINTESSENTIAL IXTAPA AND ZIHUATANEJO

Among other things, traveling south of the border doubtless has taught you that the real spirit of this country lies somewhere between an ancient ruin, the jet set glitz of an all-night disco, and a tranquil sunrise on a secluded beach. If you have tried on the requisite number of sombreros, anointed your body with coconut oil to bronze it in the tropical sun, and haggled over a colorful serape at the *mercado,* you've certainly scratched the surface. You may even have donned a scuba mask, mixed it up with a marlin, eaten an enchilada, and outstared an armadillo on Ixtapa Island. But, amigos, until you savor the places and pleasures listed below, you haven't experienced the true meaning of Mexico's Pacific Coast — most especially, Ixtapa and Zihuatanejo.

A DAY AT PLAYA LA ROPA: Ixtapa and Zihuatanejo boast some of the finest beaches of any of the resort towns along Mexico's Pacific Coast, but there's more magic at La Ropa on Zihuatanejo Bay than at any other beach in the area. You can walk here from town (it starts just a mile south of Zihuatanejo) but go early, before the sun gets too hot. If you decide to take a taxi, ask the driver to take you to the south end of the beach, or to any nearby hotel or restaurant (*La Perla* is right in the middle).

Visually, La Ropa is a nearly mile-long arc of clean, soft white sand and a calm sea ranging in color from nearly emerald green in winter to deep rich blue in summer. Depending on where you sit, you can enjoy anything from relative seclusion to in-depth mingling. Though it is never really crowded, La Ropa attracts a fascinating following of Mexicans, North Americans, and travelers — art dealers, diplomats, psychologists, fashion designers, models, musicians, painters, and restaurateurs — who congregate here for peaceful days of eating, swimming, snoozing, and good conversation. Strolling musicians and local families join them on weekends.

There are always a few energetic souls who hit the beach by 7 AM for a morning jog, but most people don't arrive until at least 9 AM, when the restaurants open for breakfast. La Ropa is a swimmer's beach; there is no windsurfing or surfing, so you can backstroke to your heart's content.

While on the beach, use sunscreen and cover-ups and sit under the shady *palapas* (thatch umbrellas) when the sun is strongest. When hunger strikes, sample the food served at the casual seafood restaurants that sit in clusters just 60 yards from the surf. It's easy and fun to move from one to the next, snacking on guacamole, seafood tacos, shrimp cocktail, and *tiritas,* succulent stips of raw fish (usually snapper) that are marinated in lime juice and served with crisp onions and fiery green chilies. (*Tiritas* don't usually appear on menus, so make a point of asking for them.) The best restaurants on La Ropa are *La Gaviota, El Marlin, Rossy, Omar's, La Perla, Villa del Sol, Catalina-Sotavento,* and the new place at the northern end of the beach that doesn't have a name.

At day's end, head to the bar and observation deck at the *Catalina-Sotavento* hotel and celebrate the sunset while sipping some surprisingly smooth mescal, "the cognac of Mexico." Sunset on the Pacific — when the sky turns a fiery gold, then melts into rosy reds and soft pinks, radiating a coppery, then deep blue, then purple sheen across the bay — is an experience that will linger long after you leave this place. As if all this splendor weren't enough, as darkness falls, thousands of stars cast their sparkling reflections on the bay.

At dinnertime (early or late, it's entirely up to you), try a tasty, tangy *huachinango* (red snapper), prepared *a la parrilla al mojo de ajo,* or rubbed in salt and grilled over a hot fire. Be sure to savor the little flakes of cheek meat that sit in small indentations near the fish's jawbone — they're considered a delicacy. As it is all day long, the mood at La Ropa is based solely on the pursuit of leisure. No one will rush you to leave your dinner table, but once you're ready to call it a day, take one last stroll on the beach — barefoot, natch. The feel of the cool sand caressing your toes and the sound of the gentle waves against the shore form the perfect way to end a perfect day.

MORNING AT THE MARKET: Zihuatanejo's large public market, a 15-minute walk from the boat pier, is not nearly as colorful and grand as the markets of Guadalajara or Oaxaca, and there are no handicrafts for sale. Instead, this busy *mercado* offers visitors a rare glimpse of the everyday life of the residents of this onetime sleepy fishing village; it is one of those places where — despite the influx of tourists — no concessions to modernity have been made. The best time to visit the market is early in the morning, around 7 or 8 AM, when the locals do their shopping, and when the freshly baked *bollilos* (small rolls) are soft and warm.

Enter from Avenida Benito Juárez and follow your nose (and the crowds) through the large main room, past baskets and tables filled with fresh food from area farms, plantations, and local waters — shiny limes, garlands of garlic, brightly colored chilies and beans, fish, salted beef, and fragrant white cheese from Oaxaca. There are several small counters in the center where you can relax over a steaming cup of *café con leche* and a roll, or if the sight of all this food has sparked your appetite, a stack of hotcakes. From this vantage point, it's possible to watch merchants and customers debating the freshness of the leeks and neighbors catching up on family gossip, as well as listen to the mariachi and salsa music that is being played in some of the stalls.

If you don't have cooking facilities at your hotel, you can still pick up some inexpensive treats and souvenirs. The colorful plastic market *bolsas* (bags) make great beach totes, and the coconut oil soap and boxes of wooden matches with mythological scenes printed on them are good gifts for friends back home.

Although it's possible to whiz through the entire market in 15 or 20 minutes, it's worth spending an hour or more roaming through the center hall, where most of the fresh-food merchants display their wares, and poking around the stalls in the corridor where canned foods, household goods, and inexpensive clothing are sold. Before leaving, walk to the other end of the market to the open-air stalls in the back, where you'll find more produce, including bananas for 3¢ apiece. The merchants start packing up around 3 PM.

DIVING OFF IXTAPA AND ZIHUATANEJO'S COAST: Most everyone knows that some of the world's best scuba and skin diving is found in the coral reefs of Cozumel and other Mexican Caribbean sites off the Yucatán Peninsula. What everyone *doesn't* know, however, is that some wonderful tropical-ocean diving spots exist on the Pacific Coast, and the best are right here. In fact, contrary to the outdated belief that local dive sites are limited to a few islands and Los Morros (a rocky islet that, because of strong surges, is suitable only for expert divers), there are 28 fine dive sites, including shallow coral beaches, rocky islets, and even a sunken wreck. Among the best are four sites at Zacatoso, off Ixtapa, where you will find stunning beds of red and green coral among rock formations, anemones (tiny cones that will grasp your finger when you touch them), nudibranchs (a form of coral that looks like fine mesh), and gorgonians (coral formations with horned branches). You're also likely to see spotted eels, and large schools of puffer fish. The best diving is in July and August, when the water temperature reaches 90F and visibility reaches 70 feet, but there's still lots to see during the winter months, when the water temperature averages 75F — everyone wears wet suits to stay warm — and visibility is about 25 to 35 feet. The best dive shops for equipment and instruction are the *Zihuatanejo Scuba Center* on the boat pier (phone: 753-42147) and *Carlos Scuba* (no phone; but the *Zihuatanejo Scuba Center* will take messages) on Playa Las Gatas.

SECLUSION ON THE SAND: Ever dream of a private swath of sand that is virtually untouched by civilization, a place that is silent except for the hypnotic sounds of tropical birds hidden among the trees, and of waves breaking near the shore? Information about such a paradisiacal day trip cannot be found in the brochures at your local tour agency (though some agents may be able to help you make arrangements); instead, head down to the *Cooperativo,* a stone building at the end of the pier in Zihuatanejo, arrange for a boat and a fisherman — and discover that dreams really can come true.

The idea is to round up a small circle of friends — or just one very special person — and hire an open 28-foot *panga* (fishing boat) and a knowledgeable fisherman to take you to one of the many secluded beaches within 30 or 40 minutes of Ixtapa and Zihuatanejo. Along the way, the boatman will troll for the fish that he will grill over an open fire or chop up for *tiritas* at the beach later on. Bring a cooler of sodas and beers, or if more fitting to the occasion, a couple of bottles of Mexican beer or domestic wine (such as Los Reyes, Don Angel, or Hidalgo), fruit, and light snacks. (Wine can be purchased in restaurants, but are not usually sold in liquor stores, which sell primarily beer and hard liquor, including tequila and mescal.) Don't forget to pack your own beach accesories — blankets, towels, suntan lotion, and snorkeling gear. You'll be on your own for the day — free to skinny-dip in a secret cove, hunt for exquisite spriral-shape shells and bits of bleached coral, read (or write) a novel under the shade of a palm tree, or sunbathe, snorkel, and enjoy a barbecue on the beach.

When arranging your trip, be sure to discuss all of the particulars, including cost (it shouldn't exceed about $35 total), pick-up time and place, and an approximate drop-off time (it will have to be before dark). Fishermen expect to be paid — and tipped — upon return.

PACIFIC SUNSETS: Pacific sunsets are among the finest on the planet, and watching the shifting light and colors — from yellow-gold to lush orange and red to pink and finally the deep blues and purples of night — is a cherished ritual among visitors to Ixtapa and Zihuatanejo. You can choose a spot in the sand and park your blanket or beach chair, or opt for a restaurant or bar above the beach. In Ixtapa, try the lobby bar at the *Westin Resort Ixtapa.* The music is a bit tacky, but the view of the shifting light and colors is magnificent. In Zihuatanejo, *El Morro Viejo,* a small but attractive restaurant-bar tucked into a tiny cove at Puerto Mío, is so ideal for viewing the sunset that one might belive that it was built solely for this purpose. The view is also exceptional at both the *Bay Club* and *Kon Tiki,* two restaurant-bars located on the hill overlooking Zihuatanejo. The *Catalina-Sotavento* hotel's sun deck affords both bay and beach views.

Wherever you are, be sure to watch for the "green flash," that sudden burst that appears just before the last rays of the sun slip beyond the horizon. Legend has it that if you see the green flash on your honeymoon, you'll live happily ever after.

DÍA DE LOS MUERTOS (DAY OF THE DEAD): Although Mexicans fear and respect death as much as any other peoples, they face it, defy it, mock it, and even toy with it more than most cultures. Never is this more apparent than on November 1, *All Souls' Day* — known in Mexico as the *Day of the Dead* — an eminently Mexican holiday perpetuating a tradition of death and rebirth.

By mid-October, bakeries and markets throughout Mexico are filled with sweets and toys created with death as their theme. Bake shops are piled high with *pan de muerto,* a coffee cake decorated with meringues fashioned into the shape of bones. Children, friends, and relatives are given colorful sugar skulls with their names inscribed on them; death figures shaped from marzipan are on sale at most candy stores. Verses called *calaveras,* containing witty allusions or epitaphs, are written about living friends, relatives, and public figures, and by the end of October, shop windows take on a macabre air, with shrouded marionettes and other ghoulish-looking figurines heralding the holiday.

On the actual date, families gather in graveyards to picnic and spend the day with their departed, bringing along their loved ones' favorite foods and drink. Graves are decorated with bright orange *zempasuchil* (marigolds), the flower of the dead; *copal,* an incense that dates back to pre-Hispanic cultures, is burned. The celebration begins with prayers and chants for the dead, and usually ends with drinks to the health of the departed. Homes are decorated in much the same way, with tables filled with marigolds and objects of which the deceased was especially fond.

One of the most moving observances of this tradition is held on Janitzio Island in Lake Pátzcuaro. Here the ceremony begins on November 1, with the descendants of Tarascan Indians gathering on the lake at dawn for a ceremonial duck hunt. Using ancient Indian weapons, they paddle their canoes into a semicircle, trapping the ducks against the shore. At a signal from the leader of the hunt, the weapons are thrown. Shortly after midnight, the women make their way to the cemetery, laden with baskets of food — including traditional dishes of duck meat — incense, bouquets of *zempasuchil,* and thousands of candles, transforming the small graveyard behind the church of Janitzio Island into a glittering outdoor cathedral. As the women and children meditate at the grave sites and the church bells toll, the men begin the slow, steady chants that they will continue through the night.

MARIACHI MUSIC: The melodies pervade all of Mexico. Groups of musicians roam the streets of cities large and small, serenading under the windows of apartment buildings and in the doorways of restaurants and shops. Students, carrying guitars and flutes on buses and subways, often play for their fellow passengers in hope of earning a few pesos on the way to and from school. Although every region of Mexico has its own special music, none is more associated with the country as a whole than mariachi (the word comes from the French for "marriage").

During Emperor Maximilian's reign, wealthy Guadalajara families, trying to imitate the customs of the court, hired musicians to entertain their guests. Today, mariachis — made up of at least one vocalist, a guitar, bass, violin, and a trumpet or two — are usually hired to serenade girlfriends or to play at special events (weddings, birthdays, anniversaries). Their vast repertoire consists of such sentimental love songs as "Si Estás Dormida," "Las Mañanitas" (the Mexican equivalent of "Happy Birthday," but sung for almost any special occasion), "Guadalajara," "La Bamba," or "Cucurrucucú Paloma." The traditional Mexican fiestas held at large resort hotels in Ixtapa usually include at least one group of mariachis, and there are a number of restaurants and bars where they provide the entertainment. Some of the best mariachis — dressed in their close-fitting pants and bolero-type jackets decorated with silver — play weekend afternoons on Playa La Ropa, and in Zihuatanejo at *La Bocana* at dinnertime, and at *Los Arbolitos,* the cluster of restaurants across from the municipal beach, on Friday afternoons.

MOLE: To an uninformed gringo reading a Mexican menu, an entrée of turkey mole conjures up visions of a drumstick topped with hot fudge. Nothing could be farther from reality. The word "mole" comes from the Nahuatl *mulli,* which means "sauce" — and this one is made of more than 30 ingredients — only *one* of which is unsweetened chocolate. Most Mexican housewives pride themselves on preparing the sauce from scratch, a time-consuming recipe that involves at least four kinds of chilies (which have to be seeded, deveined, and roasted), sesame seeds, almonds, peanuts, raisins, prunes, plantains, onions, garlic, coriander, anise, cinammon, and an infinitesimal amount of the aforementioned chocolate. Traditionally, it is served with chicken or turkey, as a filling for tamales, or as a sauce for enchiladas. If you are served mole in a Mexican household, you know you're an honored guest.

Ixtapa and Zihuatanejo's Resort Hotels

Whether your idea of a resort is a place to bake elegantly under the tropical sun, with no greater exertion than raising your wrist to sip a tall, cool drink (remember that the now-famous "swim-up" bar was invented in Mexico, 130 miles (208 km) down the coast at Acapulco's *Villa Vera*), or whether you prefer a haven that inspires you to play tennis and golf in the morning, go boating or riding in the afternoon, and dance all night, Ixtapa and Zihuatanejo are an absolutely perfect vacation choice.

All the resort hotels in the area maintain a high standard, and prices vary only slightly. Rates go up and down based on season, meal plans, special packages, and individual or group travel. Even though rates have increased dramatically in recent years (partially attributable to improvements to services and facilities), prices are almost always lower in Ixtapa and Zihuatanejo than at their Caribbean and Hawaiian counterparts.

A multitude of package and price options are available, so work with a travel agent who knows and likes Mexico, or contact the hotels yourself. (Many of them have US representatives and toll-free numbers.) When requesting information, be sure to find out if a resort offers (or requires) a meal plan, or MAP (Modified American Plan). In such cases, the price of breakfast, lunch, and/or dinner at the hotel are included in the rate. Although taking meals at the hotel can be convenient and may increase the value of the package, it robs guests of the opportunity to discover other restaurants and cafés on their own. If possible, always try to get weekly rates, as they are much more competitive than daily rates. When planned in advance, it is possible to save a fair sum.

Peak season for most of the coastal resorts is December 15 through April 15. Those who travel during the off-season (April 15 to December 15) normally can save from 40% to 80% on accommodations. The temperature may be a bit hotter and the crowd a bit less chic, but there will be fewer people, and the lower rates may permit an increase in the level of luxury and the length of stay. Although many new hotels are in various stages of development, at present the *Krystal Ixtapa* and the *Westin Resort Ixtapa* rates special mention in this section.

WESTIN RESORT IXTAPA: This modern, $63-million resort, formerly the *Camino Real,* has acres of palm trees and tropical flowers, and 24 miles of beach. The 428-room hotel's decor was inspired by neighboring coconut plantations. All of the rooms have private patios with hammocks. An 18-hole Robert Trent Jones, Jr. golf course is minutes away, and 4 lighted tennis courts are near a complex of multilevel pools and waterfalls. Facilities at the resort include 3 restaurants, a bar, shops, jeep rental, beach parties, and nightly entertainment. The hotel sits on Vista Hermosa, a first-rate beach that is frequented almost solely by hotel guests because of its secluded location. *Mailing address:* Apdo. 97, Ixtapa, Guerrero 40880 (phone: 753-32121; or Westin Hotels, 800-228-3000).

Evocative Small Hotels

The very best Mexican inns — usually called *posadas* — are a happy blend of Old World charm and New World plumbing, and one of the finest is right in Zihuatanejo.

VILLA DEL SOL: Set on Playa la Ropa, the area's best beach, this 22-room, 4-suite inn is built around a small swimming pool and a large *palapa,* which houses a bar and open-air dining area; there's also a casual, but elegant, multi-story dining room next door that offers continental fare; and the restaurants and discos of Ixtapa's big hotels are just 4½ miles (7 km) away.

This place is for those who appreciate low-key, high-style leisure, enjoy quiet conversation, and are able to unwind using their own resources — since there isn't much here besides a great beach. If you crave a posh escape from reality, this is about as good a place as you'll find anywhere. No children under 14 during the winter season. *Mailing address:* Apdo. 84, Playa La Ropa, Zihuatanejo, Guerrero 40880 (phone: 753-42239; 800-223-6510 in the US; FAX: 753-42758).

Natural Wonderlands

The best bird watching in the Ixtapa and Zihuatanejo area is at Laguna Potosí in Barra de Potosí, 8 miles (13 km) south of Zihuatanejo. Orlando Banuelos will take birders out for an hour-long tour — expect to see great blue herons, egrets, ibis, cranes, and spectacular flocks of rare roseate spoonbills. Cost is about $15 for four people. Ask for Orlando in the *palapa* restaurants at Playa Blanca, which starts at the village.

Ixtapa Island is a protected wildlife sanctuary, but the animals — deer, badgers, armadillos, rabbits, and raccoons — keep to themselves in the dense underbrush when tourists are nearby. To get here, take the 5-minute boat ride from Playa Quieta. Occasionally, local tour agencies offer trips into the mountains for visitors to observe the area's indigenous bird and plant life. Unguided ventures into these areas are not recommended.

For information about nature tours and conservation in the area, contact the Zihuatanejo and Ixtapa Ecology Association through marine biologist Juan Bernard at the *Zihuatanejo Scuba Center* (4 Paseo del Pescador; phone: 753-42147). For information about the Society for Protection of Animals, or to buy one of their attractive T-shirts as a souvenir, ask for Helen Krebs Posse in any of the shops at *El Embarcadero* on the waterfront. (Each of the shops is owned by a member of her family.)

Shopping at the Source

Ixtapa and Zihuatanejo support hundreds of shops, but many are of marginal interest to visitors. In Ixtapa, clothing boutiques offer the most diversity and quality: You can find such US designer labels as Ralph Lauren's Polo at somewhat discounted prices, and distinctive Mexican fashions in flashy colors and styles. For serious shoppers, silver jewelry fashioned in nearby Taxco is sold here at competitive prices.

Ixtapa's seven shopping centers are located next to one another, across from the resort strip. Unlike the sprawling shopping centers in the US, these are 2-story plazas boasting about 20 to 30 shops each. In fact, determined shoppers can hit all of them in just 1 day and return to the hotel laden with bags filled with T-shirts, silver jewelry, clothing by domestic and foreign designers, and arts and crafts items.

Most Zihuatanejo shops are concentrated in an 8-square-block area north of the plaza. Shoppers can stroll along Cuauhtémoc, a pleasant pedestrian mall closed to auto traffic.

Zihuatanejo's main municipal market is nowhere near as grand and colorful as the markets of Guadalajara or Oaxaca, but it still contains plenty to delight exploring visitors. Located on the south side of Benito Juárez between Calles González and Nava, the *mercado* carries food, clothing, household goods, and many unusual items — multicolored votive candles, love potions, and powders to cure arthritis, infertility, and bad luck — but very little in the way of handicrafts. The colorful artisans' market running along Cinco de Mayo from the boat pier has nearly 20 rows of stalls filled with craft items.

Although the cooler morning and early evening hours are the most comfortable for browsing, late-rising visitors tend to hit the streets in numbers closer to noon. Normal business hours for most shops are 10 AM to 2 PM and from 4 to 8 PM. Many shops have air conditioning, which provides a cool break for shoppers — and reluctant spouses.

Since last season, all beach vendors have been removed by government directive from tourist beaches throughout Ixtapa and Zihuatanejo, as well as from the rest of Mexico's Pacific Coast. This dramatic action was taken to end the increasing harassment of visitors by local vendors selling everything from beads, blankets, and silver to painted fish, peanuts, and coconut oil lotion. As an alternative, market stalls have been set up in Ixtapa south of the commercial shopping malls, and in Zihuatanejo along Cinco de Mayo, near the church, and on Playa La Ropa, just south of the *Fiesta Mexicana* hotel. These outdoor markets are worth visiting for inexpensive gift items and souvenirs like onyx wind chimes, brightly painted wooden fish, wool blankets, and bead necklaces. Prices are lower here than in shops, and are always negotiable.

Native crafts are usually less expensive in local markets than in shops. It is better to buy more expensive items — jewelry or gems — in reputable shops. And if someone offers to sell you an archaeological relic from a Mexican ruin, turn him down flat. In most cases these "relics" are manufactured by the truckload, and if by some wild chance you are being offered a genuine artifact, the sale is illegal, and the item cannot be exported from Mexico without breaking the law.

Carefully check the quality of any merchandise you are considering buying. Goods are often presented as hand-crafted that are patently machine-made — although if the price is right and the item attracts you, this is certainly no reason to refrain from buying it. But be sure you are paying what the item is worth.

Certain items are produced or crafted especially well in Mexico, though the areas in which they are found vary. Silver, pottery, woven goods, leatherwork, and copper and tin goods are all uniquely Mexican materials and are worked into enduring art by Mexican craftspeople. Well-made shoes are often an excellent buy.

Silver has been plentiful in Mexico since before the Spanish conquest. Silver items should be marked *sterling* or *.925* so that you know that there are not less than 925 grams of pure silver for every 1,000 grams of weight. If you are told that the silver in the jewelry came from local mines, be skeptical. Nowadays, all silver from Mexican mines goes to the central Bank of Mexico, where it is melted into bars and then resold around the country to craftspeople.

Pottery is one of the major crafts of Mexico. There's a lot of it — some of high artistic value — and it's usually inexpensive, but don't buy it to cook in and don't store acidic foods in it, since potentially dangerous lead compounds are often used in glazing. Each area of the country has its special designs and materials. Oaxaca pottery is satin black or has an unusual green glaze. You can choose as well from Tlaquepaque pottery, Puebla earthenware, or Mexico City's modern designs. Lacquerwork and ceramics also are often of high quality. The lacquer is made from *chía* oil (a combination of wild sage and *aje,* the remains of plant lice). Dolomite and other minerals are added to this mixture to produce a lacquer as fine as that made from the sap of the Chinese tree. Lacquer trays usually have polished black backgrounds painted with flowers or gold lacquer.

Serapes, rebozos, blankets, and other woven articles, such as the beautiful bulky sweaters of Toluca, are usually bargains. They should be handloomed from wool; examine the weave to make sure that other yarns weren't used.

You should examine leather goods also, to make sure that they are pure rawhide, not leather glued to cardboard or plastic. Other native crafts that you will see are *huaraches* (braided sandals), *huipiles* (embroidered dresses), and all sizes and shapes of baskets, hammocks, and piñatas.

Copper and tin goods can be found all over Mexico. Copper was once the most popular metal of the Mixtec and Aztec Indians. Kettles, pots, pans, and pitchers are sold in markets as well as in the more expensive shops. Again, check for quality — some articles are actually made of iron sprayed with copper-toned paint.

Be wary of gems that are sold as bargains. Jade has not been found in Mexico since the Spanish conquest; turquoise, like all other stones, should be bought only in reputable stores; and gold is not much less expensive in Mexico than in the US. Mexico does, however, have high-quality amethysts and opals and some lovely onyx and black obsidian.

Mexico is home to many working artists and craftspeople, some of whom combine new materials and design with the art of the past to produce original painting, sculpture, weaving, jewelry, and much more. In many ways, Mexico is the perfect place for an artist to live: Life moves slowly and is relatively inexpensive; also, the country's great natural beauty is inspiring. You can see the work of these artists in galleries and shops in towns and cities throughout the country. You are allowed to bring most Mexican crafts into the US duty-free under the Generalized System of Preferences (GSP) program. For complete details about customs regulations in the US, see *Customs and Returning to the US,* GETTING READY TO GO.

Bullfights: The Kings of the Rings

If you're truly interested in Mexican culture, you should experience at least one bullfight. The bullfight, a spectacle rather than a sport, dates from before the Christian era. (The people of Crete were known to have hand-wrestled bulls long before the Moors introduced bullfighting to Spain.) Modern bullfighting originated on the Iberian Peninsula during the 12th century. The Spanish brought bullfighting to Mexico just 8 years after the conquest, and the first official bullfight in the New World took place in 1529.

It should be reiterated that you do not attend a fight with the idea of rooting for the bull as though it were the home team, because the bull never wins. Some people find the spectacle of an animal being killed before a cheering crowd thoroughly repugnant. If the idea offends you, don't go. Others consider the bullfight an art form, as much a part of Mexican culture as weaving, pottery work, or onyx sculpture. In any case, the bullfight is certainly a colorful event, especially at *Plaza México* in Mexico City (1 block west of Insurgentes in the southern part of the city) — one of the best bullfighting rings in the world. Matadors, picadors on horseback, banderilleros, and helpers parade into the plaza accompanied by stirring *pasadoble* music. If your schedule allows, it's worth a stop here on your way home.

In 1989, Zihuatanejo offered bullfights on Sundays at the *Plaza de Toros* out on Avenida Morelos, but none took place last year. The unexceptional local events paired *novillero* (apprentice) matadors with second-rate bulls. Whether bullfights will resume in Zihuatanejo in the future is undetermined; inquire at your hotel travel desk.

For those who want to witness the spectacle in this area, Acapulco hosts bullfights on Sunday afternoons during the month of December and *Easter Week.* The festivities begin at 5:30 PM. Tickets and transportation to Acapulco can be arranged through Ixtapa-Zihuatanejo tour agencies. The bullring is near Caleta Beach.

For The Body

Ixtapa and Zihuatanejo's Amazing Beaches

Ixtapa and Zihuatanejo have some of the finest beaches of any of the resort towns along Mexico's Pacific Coast, and since all beaches in Mexico are public, visitors can swim and use the facilities, including those near luxurious hotels (though access to these resort strips may prove awkward or difficult). Beaches that are designated "public recreational areas" are maintained by the government and are much used by resident Mexicans. Although Playa Palmar is the main hotel beach in Ixtapa at present, there are plans for development (hotels and restaurants) along a total of 14 local beaches. Running from north to south, they are Varadero, Cuachalate (on Ixtapa Island), Pequeña, Carey, Larga, Linda, Oliverio, Quieta, Cuata, Don Rodrigo, Don Juan, Don Juan de Dios, Palmar, and La Hermosa. For now, however, here are a few of our favorite strands.

ISLA IXTAPA: A 5-minute boat ride ($2 round-trip) from Playa Quieta takes you to this small, wooded isle, a protected wildlife sanctuary where iguanas and raccoons roam free (although they tend to stay in the dense underbrush out of the visitor's view). Each of the four primary beaches on the island, all within easy walking distance of one another, is quite different, with a variety of sand, shell, or pebble surfaces. Playa Carey's waters boast red and green coral formations and schools of tiny fish, making it the best beach for snorkeling. Of the handful of seafood restaurants, *El Marlin* (close to the boat dock) is our choice. Some of the beaches get crowded on weekends, but those seeking seclusion need walk only 15 to 20 minutes in either direction from the spot where the boat drops passengers off.

PLAYA BLANCA: This exquisite length of beach begins at Barra de Potosí, a tiny fishing village about 8 miles (13 km) southeast of Zihuatanejo, and continues uninterrupted and nearly deserted for 10 miles (16 km). In Barra de Potosí, a row of casual *palapa* (thatch-roofed) restaurants serve the day's catch and handmade tortillas; try the last restaurant to the north — the food is good, and the views, which span all the way to Zihuatanejo, are spectacular. Development along this pristine beach appears inevitable — a few new structures already dot the coastline — so enjoy it while you can. To get to Playa Blanca, take Highway 200 to the exit for Los Achotes, then head west on the dirt road for about 7 miles (11 km).

PLAYA LAS CUATAS: The two almost identical beaches in Ixtapa that make up Las Cuatas (The Twins) are separated by big rocks, and offer some of the best body-surfing waves in Mexico. For optimum conditions, visit in the late afternoon from December through February. Waves usually average about 4 to 5 feet, but occasionally they get as high as 15 feet, at which point surfing, swimming, or even standing in the water can be perilous. Check conditions, don't exceed your capability, and if you're unsure, stay out of the water altogether. Easy footpaths run between the two beaches; there are also several other footpaths north of Cuatas that lead to a beautiful cliff-top overlook offering a grand view of the crashing waves of the beaches and the calm waters of the secluded coves below. In the haze to the south are Ixtapa's resort hotels. There are rarely more than a few couples at Las Cuatas, and topless sunbathing is permissible. Las Cuatas is 3 miles (5 km) from the Ixtapa hotel zone; turn left just before the parking lot at Playa Quieta.

PLAYA LAS GATAS: Worth visiting, regardless of whether or not you believe the charming tale that the coral reef was formed to provide a shallow swimming spot for the daughter of a Tarascan king. Las Gatas (The Cats) supposedly refers to the whiskered nurse sharks that used to slumber here. Composed of fine white coral sand with wide, shallow waters and gentle waves, it's ideal for small children and beginning snorkelers (watch for sharp rocks when entering the water). Access is by boat from the pier in Zihuatanejo. The scenic 5-minute ride across the bay costs about $2 round-trip. About a dozen casual *palapa* restaurants line the beach. Avoid the rocky footpath between Playa La Ropa and Las Gatas; it's a deserted stretch and a favorite lair of bandidos.

At the far end of Las Gatas is the jungle-like guest compound of Owen Lee, a longtime resident, and author of several definitive handbooks on scuba diving (Lee accompanied Jacques Cousteau on some of his earliest dives). Some of the area's best surfing is at the south end of this beach, where skilled surfers can catch some impressive waves. (Surfers unfamiliar with Las Gatas should be aware that the water is quite shallow in spots.) About a dozen casual *palapa* restaurants line the beach.

PLAYA LA MADERA: This small, secluded beach with gentle waves is tucked into the crook of Zihuatanejo Bay, and is used primarily by guests of the bungalows and small hotels nestled on the hillside. Between town and Playa La Ropa.

PLAYA MAJAHUA: An attractive, relatively isolated beach midway between Ixtapa and Zihuatanejo, it has some big waves, but beware of undertows. No restaurants, no restrooms. If you're driving here, take the road that runs along the north side of the lagoon in Zihuatanejo, then turn right at the intersection after the water filtration plant; when the road splits three ways, stay to the right and follow this road until you reach the beach. Alternatively, take a taxi and arrange for the driver to pick you up at a prearranged time.

PLAYA PALMAR: A straight, wide swath of white sand beach on which all the main beachfront hotels (except the *Westin Resort Ixtapa*) sit. A picture-perfect beach with often deceptively heavy surf and tricky undertows, Palmar is more for sunning, strolling, and admiring than for swimming. Red flags fly almost constantly to warn of dangerous conditions.

PLAYA QUIETA: Far more lively than its name implies, this stretch of soft, dark sand, home of *Club Med,* is the jumping-off point for the 5-minute boat trip to Isla Ixtapa. At Quieta, sailboards and small sailboats are available for rent, and novice windsurfers can test their skills against the small bay's gentle waves. Though a staggering array of vendors greet visitors from stalls in the small parking area, this is still a pleasant place to spend a few hours in the sun; there are no restaurants, and only one public restroom, which costs about 30¢ to use. Located 3 miles (5 km) north of the Ixtapa hotel zone.

PLAYA RISCAL: This isolated, block-long beach is about 8 miles (12 km) south of Zihuatanejo, off Highway 200. Just past the town of Coacoyul, turn right on an unmarked dirt road into a coconut plantation, then head toward the sea. Riscal is a small, sandy strip bordered by an impressive rocky cliff.

PLAYA LA ROPA: The real gem of the area, La Ropa is a stunning, nearly mile-long arc of sea and sand in Zihuatanejo that is ideal for swimming, strolling, jogging, sunning, and napping. The bay is pleasant enough to play at for hours, but keep an eye out for occasional show-offs on jet skis and for speedboats that race dangerously close to swimmers. Hotels, bungalow compounds, and attractive villas stand tastefully back from the beach. A favorite with families on weekends, packed at *Christmas* and *Easter,* but relatively unpopulated during the week. Great for sunsets, suntans, and daydreams — find a hammock, lie back, and enjoy the view of the bay.

Legend has it that the name La Ropa, "the clothes," originated when a Spanish ship from China sank in the bay and clothes from the wreck washed up onshore. The bay's most notable modern-day wreck is the sunset cruise ship *Fandango,* which sank here while on an empty run in 1990. Before it was a cruise ship, the *Fandango* served as a World War II minesweeper and then belonged to actor John Wayne. Authorities are considering removing the vessel from the bottom of the bay — where it lies in three separate pieces — but for now, scuba divers are taking advantage of the underwater habitat it has spawned.

La Ropa is an easy half-hour walk from downtown. If you prefer to take a taxi, tell the driver what part of the beach you wish to visit: *La Perla* restaurant is at the midway point. For the best photographs of La Ropa, go to the expansive sun deck balcony of the *Catalina-Sotavento* hotel.

PLAYA VISTA HERMOSA: Natural rock formations and the exquisite *Westin Resort Ixtapa* hotel (which is artfully terraced into the hillside) combine to create this idyllic crescent-shape cove that is shielded from the rest of the world by dramatic black rocks. Guests can lounge in the soft, clean sand under *palapa* shades, enjoying the pleasing views and signaling the waiters' attention by running a small red flag up the *palapa*'s pole. Waves vary from gentle surf to fun little rollers that push you along but won't push you down. There's snorkeling along the rocks and some parasailing, although the hotel posts a sign advising against parasailing because of the danger involved.

Scuba and Skin Diving: Best Depths

When it comes to scuba and skin diving in Mexico, divers tend to think only of Cozumel and the crystalline waters of the Caribbean Sea off Mexico's Yucataán Peninsula. Caribbean diving is justifiably famous, but this one-coast mindset neglects the rewarding (sometimes incredible) diving possibilities along Mexico's southern Pacific Coast.

Divers and snorkelers in Ixtapa and Zihuatanejo are especially fortunate, because the mix of ocean currents off the coast creates an ideal environment for myriad species of marine life and affords some of the best diving conditions in Mexico. During the winter, diving visibility is 15 to 20 feet, humpback whales can be sighted, and schools of porpoises frolic with the boats that ply these waters. From May through December, Zihuatanejo Bay turns deep shades of blue, quite a noticeable change from the gray-green of winter. Visibility peaks at 35 to 40 feet during the rainy months of July and August.

There are at least 28 fine dive sites in the area. Among the best are the four sites at Zacatoso, off Ixtapa, where stunning beds of red and green coral nest among great rock formations teeming with tropical fish, and huge lobsters are not uncommon sights. Visit early in the morning when the sea is calm and this underwater world is in full swing. Other sites include the surging rocky upthrusts of Los Morros (for expert divers only) and the shallows at Yunque, Chato, and Borracho.

The best dive shop in the area is *Zihuatanejo Scuba Center* (on the boat pier in downtown Zihuatanejo, 4 Paseo del Pescador; phone: 753-42147). Director Juan Bernard is a skilled marine biologist and expert dive master. The price for two-tank dives starts at $60. Instruction, night dives, marine biology tours, underwater photography tours, and dive videography are available. Also on Paseo del Pescador is the Escuela de Buceo (Diving School), part of the *Casa del Mar* dive shop (phone: 753-42119).

Carlos Scuba (on Playa Las Gatas) specializes in shallow coral beach dives, resort courses in the bay (for beginners), and trips outside the bay. Two-tank dives start at $55. Las Gatas diver Owen Lee also teaches here (no phone).

In Ixtapa, *Club de Playa del Palmar* offers diving instruction.

Those who aren't certified divers can either inquire about certification at the dive shops or settle for excellent snorkeling along the coast, especially off Playa Las Gatas, Isla Ixtapa, and Playa Majahua. Snorkel gear can be rented at most resorts.

Surfing

Although surfing is not a Mexican sport, American surfers claim that Mexico's Pacific coastline — with its abundance of reef breaks, point breaks, and river-mouth breaks — offers some of the best virgin surfing waters in the world. Despite the dangerous undertow in many areas, as well as a distinct lack of appreciation of surfers on the part of most Mexicans, dedicated American surfers readily travel up and down the Pacific Coast to try waves at beaches big and little. Windsurfing has recently become a popular sport at most resorts.

The single most popular surfing spot in Ixtapa and Zihuatanejo is on the southern tip of Zihuatanejo Bay, just beyond Playa Las Gatas. This riffling reef break runs constantly and attracts expert surfers who make riding the waves look easy. Novices are advised to inspect the shallow reef before taking to the board. Surfers also ply the strong surf at Playa Blanca, 12½ miles (20 km) away at Barra de Potosí. Surfboards can be rented at both Las Gatas and Playa Quieta. A note of warning: American boards are prime targets for theft.

Sailing: Mexico Afloat

Mexico's southern Pacific Coast plays host to sailboat races and regattas throughout the year; recreational sailors from the States venture to the Pacific Coast during the winter season, and many resort hotels rent small sailboats to guests. For exact dates of regattas and competitions, as well as general information, write the Mexican Sailing Federation, 42 Córdoba at Puebla, México, DF 06700 (phone: 5-533-3412 or 5-533-4664).

The big news for sailors in Ixtapa and Zihuatanejo is the development of two new marinas, one in each resort town. Marina Ixtapa will have 500 new slips for boats within a year or two, and a smaller marina is under construction in Zihuatanejo Bay. In the meantime, pleasure boats tie up in the bay; sailboats, sailboards, and surfboards are rented in Ixtapa at Playa Quieta and on Isla Ixtapa and in Zihuatanejo at Las Gatas; sailboards can also be rented in Zihuatanejo on Playa La Ropa near the *Villa del Sol;* and small sailboats are available for rent in front of the *Catalina-Sotavento* hotel. Zihuatanejo Bay is an ideal place to learn basic windsurfing skills as long as you don't drift too far from shore.

Tennis

Although Acapulco remains Mexico's tennis capital, the major resorts in Ixtapa and Zihuatanejo maintain first class tennis facilities. For more specific information, write the Federación Mexicana de Tenis (Mexican Federation of Tennis), 953 Miguel Angel de Quevedo, México, DF 04330 (phone: 5-549-1618 or 5-514-1956). Below, some of the best:

CLUB MED: 12 composition courts, 4 lighted (phone: 753-30944 or 800-CLUB-MED).

DORADO PACÍFICO: 2 lighted cement courts (phone: 753-32025).

HOLIDAY INN: 2 lighted cement courts (phone: 753-31186 or 800-HOLIDAY).

IXTAPA GOLF CLUB: 5 lighted hard-surface courts (phone: 753-31163 or 753-31062).

KRYSTAL: 2 lighted cement courts (phone: 753-30333).

SHERATON IXTAPA: 4 lighted hard-surface courts (phone: 753-31858).

STOUFFER PRESIDENTE: 2 lighted cement courts (phone: 753-30018).

VILLA DEL SOL: 1 lighted cement court, in Zihuatanejo (phone: 753-42239).

WESTIN RESORT IXTAPA: 4 lighted Laykold courts (phone: 753-32121).

Good Golf

Although many of the best Mexican courses are part of private country clubs or resort hotel complexes, it is possible to play on some of them. Currently, the only golf course in Ixtapa is the *Ixtapa Golf Club.* The club doesn't take reservations, so get here early to ensure your desired tee-off time.

IXTAPA GOLF CLUB: Formerly the *Palma Real,* this Robert Trent Jones, Jr. 18-hole course is considered one of the best in Mexico. It is managed by Manuel Domínguez; Eualalio Medina is the pro. All golfers are required to use a caddy or cart. In the early evening (until 7 PM), the club bar serves as a gathering place for golfers and non-golfers alike. The pro shop sells a wide variety of sporting goods. There are also 5 lighted tennis courts (phone: 753-31062 or 753-31163).

Fishing Ixtapa and Zihuatanejo's Rich Waters

The best season for game fishing in the Ixtapa and Zihuatanejo area is December to March, when fishermen will find sailfish, marlin, wahoo, dorado, red snapper, yellowtail, roosterfish, mackerel, and bonito. Arranged through a tour agency, deep-sea and small-game fishing excursions will run about $250 per day; contact *Ixtamar Tours* in Zihuatanejo (phone: 753-43590); *Paseos Ixtapa* (phone: 753-30343); or *Rapala Fishing Charters* (phone: 753-42119). It will cost less if you arrange the trip on your own down at the pier (expect to pay about $100 to $150 per day, or about $80 per person), but you risk ending up with a less than professional fisherman who may decide to bring you back to shore by mid-morning after you have caught just one or two fish. Ask employees at local seafood restuarants and dive shops to recommend a captain (don't arrange fishing trips with unauthorized agents who approach you on the street). The *Zihuatanejo Scuba Center* (phone: 753-42147) recommends Luis Roberto Maciel. Fishing permits are mandatory and can be obtained for the day or length of stay at local tackle shops.

Sport fishermen should be reminded that increasing concerns about protecting marine species have resulted in a voluntary catch-and-release program. The boat captain and mate will comply if requested, although some will be less than enthusiastic because they would prefer to sell your catch in the market. For free catch-and-release guidelines, contact the National Marine Fisheries Service, 9450 Koger Blvd, St. Petersburg, FL 33702 (phone: 813-893-3141).

Ixtapa and Zihuatanejo on Horseback

Rancho Manzanilla offers horseback riding tours in Zihuatanejo from Playa La Ropa to Playa Las Gatas by way of an upper road that offers sweeping views of the bay, with a stop for swimming, snorkeling, sunning, and snacking. The fee is about $30, and includes hotel pickup and drop-off. Some of the horses show more pep than others, so make it known if you would prefer a feistier one. Arrange with *Ixtamar Tours* (phone: 753-43590), or with Pedro Serrano after 6 PM at *El Marlin* restaurant on Playa La Ropa. Beach rides on Playa Linda can be arranged through any of the area tour agencies. Sunset rides are just as magical as they look in the movies.

DIRECTIONS

Introduction

The pleasures of travel to such resort areas as Ixtapa and Zihuatanejo have broadened in recent years, as more and more visitors to these serene jewels along Mexico's Pacific Coast discover that — if they choose — there's much more to a vacation here than what lies along its beaches. Exploring the regions around and beyond — the cities, small villages, nature preserves, archaeological treasures, dramatic history, spectacular scenery, and, yes, even more beaches — has proved pure pleasure for those folks willing to do a bit of roaming on their own.

Our routes traverse Mexico's excellent Highway 200, following the Pacific Coast — with its wealth of magnificent beaches — all the way to the Bays of Huatulco; the northern route to Oaxaca is rich in scenery — and history. For those who prefer to use Ixtapa and Zihuatanejo as a base, we offer day trips to neighboring beaches and fishing villages, as well as an option for a 3½-hour jaunt to Acapulco.

Entries describe the highlights of each route, including useful suggestions for sightseeing and dining, plus descriptions of the driving conditions and approximate timetables for coming and going. *Best en Route* lists suggested accommodations at the best hotels and inns along the way. Detailed maps introduce each itinerary and note the major reference points along the route.

We've made our route selections based on our opinions of the most memorable sites and sights along Mexico's Pacific Coast, and into the mountains of Oaxaca. It's possible to string two or more of these itineraries together for more extensive exploration. For those with less time, following any single itinerary will cover the most notable points of interest (and the most attractive accommodations) in a given area.

One word of caution about driving in Mexico: It's always wise for travelers who will be driving on remote country roads to allow sufficient time to reach their destinations well before dark. Driving secondary roads in Mexico after dark is not something we recommend; as a matter of fact, it's a risk we earnestly advise readers to avoid. Naturally, before your journey, be sure your vehicle is in top mechanical condition and include an extra fan belt and quart of oil for good measure. Should your car break down, don't abandon it; Mexico has a wonderful system of "Green Angels" who patrol the highways to help stranded motorists. They will repair your car on the spot if possible, or tow you to the nearesst garage. The only cost to you is for repairs and/or gas.

Finally, as anywhere in the world, picking up strangers, camping on lonely beaches, or sleeping in a car in some isolated area can invite serious trouble. It only takes a little common sense, and some very basic planning, to make a driving tour along Mexico's Pacific Coast both a safe and an especially memorable travel adventure.

Ixtapa and Zihuatanejo to Acapulco

If basking in the sun beside a sparkling blue-green sea by day, sipping *coco locos* at sunset, and dancing the night away under starlit skies is your idea of heaven, then Ixtapa and Zihuatanejo are perfect vacation choices. Chances are you may never tire of their sybaritic splendors, but if you do, there's a whole other Mexico — from resorts to ruins — just a few days' drive from your lounge chair. And if you're restless, but still in a tanning mode, Acapulco is a logical extension of a beach-bound vacation. Less than 4 hours away, it offers a livelier atmosphere, but with no interruption of the pampered lifestyle to which you've become accustomed.

Those who prefer to restrict their roamings to short day trips, using Ixtapa and Zihuatanejo as a base, can visit the charming fishing village of Barra de Potosí, the fine church at Petatlán, and the little-known town and beach at La Barrita, all to the southeast, or the sand and sounds of music at Playa Azul to the northwest — all within easy reach. (All but the last of these sites are also short detours on the way to Acapulco.)

The 130-mile (208-km) strip of Highway 200 between Ixtapa-Zihuatanejo and Acapulco boasts the most spectacular ocean views of any stretch along the Pacific Coast. You can drive straight through in 3½ to 4 hours, or stop along the way at a secluded beach, a village market, a peaceful lagoon — or a coconut plantation. Most of the two-lane highway is well maintained, but beware of the *topes,* asphalt speed bumps used to slow traffic in populated areas. Signs precede most bumps, but some of them are unmarked and can be hard to spot, especially at night. In general, travel along this route should be avoided at night, on weekends (when there is always a lot of traffic), and during *Christmas* and *Easter,* when *everyone* — Mexicans and tourists alike — heads for the coast.

DAY TRIP 1: BARRA DE POTOSÍ, PETATLÁN

Three miles (5 km) south of Zihuatanejo, just past the town of Coacoyul (pronounced Ko-a-ko-*yule*), is the little-known Temple of the Virgin of Guadalupe, worth a stop on the way to Barra de Potosí. About 500 yards south of Coacoyul Bridge, just before a roadside stand with a hand-painted red sign that says *Miel,* or "honey" (which is sold here), turn left onto the dirt road. Take the next left, park your car, and follow the footpath over the pond to the temple.

Set in the center of a lovely lake filled with floating lily pads, the gleaming white chapel was built 20 years ago by neighboring townsfolk; some — especially the blind fisherman who spends his days sitting outside the church — say it was divine intervention that caused the church to be built. According to the fisherman, he heard a voice

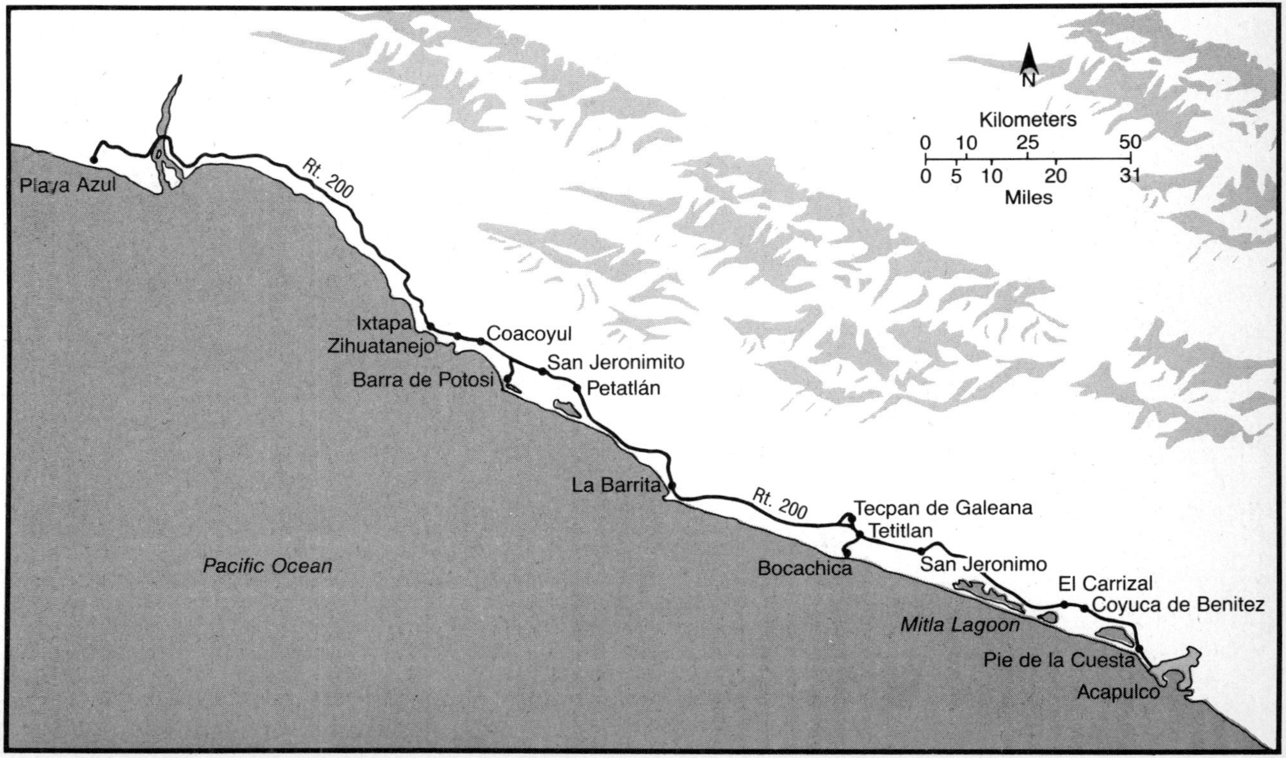

N
Kilometers
0
10
25
50
0
5
10
20
31
Miles
Playa Azul
Rt. 200
Ixtapa
Zihuatanejo
Coacoyul
San Jeronimito
Barra de Potosi
Petatlán
La Barrita
Rt. 200
Tecpan de Galeana
Tetitlan
Bocachica
San Jeronimo
El Carrizal
Coyuca de Benitez
Mitla Lagoon
Pie de la Cuesta
Acapulco
Pacific Ocean

instructing him to build a temple on this site and convinced his neighbors to help him. Though rarely used for formal services (an occasional wedding or baptism is conducted here), the church stands ready to receive worshipers. The interior is festooned with colored paper streamers, glittering tinsel, glowing candles of white, yellow, red, and green, and throughout, framed portraits of the Virgin. A large, pointed rock juts from the floor, and on another larger boulder behind the shrine is a tiny painted image of the Virgin, viewable only through a magnifying glass, which is provided. Zihuatanejo residents often come here to pray for ailing relatives. It is customary to leave a small donation in the collection box beside the shrine. Return to Highway 200 and continue south for about 9 miles (14 km) to Barra de Potosí.

BARRA DE POTOSÍ: This small fishing village boasts part of Playa Blanca, a gorgeous 10-mile-long beach that is rarely populated by more than a handful of people. In the village, there is a row of informal *palapa* (thatch-roofed) restaurants where meals cost at least 50% less than those at comparable dining spots in Ixtapa and Zihuatanejo.

According to local legend, there is a cache of pirate treasure buried somewhere on the back side of the mountain directly south of Barra de Potosí's "restaurant row." Several years ago, after a local resident found a gold doubloon on the hillside, treasure seekers started digging here; to date, no further discoveries have been reported.

An ideal visit to Potosí includes a stroll along Playa Blanca, a refreshing swim (watch out for the bay's rolling waves), and a leisurely seafood lunch. None of the restaurants have names, but the food at the northwesternmost eatery, on the far right when facing the sea, is consistently good. Recommended are fish filets and red snapper prepared *a la talla* (pronounced *ta*-ya), wrapped in woven plant fibers and grilled. In addition, the view to the northwest is uninterrupted — in the distance is the lighthouse on Zihuatanejo Bay — and there are plenty of hammocks for relaxing after lunch.

Potosí Lagoon — which starts less than 100 yards south of the restaurants and continues as far as Petatlán — offers some of the best bird watching along Mexico's Pacific Coast. March is the best month for birding, but any time during the winter season can be exceptional.

Orlando Banuelos conducts hour-long boat tours of the lagoon for about $7 per person (ask any of the locals to point him out). Though he's short on commentary (his English is poor, at best), the spectacular show — great blue herons, egrets, ibis, and cranes, plus spectacular flocks of rare roseate spoonbills whose glowing rosy-pink hue makes flamingos pale by comparison — speaks for itself. Since the lagoon is teeming with fish, you'll probably also see pelicans, sea gulls, and frigate birds diving for meals, as well as fishermen casting their nets in the ankle- to chest-deep water. Be sure to bring binoculars. Return to the highway and continue for about 9½ miles (15 km) southeast to Petatlán.

PETATLÁN: A medium-size town (pop. 60,000), Petatlán offers absolutely no tourist trappings — and boasts one "miraculous" church. Although prices at the produce market and surrounding shops are not significantly lower than those in Zihuatanejo, this commercial center makes a pleasant change from the resort scene, and is a popular outing for Zihuatanejo residents.

To enter the town, cross the bridge and make an immediate right turn at the sign that reads "Valentín 10." Follow the paved road to the Cristo de Petatlán church, with its exquisite wooden statue of Christ that dates back to the 16th century (in fact, this is one of the few churches along the Pacific Coast that glorifies Christ rather than the Virgin). On the big board in back, worshipers hang packets of *milagros* (tiny charms depicting animals' eyes, hearts, and other body parts) and written prayers for sick relatives or animals. Many stories of miracle cures are linked to this church: In the late 1980s, a wealthy local businessman pledged to refurbish Cristo de Petatlán if his prayers for a cure of his daughter's blindness were answered. Worshipers reported that the statue actually wept for the father and child; and when medical treatments proved successful, the man donated the pews, the beautiful cedar tongue-in-groove altar, and the marble-tiled floor that now grace this house of worship.

The statue of Christ, which is believed to have come from a ship that sank off the coast, was discovered in a dry creek bed around the time that the Spanish arrived in Mexico. About 30 years ago, a priest found sand on the statue's feet and told his congregation this was a sign that Christ was watching over the local fishermen.

LA BARRITA: A tiny fishing village 35 miles (56 km) southeast of Zihuatanejo, right off Highway 200, La Barrita makes an ideal day trip or overnight excursion. Spend all day at the beach, with its rolling, curling waves, dine at one of the local seafood restaurants (*El Frizo* is one of our favorites), and spend the night in one of the ocean-view, thatch-roofed bungalows on the right on the way into town. La Barrita is nearly deserted on weekdays, and is never deluged by tourists — probably because not many know about it. Take Highway 200 north back to Ixtapa and Zihuatanejo; for those who are continuing along the route to Acapulco, take Highway 200 south.

DAY TRIP 2: PLAYA AZUL

This low-key beach resort (70 miles/112 km and 2 hours northwest of Ixtapa and Zihuatanejo on Highway 200) is popular with Mexicans who come here on weekends; during the week it's virtually deserted, making it an ideal place for those seeking solitude. Though the ride out here is not easy — roads are narrow and rutted, and traffic is heavy — even on weekends there's plenty of room for everyone on the beach (though gringos may find themselves the object of curiosity).

More than 50 *enramada* (arbored) restaurants, many named after women or sea themes — among them, *La Sirena* (The Mermaid) or *Roca Mar* (Sea Rock) — crowd the 2-mile-long beach, but fortunately, there is plenty of sand between the eateries and the surf. On Sundays, the strand resounds with live music from strolling minstrels, mariachis, marching bands, and salsa groups (complete with eardrum-shattering amplifiers). There is little of interest in the shops, but beach vendors — who sell everything from onyx wind chimes to coconut oil and peanuts — make up the difference. Those who wish to linger can spend the night at the 80-room *Playa Azul,* which offers moderately priced accommodations (about $22 per night for two). Day-trippers should return south on Highway 200 to Ixtapa and Zihuatanejo, the starting point for our extended route to Acapulco.

En route from Ixtapa – Take Ixtapa Boulevard south to Zihuatanejo and Highway 200. Three miles (5 km) southeast of Zihuatanejo is the little town of Coacoyul, and just south of the Coacoyul Bridge (Puente Coacoyul) on the left side is the turnoff for the chapel to the Virgin of Guadalupe (see *Day Trip 1: Barra de Potosí, Petatlán,* above). On the left, just before the village of San Jerónimito, is one of the most beautiful cemeteries along the Pacific Coast: Set on a hillside above the highway are tiered rows of monuments and small chapels. Farther on, horses graze in the town square, and children can be seen playing volleyball in the local schoolyard.

Continue on Highway 200 for 10 miles (16 km) to the Las Salinas saltwater evaporation plant, where workers tend acres of low, square pools from which salt is recovered and dried; stacks of plastic bags filled with salt are sold at roadside stands.

Farther along Highway 200 are lush coconut plantations with 60-foot palms, dry, rolling terrain, and wide river basins, and off to the left, splendid vistas of the ocean and the Sierra Madre range. At the unmarked fork just past Km 125, bear left where the highway curves. (The straight road leads to the village of Nuxco.)

Ten miles (16 km) farther on (just over halfway to Acapulco), the highway passes through the center of Tecpan de Galeana, a busy commercial center and fishing town. On the way out of town is an imposing church on the left and a large cemetery with many aboveground crypts on the right. For a beach break, drive 3 miles (5 km) south to Tetitlán and follow the dirt road to Bocachica.

The last third of the journey to Acapulco is relatively uneventful. About 12 miles (19 km) beyond the turnoff to Bocachica is the town of San Jerónimo, where life centers around the immense Hacienda de Cabañas coconut plantation. There are no organized tours, but it is possible to drive through the plantation and watch local folk harvesting and processing the coconut and its sweet milk. At the end of this winding road is Mitla Lagoon, where *pangas* (fishing boats) transport visitors to the relatively untouched beaches of Playa Paraíso. While Playa Paraíso has its devotees who swear by its beauty and isolation, a trip there means having to leave your car unattended on the plantation side of the lagoon and having to return in time to drive on to your final destination before nightfall (there are no accommodations on Paraíso).

About 15 miles (24 km) before Pie de la Cuesta and the outskirts of Acapulco is the small beachside village of El Carrizal, a pleasant stop for a cool drink before braving the inevitable traffic on the way into the city. Three miles (5 km) farther on is the large town of Coyuca de Benítez. Use caution along the curves at the south end of town; numerous white crosses along the roadside indicate traffic fatalities that have occurred here.

Entering Acapulco can be a shock to a system soothed by the relatively traffic-free silence of Ixtapa and Zihuatanejo. Don't despair: Once you've gotten through the maze, the rewards of the city on the bay are well worth the effort spent getting here. From Highway 200, follow the general flow of traffic, keeping to the right. At the first major intersection, look for signs that read "Mexico left, Caleta right," and turn right onto the Costera Miguel Alemán. This main boulevard, where aggressive taxi drivers vie for space with slow-moving city buses, passes downtown markets, marinas, boutiques, and high-rise hotels.

ACAPULCO (pronounced Ah-ca-*pul*-co): The mere mention of Acapulco usually causes a string of extravagant images to come to mind. Whether or not you consider these superlatives justified, Acapulco's reputation as an international beach resort borders on legendary. Throughout the year, and especially in the winter, tourists from all over the world descend on the hotel-lined gem of a bay facing the Pacific Ocean, generating a momentum that is in itself a kind of homage to this resort's reputation.

How you personally feel about Acapulco will depend, in large part, on your reaction to the sheer number of tourists around you — almost 5 million people visited Acapulco last year. It is definitely not a place for "getting away from it all," if by that you mean getting away from all the other people who are also trying to get away from it all. It is not, in fact, a place where you can get away from much of anything, except the rest of the world's rotten weather and your own daily routine. But if you don't mind sharing the pleasures of the sun — and the flesh — with lots of other similarly inclined folk, the beaches and pools in and around Acapulco can be among the most compelling tourist destinations in the western hemisphere.

The prime reason anyone comes to Acapulco is the weather — that perfect weather that simply can't be duplicated in any sun-drenched spot within the same distance of the United States. When a winter-paled body makes its hegira to Acapulco, it knows it's going to return home beautifully browned, sporting an even tan devoid of imperfections.

It is possible to enjoy Acapulco without getting into a hectic round of nightclubs, discos, and parties. You can get up early in the morning and have the eastern beaches all to yourself, although it's common to joke that the only people in Acapulco who get up early in the morning are those who go deep-sea fishing. (*A sun warning:* Be very careful if you have sensitive skin. Two hours on an Acapulco beach in the morning can roast you — to say nothing of the afternoon, when the sun is even stronger.)

In the afternoon, it's far better to take a siesta between 1 and 4 PM. Even Acapulco residents stay out of the sun in the middle of the afternoon. In late afternoon, watch the sunset while sipping tequila concoctions. Places like Pie de la Cuesta Beach, just outside town, are traditional dusk headquarters, though in recent years they've become inundated by native peddlers so you'll now have to venture farther off, or to hotel beaches, to escape the harassment of vendors and beggars. After dusk, return to your hotel and get ready for a quiet, leisurely dinner. Acapulco doesn't have to be frenetic.

But for most of the people who come here, Acapulco means party. A lot of people, Mexican as well as foreign, wouldn't be caught anywhere near a beach until one or two in the afternoon, after they've had a chance to sleep off the night before. The afternoon beach used to be Los Hornos, and Caleta the morning beach, but times have changed. Caleta is not as classy (or as clean) as it used to be, and the action has moved farther east, from Los Hornos to La Condesa, which is the stretch of beach between the *El Presidente* and the *Continental Acapulco* hotels.

There are two things to heed on this stretch of beach: the Pacific Ocean, which can easily toss you upside down, and the swarm of vendors of all ages who work the strip (except the hotel beaches). The surf, however, never discriminates. At Condesa, things don't get going until noon and don't really start swinging until after one in the afternoon. Lunch is served around 2 PM. Take your time. People don't start drifting back to the beach until late afternoon. Dinner in Acapulco is served around 9 or 10 PM.

More than any other Mexican city, Acapulco reeks of sensuality. This, too, accounts for its popularity. Acapulco's sexiness is part of its legend, and one of the first things you're almost bound to notice is that no one ever wears more than bathing trunks or a bikini during the day. People are constantly flaunting their bodies, even on the city's buses or in supermarkets.

At night, the sounds of tropical guitar and rock music drift through the air, mingling with the music of the ocean, the leaves blowing in the soft, humid wind, and the murmur of gentle conversations. There is something languorous in the air, and it can prove disastrous to one's inhibitions. In addition to mellowing people, the sexual atmosphere serves to level differences in social class. There's no way to tell the difference between a genuine jet setter and an Oklahoma secretary or Omaha insurance salesman when everything is pared down to the bare essentials. You can get down to basics very quickly in Acapulco.

The spectacular beauty of Acapulco's bay has been appreciated for centuries, but for years the isolation of the area kept the city from participating in much of Mexico's history. It was founded in 1530 by the Spanish, who cut a sort of horse path through the rugged mountains to it from Mexico City. Today, the drive takes 5½ hours on a road that was blasted through the mountains in 1955. It used to take weeks.

A few years after Acapulco was settled, the Spanish built two boats and began sailing up and down the coast making charts of the shoreline. By 1565, they learned (thanks to Magellan's crew) that it was possible to sail *east* from Spain and reach Mexico. Trade routes from the Orient to Mexico were opened, and Acapulco's beautiful harbor came into its own. Luxury items such as silk, porcelain, and ivory were transported by boat from China and Japan to Acapulco, then carried by mule train to Mexico City. From the capital, they were sent on to Veracruz for shipment to Spain. Acapulco soon grew to about 10,000 people (it has more than 1.2 million residents today), but this profitable trade did not go unnoticed by the English pirates. Sir Francis Drake, among others, began to prey on the Spanish galleons. Acapulco's Fort San Diego was constructed to defend the port city against pirate raids. Destroyed in 1776 by an earthquake, it was rebuilt and still stands today.

After Mexico's War of Independence began in 1810, trade with the Orient ceased. Acapulco became a forgotten fishing village until a paved road was finally built from Mexico City in 1922, but even then it took another 10 years for it to get its first tentative start as a beach resort. An international port city since 1945, it really came into its own toward the end of the 1950s, when it began to be known as "The Riviera of the West."

Since then, Acapulco's reputation as a resort has dipped and soared like the waterskiers-cum-parachutists who take off from Condesa Beach. At the moment, it is on a plateau after several years of decline — due in part, at least, to the studied opinion of well-heeled travelers that Acapulco was no longer a prime choice among the world's most stylish tropical destinations. The rich and famous still go to Acapulco — religiously, every winter, to soak up sun at their villas in the surrounding hills — but they just don't talk about it the way they used to. More important, the stress of coping with such huge numbers of visitors (and the concomitant growth of the resident population, making Acapulco one of the fastest-growing cities in the world) overtaxed the city's resources.

Several years ago, the Mexican government invested $300 million in restoring and revitalizing Acapulco and the surrounding area. A superhighway, scheduled to be completed by this year, joins Cuernavaca and Acapulco, cutting driving time from Mexico City to 3½ hours. Acapulco's main street, Costera Miguel Alemán, is now a well-maintained seaside avenue, and the beaches are better maintained than they've been. The government has made a real effort to clean up its act, literally and figuratively, and to solve the problem of constant harassment by street vendors. At press time, the beach around the bay was being cleaned each morning — as were the streets — and the peddlers were being kept away; the hope is these efforts will continue. The state and municipal governments have set up open-air markets on vacant lots around the city; though the markets aren't attractive, they have helped get many vendors off the streets and beaches — for a time at least. Uniformed "tourist police" also have begun to patrol the Costera and to provide visitors with information. There is still room for improvement, especially in town and up in the mountains, where the majority of people live in substandard conditions. Still, there is too much about Acapulco to be prized and protected for the city to lose its luster entirely. You have only to look down on the city at dusk from the heights of a casita in the luxurious *Las Brisas* hotel complex to appreciate that you are in a unique place. The lights flicker like pearls on an endless necklace, and the dark water provides a muted reflection of the blinking brightness. Outside town, only the most blasé can turn down a ride on an Indian pony down the Revolcadero Beach and beyond.

It may be that Acapulco can regain its former place at the top of the pedestal of resorts that appeal to determined hedonists. Surely if money alone could cure overdevelopment, the city would already be all the way back to its former preeminence. The physical surroundings remain awesomely appealing: Just look at those green mountains rising from the white, sandy beaches surrounding the blue bay on three sides, and listen to the palm trees rustling in the Pacific wind. Add to this more than 300 hotels of every description, dozens of restaurants, nightclubs, discotheques, and beaches with skin diving, snorkeling, water skiing, parasailing, and swimming, and you have Acapulco — a very tempting tropical resort.

The setting is magnificent, for Acapulco is built where the mountains meet the sea. The first breathtaking view for most people appears at the high point of the hill above the southern border of the city (at the entrance to *Las Brisas* hotel). The road south to the airport is known, for good reason, as the Carretera Escénica — the Scenic Highway. And almost every hotel balcony offers an unforgettable view. For a special look, try dining at one of the high-rise, roof garden restaurants, or go parasailing. The nicest time to soak up the scenery is at sunset, when the sky turns bright pink and gold, the city lights begin to twinkle, and the first stars come out.

These days the action in Acapulco centers along the Costera Miguel Alemán, the broad avenue that runs along the bay. To the left (as you face the ocean) beyond the southwestern headland is Puerto Marqués and then the open sea, as well as the fashionable *Acapulco Princess* and *Pierre Marqués* hotels. To the right is Caleta, where many of Acapulco's first hotels were built, and still operate, albeit many in rather run-down fashion now. Since the sea is Acapulco's prime attraction, look first at the beaches. Remember that there are no private beaches in Mexico. All are federal property, and the hotels have no jurisdiction over them. Itinerant vendors are everywhere on the popular beaches, and their petitions can be wearisome, but for safety's sake it's best to avoid completely isolated beaches. Remember that there are no private beaches in Mexico. All are federal property, and the hotels have no jurisdiction over them. Itinerant vendors are everywhere on the popular beaches, and their petitions can be wearisome, but for safety's sake it's best to avoid completely isolated beaches.

More and more foreign tourists are coming to know about Pie de la Cuesta, so it's no longer the private turf of Acapulco regulars. Swimming is dangerous at this beach 8 miles (13 km) west of the city proper, but it's a wonderful place to order a *coco loco* (perhaps at *Steve's Hideaway*), cuddle up in a hammock, and cement friendships as the sun goes down. Continue to *Club de Playa Maebba,* where visitors can enjoy a buffet and use the pool, tennis court, and hammocks for a small fee. There's also *Cadenas Ski Club,* which offers water skiing and jungle boat rides with delicious meals.

A primitive freshwater lagoon, Laguna de Coyuca (a little northwest of Pie de la Cuesta) is a bird sanctuary bordered by coconut palms and full of water hyacinths. The waters teem with catfish, mullet, and snook. The *Club de Playa Maebba* offers a tour, including transportation to and from Acapulco proper; a visit to a coconut, pineapple, or banana plantation; a half-hour boat trip on the Coyuca Lagoon; lunch; and a few hours at the club — all for about $22 (phone: 74-858515).

Back in the days before air conditioning, when the best hotels were built on the adjacent hillside to catch the breeze, La Caleta was where everyone began his day: Caleta was the morning beach. It's not so elegant now, and some segments are polluted, although it does attract the traditionalists and those who like their ocean as calm as a pond. Here the thing to do is rent an inner tube and just paddle around. The small aquarium here, which was opened in 1990 to attract more visitors to the northern end of town, is popular with children.

Roqueta, the uninhabited island across from Caleta, has a beach populated by beer-drinking donkeys; it has a certain vague Robinson Crusoe charm. Boats ferry bathers from and to Caleta throughout the day. There is a direct route as well as a more scenic one, which takes 45 minutes; buy tickets from the kiosk on the beach. Snorkeling and windsurfing are good, and there are boards for rent.

Near the docks, south of Caleta, Los Hornos was once the fashionable spot for late-afternoon sunbathers. The water here is calmer, though not very clean; *palapa*-topped (thatch-roofed) eateries line the beach.

Running from the *Continental Acapulco* to the *El Presidente* hotel, La Condesa is the most tourist-infested stretch of sand these days. It's also where the scantiest bikinis are found. One section of the beach is dominated by gays. La Condesa has the most pounding surf on the bay, and up by the Costera are a number of nice luncheon spots with music for dancing.

Icacos's sheltered waters are calm and quiet and the beach less hectic. *La Palapa* and the *Hyatt Regency* hotels share the sands, the last stretch of true Acapulco Bay beach before the road heads south to the airport.

Located on the open Pacific, Revolcadero Beach (in front of the *Acapulco Princess* and *Pierre Marqués* hotels, and off to either side as well) is great for body surfing (beware of the sometimes vicious undertow), and it's a favorite of the rich and pampered. Indian ponies are available for those who enjoy a canter on the sand.

Among the Acapulco region's best strands is Barra Vieja, a long stretch of beach about 24 miles (38 km) southeast of the city, where Tres Palos Lagoon meets the Pacific. The water on the Pacific side is too treacherous for swimming, but small boats are available for exploring the lagoon, which is fringed with palm and banana trees and populated by tropical birds. *Pescado a la talla* (whole fish char-broiled on a spit) is said to have originated here, and is available at any one of the small restaurants along the beach.

Besides its beaches and lagoons, Acapulco offers many other sites and sights to delight travelers.

A wonderful way to see the city is to hire one of the *calandrias,* little horse-drawn carriages, decorated with brightly colored balloons, that run up and down the Costera Miguel Alemán, the avenue that skirts the bay. The standard ride is a tour of the town, but *calandrias* also can be hired as taxis. If you're not in a hurry (and who is in Mexico?), they are more fun, albeit more expensive.

The Centro Internacional Acapulco, formerly the convention center, has been completely remodeled and renamed, and is once again a center of urban activity. For evening entertainment there are folkloric performances in the plaza Mondays through Saturdays ($35 includes dinner and open bar), along with the *Disco Laser* restaurant (no cover charge), a movie theater, and occasional special productions in the *Juan Ruiz Alarcón* theater. 4455 Costera Miguel Alemán (phone: 74-847050).

On the beach across the street from the *Embassy* hotel is *CICI Park,* a small, well-maintained amusement park that has trained dolphins and seals, a pool with manmade waves, two water toboggans, three dolphin shows daily, several bars and restaurants (including a gigantic seafood restaurant), a beach club (accessible from the beach), and seagoing motorcycles. There is also a day-care center where infants and young children will be entertained and cared for by experts while parents play (phone: 74-841970).

Art lovers will appreciate Acapulco's Diego Rivera mural, a spectacular and little-known work by one of Mexico's most famous artists, which surrounds a private home up in the hills of Acapulco. The house is not open to the public, but the mural may be seen by taking the road that leads up to the *Casablanca* hotel (at the gas station about 4 blocks past the zocalo, the main plaza). Bear left at the fork and keep going up; it shouldn't be missed.

No visit to Acapulco would be complete without seeing the cliff divers, or *clavadistas,* perform — especially at night. They plunge from a 150-foot cliff into a shallow inlet, and each dive must be perfectly timed to coincide with a wave coming in or the diver risks being crushed on the jagged rocks. There is no trick to it, nor are they in any way faking. The exhibition takes place on the cliffs of La Quebrada, adjoining the *Playa las Glorias El Mirador* hotel. Viewers can sit on the terrace or in the hotel's *La Perla* nightclub and have a drink while watching, or pay a small admission to get closer, but it is a spectacle worth seeing at least once. Shows (one dive per show), with torch processions, at 1, 7:15, 8:15, 10 and 10:30 PM..

Another must-see is Acapulco's *Flea Market.* That's what the locals call it (try saying it with authentic Spanish pronunciation), and it's where handicrafts and Mexican curios are sold. The *Flea Market* is about 5 blocks from the zocalo, and the way is well marked with signs. It's a good place to browse and bargain. Open daily.

El Fuerte de San Diego (Fort San Diego), the most historic spot in Acapulco, was first built centuries ago to protect what was then a major port from pirate attacks (and rebuilt after an 18th-century earthquake). Here the insurgents defeated the royalists in the early 1800s. It has been converted into an interesting museum dedicated to the history of Acapulco from pre-Hispanic times through the conquest of the southern seas, trade with the Orient, piracy, and the war of independence from Spain. Closed Mondays. Admission charge. The fort is a few blocks to the left of the zocalo, just across from the piers and customs house (phone: 74-823828).

On the grounds of the old *Papagayo* hotel, the delightful 60-acre *Papagayo Park,* straddling Costera Miguel Alemán, has cable cars, bumper cars, a Ferris wheel, a carousel, an artificial lake, boats, a small zoo, and a lakeside restaurant.

Getting away from the beaches, Plaza Juan Alvarez (the zocalo) is the heart of Acapulco proper, the main plaza near the piers and docks for deep-sea fishing boats. The zocalo is dominated by the Acapulco Cathedral, an oddity built in 1930 with Byzantine towers and a mosque-like dome. Opposite, at the waterfront, stands a monument to national heroes Guerrero, Morelos, Hidalgo, Juárez, and Cuauhtémoc (the last Aztec emperor).

If the zocalo is the city's heart, some might argue that the Old Town is Acapulco's soul. Enter from Azueta at the north end of the Costera and wander among crowded, narrow streets filled with wandering musicians, shopkeepers, and residents. *El Amigo Manuel* restaurant, 1 block off the Costera (31 Benito Juárez; phone: 74-836981) serves delicious ceviche and grilled grouper filets with crunchy garlic, at a fraction of the cost of a meal in a hotel; take a table upstairs for the breeze, ambience — and view. For shopping that's a world away from the Costera's chic boutiques, head south a few blocks to find the central market on the other side of the wide canal, where blocks and blocks of clothing, crafts, household goods, and curiosities will tempt you.

For a pleasant day's outing, visit Puerto Marqués, a village about 8 miles (13 km) southeast of the center of the city, along the Carretera Escénica (the Scenic Highway), past *Las Brisas,* where the jet setters sequester themselves in villas with private swimming pools and descend only for an occasional jaunt into town in *Las Brisas'* famous pink-and-white-striped jeeps. At the traffic circle just past *Las Brisas* (in the direction of the airport), turn right and you'll find yourself in the fishing village of Puerto Marqués, where the bay is so calm it hardly shows a ripple. You can rent paddle, sail, and water-ski boats. There are also many seafood restaurants lining the beach and the opposite side of the road. *Pipo's,* one of the best (see *Eating Out*), has a small marina with fishing boats for hire. Punta Diamante, the adjacent headland, is slated to be the next major resort and condominium complex in the area (though at press time, work had barely begun).

Southeast of Acapulco is Costa Chica, a 136-mile (218-km) stretch of coast, lined by a paved road that is passable most of the year. (During the rainy months, sections occasionally get washed out.) The road runs through dramatic, uninhabited terrain of lagoons and rocky cliffs. Along this route, in the shadow of the Sierra Madre, several rivers run into the sea. South of the small mining village of Ometepec, Cuajinicuilapa (about 140 miles — 224 km — from Acapulco) is inhabited by the descendants of Bantu tribespeople who were brought to the New World as slaves. The road continues all the way to Guatemala, passing the beaches at Puerto Escondido and Huatulco (see *Ixtapa and Zihuatanejo to Huatulco,* DIRECTIONS).

For tourist information in Acapulco, contact the State Tourist Office (Centrol Internacional Acapulco; phone: 74-847050). It's large and the staff is extremely helpful. The consumer protection bureau, in the same building, can aid in ironing out disputes (phone: 74-846136). They're open from 9 AM to 10 PM daily. A smaller, but much more helpful, Federal Tourist Office is at Hornos Beach (187 Costera Miguel Alemán; phone: 74-851041); and several information kiosks line the Costera. There is also an Acapulco Tourist Office (10 Privada Roca Sola; phone: 74-847621 or 74-847630).

To keep abreast of what's happening in the outside world, go to the tobacco shop in the *Acapulco Plaza* or almost any of the other classier hotels, which sell the *International Herald Tribune,* the *Los Angeles Times, The New York Times, USA Today,* and the English-language *News,* published in Mexico City. They're also available at *Sanborn's* (Costera Miguel Alemán) for considerably less than the hotels normally charge. *Acapulco News* and *Adventure in Acapulco,* local weekly and monthly publications respectively, give tips on local happenings in English.

Getting from one place to another in Acapulco is not difficult. Buses run up and down the Costera all the way from Puerto Marqués to La Caleta Beach and are inexpensive. With newer vehicles in operation, service is much improved — but do watch out for pickpockets when it's crowded.

Acapulco cabs don't have meters, which means that you have to give the driver your destination and agree on a price before getting in. There are cabstands in front of most of the hotels, and you can ask the doorman about reasonable prices. If you flag down a cab in the street, you'll have to do your own haggling. The going rate should be no more than $2.50 from the Costera area near the *El Presidente* hotel to the zocalo, in the center of downtown. The ride from the *Hyatt Regency,* at the far eastern end of the Costera, to La Caleta Beach should cost about $5. No trip within Acapulco proper should cost more than $7, although the fare will be higher when the destination is Revolcadero Beach or Pie de la Cuesta, both a bit out of town.

The more adventuresome can rent Honda Elite motorcycles at *CICI* (phone: 74-841970) for $15 to $20 for up to 4 hours; daily rates are also available. On the beach across the street from the *Embassy* hotel.

Acapulqueños love a good celebration. *Carnaval* (Mardi Gras), just before *Lent,* is Acapulco's biggest fiesta. The *International Billfish Tournament* is held in late November or early December; an inter-club tournament is held in February. *Guadalupe Day,* December 12, something of a national holiday, is celebrated with special fervor in Acapulco. December 12 is also the date of the *International Diving Championship,* which is held at La Quebrada, the cliff at *Playa las Glorias El Mirador* hotel (74 Quebrada). Also, there are fiestas throughout the year in the many villages near Acapulco. The government tourist office has data about what's in the offing.

One of the most popular activities in Acapulco is shopping. Frequent visitors arrive with little more than a toothbrush in their luggage, since resortwear and sports clothes are an Acapulco specialty. Stores also offer a wide selection of Mexico's best handicrafts. For a productive shopping outing, or just some enjoyable browsing, simply stroll Costera Miguel Alemán from the *Fiesta Americana Condesa* hotel to the *Acapulco Malibu.* One of the newest shopping complexes, completely enclosed and air conditioned, is the *Plaza Bahía Mall,* next to the *Acapulco Plaza* hotel. The *Marbella Shopping Center,* done in white marble, is on the Diana Circle. For some of Acapulco's more elegant shops, visit *La Vista Shopping Center* (on Carr. Escénica, 2 miles/3 km before the *Acapulco Princess,* heading southeast toward the airport). Observing the siesta tradition, many shops close in the early afternoon, reopening at 4 or 5 PM. Here are some of the better places to make a purchase:

Aca Joe – Now trying to prosper in the US, it carries stylish casual T-shirts and togs for teens. 1999 Costera Miguel Alemán and the *Galería Plaza* (phone: 74-848645).

Artesanías Finas Acapulco – A vast selection of handicrafts, jewelry, leather goods, and clothing from all over Mexico. Open daily. Horacio Nelson and James Cook (phone: 74-848049).

Benny – At last, a fashionable shop devoted to men. On Costera Miguel Alemán, 15 Horacio Nelson (phone: 74-841547), and at *La Vista Shopping Center.*

Casa Aries – Luggage and leather goods ranging from wallets to skirts and jackets. *Las Brisas Hotel* (phone: 74-841580).

La Colección de Sergio Bustamante – The world-renowned artist's fantastical eggs, animals, and people in ceramics, papier-mâché, and brass are displayed here. The *Princess* arcade and 711-B Costera Miguel Alemán (phone: 74-844992).

Galería Rudic – Paintings and other works of art by the finest Mexican artists. Costera Miguel Alemán and Yañez Pinzon (phone: 74-841104).

Gucci – Decent knock-offs of the real Gucci shoes and accessories of Italy, at fairly reasonable prices. On the Costera across from the *Galería Plaza* and at *El Patio Shopping Center* (phone: 74-840969).

Marietta – Eye-catching fashions and accessories for women. In *Torre de Acapulco* on Costera Miguel Alemán and at the *Princess* (phone: 74-843100).

El Mundo de Esteban – Very high-fashion, New York–style clothing for men and women, chic Acapulco wear, lovely hats and tunics, and glamorous evening dress. 2010 Costera Miguel Alemán (phone: 74-843084).

Polo Ralph Lauren – Men's and women's sportswear and accessories by the famed designer. In the *Acapulco Princess* hotel, Costera Miguel Alemán, across the street from the American Express office (phone: 74-843325).

Ronay – If silver jewelry is your delight, this is the place. Costera Miguel Alemán, beneath *Carlos 'n' Charlie's* restaurant (phone: 74-843343).

Rubén Torres – Stunning sportswear for men and women. 1999 Costera Miguel Alemán (phone: 74-840786).

Suzett's – Striking gold designs, especially in rings with precious stones. At the *Hyatt Regency* (phone: 74-842888).

Tane – Silver jewelry, flatware, and objets d'art of impeccable design and quality. At the *Hyatt Regency* (phone: 74-859648).

Taxco el Viejo – A most imaginative silver shop that also sell items in gold, leather, wool, wood, and ceramic. A block from the cliffs from which the famous divers leap, at 830 Quebrada (phone: 74-837300).

For those interested in sports, Acapulco is mostly a town for participants, not spectators, but there is something here for virtually every taste. Just don't neglect the sun protection!

Of all the athletic activities available here, water sports are the most prevalent. Scuba diving lessons and equipment are available at all the major hotels. The Arnold brothers run a school (205 Costera Miguel Alemán, in front of *Las Hamacas* hotel; phone: 74-820788). *Divers de México,* which is owned by a very helpful American woman, has dive packages that include pool instruction and lunch (phone: 74-821397/8). Most dives are made in the waters off Roqueta Island.

Surfing, though limited in Acapulco, is possible at the *Copacabana* and *Princess* hotels' beaches, and a half-mile south of the *Princess* at Revolcadero Beach. Although surfing is not allowed in the bay area, inner tubes may be rented at Caleta for paddling around the bay.

Parasailing, going aloft in a parachute pulled by a speedboat, is available on every beach. The cost is $10 to $20 for up to 10 minutes. *Be warned:* It can be dangerous.

Far safer is water skiing, and Acapulco is the ideal place to learn or to perfect your skills. Boats are available at all the major hotels. Caleta Beach and Puerto Marqués are especially good places to start, since the water is calmer there. Prices run about $25 to $40 per hour. At Coyuca Lagoon visitors can watch demonstrations of barefoot skiing.

One of the best ways to go sightseeing in Acapulco is on the water. Several motor yachts and a catamaran make the 3½-hour cruise around Acapulco Bay, Puerto Marqués, and La Quebrada cliffs, with a running commentary on the way, for about $35, including lunch or dinner, disco dancing, open bar (local drinks only), and a show in the evening. There are moonlight cruises — even when there's no moon — which include an open bar and performances by Argentine dancers, for about $12. The *Bonanza* and *Fiesta Cabaret* offer morning and afternoon trips, as well as starlight cruises (the stars are almost always out) that include an open bar, music, and dancing;

evening departure time is 7:30 PM and return is at 10:30 PM (phone: 74-822055). *Divers de México* runs a 3-hour champagne sunset cruise with a show provided by the cliff divers at La Quebrada, as well as a daytime *Buccaneer* cruise with the crew dressed up as pirates, each for about $25 (phone: 74-821397/8). No-frills cruises leave at 11 AM and 4:30 PM and cost about $10. A shorter ride can be taken in the glass-bottom boats that leave Caleta all day long and pass over the underwater Shrine of Our Lady of Guadalupe. Tickets for yacht cruises are available at hotel tour desks.

Charter boats for deep-sea fishing leave around 8 AM and return around lunchtime. The Pacific waters yield pompano, bonito, barracuda, yellowtail, red snapper, and shark. A few miles southeast of the city in the Tres Palos Lagoon, and at Coyuca Lagoon near Pie de la Cuesta, you can rent small boats with awnings, and fish for freshwater catfish. *Divers de México* (phone: 74-821397/8) has nine American yachts, some air conditioned, all Coast Guard–approved and with uniformed crews, costing $220 to $500 per day for 4 to 30 passengers, or $50 per chair. *Club de Esquies Beto* has speedboats, from which five can fish, that rent for $25 per hour, with a minimum of 3 hours, and fishing boats for four for $150 (phone: 74-822034). Freshwater fishing costs about $35 an hour, including equipment, with a 3-hour minimum.

Acapulco boasts three golf courses: the 9-hole public course next to the Centro Internacional (on Costera Miguel Alemán); an 18-hole course at the *Acapulco Princess* (Revolcadero Beach); and an 18-hole course at the *Pierre Marqués Club de Golf* at the hotel adjoining the *Princess,* also on Revolcadero Beach. All have resident pros and charge greens fees. Reservations for starting times are advised during the winter season. The *Pierre Marqués Club de Golf* is the longest and most challenging; the *Acapulco Princess* layout usually is in the best condition.

The city also boasts a number of tennis clubs, some with indoor, air conditioned courts as well as outdoor courts; others have lighted courts for night play. Altogether, there are about 30 courts in town. In addition to those at the *Acapulco Princess, Acapulco Plaza, Las Brisas, Hyatt Regency,* and *Puerto Marqés* hotels, there is a tennis club at *Villa Vera* (35 Lomas del Mar), and at the golf club in town, *Club de Golf Acapulco* (next to the Centro Internacional).

For equestrians, Revolcadero Beach is the place to go for a canter astride a smallish Indian pony; ask for Mundo or Carlos, who will take the time to find you the best horses. Some horses are also available at Pie de la Cuesta.

Wrestling matches are held Wednesday and Sunday nights at the *Coliseo Arena,* which draws a rough crowd. There often is more fighting in the stands than in the ring.

Bullfighting is a spectacle, not a sport, according to aficionados, but in any case, established matadors perform Sunday afternoons starting at 5:30 PM during December and *Easter Week.* Hotel travel desks have the details and the tickets. The bullring is near Caleta Beach. Tickets cost from $10 to $25.

If traditional Mexican entertainment is what you're after, Acapulco has its share of Mexican fiestas. Slightly corny, but great fun, the fiestas usually feature mariachi music, folkloric dancing, a Mexican buffet, and an open bar. Each place offers some variation on the same Mexican theme. Fiestas at the Centro Internacional Acapulco and the *Marbella Shopping Center* feature the spectacular *Flying Indians of Papantla.* Javier de León's excellent folkloric ballet performs at the *Calinda* hotel (1260 Costera Miguel Alemán). At *Las Brisas' El Mexicano* restaurant, the festivities begin with a *tianguis* (marketplace) of handicrafts and end with a spectacular fireworks display. The fiestas cost $25 to $30 per person, and reservations can be made through most hotel travel desks.

Acapulco really gets going after dark — *well* after dark. The discos don't get crowded until after 11 PM, so one way to get a table is to arrive around 10:30. The big hotels usually have several places to fill the evening hours, depending on your mood, and they often feature live entertainment. *A fashion note:* As casual as Acapulco is both day and night, its nightspots do not look kindly on shorts, old jeans, or bare feet.

Aca Tiki – The floating dinner party aboard this huge trimaran begins with cocktails on the top deck and a cruise around the bay, followed by a formal dinner, a Latin American floor show, and disco music for dancing — a very enjoyable experience. The trimaran leaves from the pier across from Fort San Diego at 7:30 PM and gets back around 10:30 PM (phone: 74-846140 or 74-846786, for reservations).

Atrium – The old *Boccaccio* club has been renamed and redecorated: no tables, no chairs — just bars, a dance floor, and a DJ spinning disco recordings. $25 covers all drinks (except champagne and cognac) and snacks. Closed Mondays and Tuesdays. 5040 Costera Miguel Alemán (phone: 74-841900).

Baby'O – One of Acapulco's top discos, imaginative and fashionable, it looks like a stylized mud hut from the outside. A pajama party is held annually. Opens at 10:30 PM, and the beat goes on until 5 or 6 AM. Costera Miguel Alemán, out where it begins (phone: 74-847474).

Cat's – A laser show in the early hours of the morning is the main attraction. Open Thursdays through Saturdays. 32 Juan de la Cosa, across the street from the *Acapulco Plaza* (phone: 74-847235).

Le Dome – One of the port's original discos, its interior is the most compelling attraction. 402 Costera Miguel Alemán (phone: 74-841190).

Eve – It's practically on the water, and one of the prettiest discos in town. 115 Costera Miguel Alemán (phone: 74-844777).

Extasis – Built on the water's edge, it offers a great view of the ski show at the *Colonial* next door. 200 Costera Miguel Alemán (phone: 74-833090).

Extravaganzza – Aptly named, the club is huge, modern, and posh, with an immense glass wall providing an awesome view of the entire bay. Truly spectacular, it shouldn't be missed, even by non-discophiles. Next door to *Los Rancheros* on the Carr. Escénica, headed to *Las Brisas* (phone: 74-847165).

Fantasy – The façade sparkles with a cascade of tiny lights; the interior is like a glass ship. *La Vista Shopping Center* (phone: 74-846764 or 74-846727).

El Fuerte – This Spanish-style nightclub claims to have the best flamenco show this side of Seville. Shows at 10 and 11:30 PM, except Sundays. In *Las Hamacas Hotel,* 239 Costera Miguel Alemán (phone: 74-826161).

Gallery – A disco and show bar where the 11 PM and 1 AM shows star female impersonators. The entertainment is surprisingly good. 11 Av. Deportes, across the street from the *Holiday Inn* (phone: 74-843497).

Hard Rock Café – At this south-of-the-border branch, dancing is in air conditioned comfort, day and night, but the live music — and real fun — begins at 11 PM when everyone — waiters and customers alike — gets into the act. Good food, too. 37 Costera Miguel Alemán (phone: 74-846680).

Jackie'O – No longer the new, chic disco in town, it still attracts a young and energetic clientele. Costera Miguel Alemán, at *El Patio Shopping Center* across from the *Continental Acapulco* (phone: 74-840843).

Magic – A selective door policy has made this one disco everybody wants to get into. People come here to be seen as much as to dance. Costera Miguel Alemán at Fragata Yucatán (phone: 74-848815).

News – One of Acapulco's largest and most popular dance spots, it seats 1,200 people in booths and love seats (no chairs). On the Costera across the street from the *Hyatt Regency* (phone: 74-845904).

La Perla – On the cliffs overlooking the sea, this is a supper club where the floor show is provided by the famed Acapulco divers. There are two orchestras for dancing. The first evening show is at 7:15 PM. La Quebrada (phone: 74-821111).

Poseidon – Some of Mexico's best nightclub performers appear here. At the *Torres Gemelas Hotel* on the Costera (phone: 74-844828).

Tiffany's – Victorian decor, with plush upholstery and all that. The sound system allows guests seated at tables to actually carry on a conversation. At the *Acapulco Princess* (phone: 74-843100).

EATING OUT: Acapulco has more restaurants than you'll be able to test even if you plan to stay as long as 2 weeks. Many of the finest are in the best hotels (including the *Hyatt Regency* and the *Acapulco Plaza*). Dining out here is relatively costly. Expect to pay $80 for two at those places we've listed as very expensive; $50 to $60, expensive; up to $40, moderate; under $30, inexpensive. Prices do not include drinks, wine, or tips. Most restaurants below accept MasterCard and Visa; a few also accept American Express and Diners Club.

Casa Nova – With modern decor and a wonderful view of Acapulco Bay, this spot serves pasta, antipasto, and Italian renderings of shrimp and fish. Open daily. Reservations necessary. 5256 Carr. Escénica, across the street from *Las Brisas Hotel* (phone: 74-846819). Very expensive.

Coyuca 22 – A great place for a pre-dinner drink and conversation, it looks like the set of a romantic Hollywood musical extravaganza of the 1940s. You almost expect to see Fred Astaire and Ginger Rogers come dancing around the pool. The menu includes lobster thermidor; a highlight of the decor is a handsome unicorn sculpture by Victor Salmones. Open daily for dinner only. Closed May through October. Reservations necessary. 22 Coyuca (phone: 74-835030). Very expensive.

Bella Vista – Set atop a hill overlooking the entire city and bay, the prime eating place at the *Las Brisas* hotel provides a wonderful view. Menu items include lobster thermidor, fresh fish, and shrimp served with coconut and rice. Open daily for breakfast and dinner. Reservations necessary. Carr. Escénica, 8 miles southeast of Acapulco (phone: 74-841580 or 800-228-3000). Expensive.

Black Beard's (also known as Barbas Negras) – Not surprisingly, the decor is early pirates' den. The menu concentrates on steaks, lobster, chicken, baked potato with sour cream, and a salad bar. It's next to Condesa Beach, and you usually have to wait for a table. Open daily for dinner only. No reservations. Costera Miguel Alemán (phone: 74-842549). Expensive.

El Campanario – A beautiful bell-tower dining room with colonial decor atop a mountain, with a panoramic view of Acapulco and very well prepared international dishes and seafood. Open daily. Reservations advised. Calle Paraíso (phone: 74-848830). Expensive.

Dino's – Homemade Italian bread is what makes this place special, and dining on the terrace makes things even more pleasant. You can get some continental dishes, but standard Italian-American fare characterizes most of the menu. Open daily. No reservations. 137 Costera Miguel Alemán (phone: 74-840037). Expensive.

D Joint – Also known as "DJ's," it's the best place in town for roast beef. An excellent place for sandwiches and chili, too. Open daily. Reservations advised. 79 Costera Miguel Alemán (phone: 74-843709). Expensive.

Embarcadero – A showplace with a South Seas motif, it offers such temptations as charcoal-broiled mahimahi with rice and bananas. Open daily (closed Mondays in summer). Reservations advised. Costera Miguel Alemán near *CICI Park* (phone: 74-848787). Expensive.

Hard Times – Trendy and fun, it's a place where you can select your meal from an international menu — or just order tacos and beer. The salad is marvelous, with artichoke leaves, avocado, beets, cauliflower, red cabbage, and much more. As you may have guessed, the motif is Depression era. Dinner only. Closed Sundays. Reservations advised. 400 Costera Miguel Alemán (phone: 74-840064). Expensive.

Kookaburra – With romantic dining under the stars and a stunning view of the bay, this spot specializes in seafood, steaks, and barbecue. There is also a wonderful ceviche bar (Mexico's answer to sushi). Dinner only. Open 6 PM to midnight; closed Sundays. Reservations advised. Carr. Las Brisas (phone: 74-844418). Expensive.

Madeiras – A pretty place with terrace dining and a view of the bay, it drips ferns and sophistication. The prix fixe menu includes baby lamb chops, sea bass, red snapper baked in sea salt, Cornish hen, and frogs' legs in white wine or garlic sauce. Dinner only. Closed Sundays. Reservations advised. Carr. Escénica, in *La Vista Shopping Center* (phone: 74-846921). Expensive.

Miramar – Elegant, yet cozy, it too offers a spectacular view. Diners sit on multilevel terraces, and enjoy fine French fare. The *pato a la naranja* (duck with orange sauce) is crisp and beautifully presented. Closed Sundays during the summer. Reservations necessary. In *La Vista Shopping Center* (phone: 74-847874). Expensive.

Normandie – Easily the best French restaurant in Acapulco and perhaps in all of Mexico, it is run by Nicole Lepine, a Gallic lady, and her daughter. Open daily. Dinner only. Closed May through October. Reservations advised. In town at Costera Miguel Alemán and Malespina (phone: 74-851916). Expensive.

Suntory – Operated by a leading distiller of Japanese whiskey, this fasionable place offers authentic Japanese food. Open daily. Reservations advised. 36 Costera Miguel Alemán (phone: 74-848088). Expensive.

Beto's – Right on Condesa Beach, it's very popular for breakfast, lunch, live music, and good seafood. Open daily. Reservations advised. Costera Miguel Alemán, at Condesa Beach (phone: 74-840473). Moderate.

Carlos 'n' Charlie's – The atmosphere is lively, but expect to wait in line half an hour or more. House specialties include charcoal-broiled spareribs and stuffed shrimp, and good sangria. Open daily for dinner only. No reservations. 999 Costera Miguel Alemán (phone: 74-840039). Moderate.

Chez Guillaume – Quiet and elegant, it serves well-prepared continental dishes including seafood crêpes, soufflés, and scampi. The bar attracts an international crowd. Open daily for dinner only. Reservations advised. 110 Av. del Prado (phone: 74-841231). Moderate.

Hard Rock Café – A combination rock 'n' roll hall of fame, bar, restaurant, dance hall, and boutique. The food, everything from shrimp *fajitas* to filet mignon, is tasty, and portions are generous. Live rock music is played from 11 PM to 2 AM. Service is friendly. There's always a line at the boutique, which sells sportswear bearing the familiar *Hard Rock* logo. Reservations advised. 37 Costera Miguel Alemán, next to *CICI Park* (phone: 74-846680). Moderate.

Huachinango Charlie's – *Huachinango* means red snapper, one of the best dishes served at this relaxed, informal seafood house. Open daily. Reservations advised. 115 Costera Miguel Alemán (phone: 74-840029). Moderate.

Mimi's Chili Saloon – Behind a bird's-egg-blue façade, it offers hamburgers, burritos, fried chicken, frozen margaritas, and a lovely view of the ocean. Closed Mondays. Reservations advised. Costera Miguel Alemán; next to *Black Beard's* (phone: 74-842549). Moderate.

Paraíso – Serving delicious red snapper right on Condesa Beach, this spot is similar to, but wackier than, its neighbor *Beto's* (see above). Open daily. Reservations advised. Costera Miguel Alemán, at Condesa Beach (phone: 74-845988). Moderate.

Shangri-La – An Oriental garden with lily pond and bridge is the setting and, as you might expect, the fare is standard Cantonese. If you can't live without egg foo yong and fried rice, this is your best bet in Acapulco. Open daily for dinner only.

Reservations advised. Just off the Costera at 5 Calle Piedra Picuda (phone: 74-841300). Moderate.

Villa Demos – A beautiful garden restaurant specializing in homemade fettuccine and other Italian dishes; we think it's the most romantic eatery in town. We recommend the veal *piccata.* There is a terrace for outdoor dining, as well as indoor service. Closed Mondays in the off-season. Reservations advised. 6 Av. del Prado, off Costera Miguel Alemán (phone: 74-842040). Moderate.

Pipo's – There are three of them; each one looks raunchy, but regulars insist that they serve the best seafood on the Mexican Pacific. Open daily. Reservations unnecessary. Across from the sport fishing docks, at 3 Almirante Bretón (phone: 74-822237); Puerto Marqués (phone: 74-846343); 105 Costera Miguel Alemán (phone: 74-840165). Branch on the Costera, moderate; all others, inexpensive.

Acapulco Fat Farm – Also known as *La Granja del Pingüe,* this cozy little eatery is run by high school and college students who formerly lived at the Acapulco Children's Center, an orphanage. The name points to the ice cream, pastries, and pies that are the specialties here, but there's less-fattening fare, too — good soups, sandwiches, and Mexican food. There's a book exchange, and live music is played Thursdays through Tuesdays. No reservations. No credit cards accepted. 10 Juárez, 2 blocks west of the zocalo (phone: 74-835339). Inexpensive.

El Fiaco – An informal place where barbecued meats are done to a turn. The menu has some other interesting touches — fondue, for example. Lots of people come here to relax and drink beer and enjoy a snack. Open daily. Reservations unnecessary. No credit cards accepted. 235 Hornitos (phone: 74-830557). Inexpensive.

Los Rancheros – Easy to overlook for its hilltop location, this is a good place to sample authentic Mexican food while gazing out at the Pacific. Open daily. Reservations unnecessary. On Carr. Escénica en route to *Las Brisas* (phone: 74-841908). Inexpensive.

BEST EN ROUTE

It's best to arrive in Acapulco with a prepaid reservation directly from your hotel, including a written confirmation stating the price. Overbooking is a frequent risk, so if there's trouble, make a scene, demand to talk to the reservations manager, and/or threaten to call the Tourism Ministry (5-250-0123 in Mexico City, day or night). The loudest squeaking wheel usually gets the oil, and noisy, demanding guests usually get service. Winter rates are often more than double summer rates. In winter expect to pay up to $250 for a double room in very expensive hotels, $145 to $175 for expensive, about $100 for moderate, and $70 or less for inexpensive.

Acapulco Princess – Designed to evoke the most dramatic elements of Mexico's Aztec and Maya heritage, the shape of its main building is pyramidal, with exterior balconies hung with exotic tropical blossoms. Try to arrange for accommodations in this building if you want to be near the action. A fine 18-hole course serves as a prime lure for golfers. There are also 5 swimming pools (one with a bar under a waterfall), a beach, a sauna, 11 tennis courts, jeeps, parachute rides, 7 restaurants (of which the *Hacienda* is best), a lobby bar, and a disco. 1,019 rooms. Rate includes breakfast and dinner. Carr. Escénica, 12 miles (19 km) southeast of Acapulco (phone: 74-843100; 800-223-1818 in the US; FAX: 74-843664). Very expensive.

Las Brisas – One of the truly unique resort hotels of the world and still our favorite in Acapulco, this striking amalgam of lovely casitas, built in 1957, has been carved into the side of the tallest of the hilltops surrounding Acapulco Harbor, offering a superb view as well as superb accommodations. Privacy is paramount here, and the service is mostly splendid, with a private beach club (at the foot of the steep hill) that satisfies the desire for swimming in the Pacific. There are 300 rooms — including some 1-, 2-, and 3-bedroom suites, as well as 4- to 6-bedroom homes — most with private or semiprivate swimming pools strewn with fresh blossoms each day. Try to arrange for a room with your own pool. There are 2 saltwater pools (at the beach club), 5 lighted tennis courts, water sports, golf and fishing nearby, and private restaurants open to hotel guests only. Rate includes continental breakfast and membership in the hotel's private *La Concha Beach Club,* which serves some of the best ceviche in Mexico. The *Bella Vista* restaurant serves good seafood (see *Eating Out*). Carr. Escénica, 8 miles (13 km) southeast of Acapulco (phone: 74-841580; 800-228-3000 in the US; FAX: 74-841580). Very expensive.

Hyatt Regency – The sight of towering ceiba trees and graceful fountains welcomes guests as they approach. It offers 700 large, comfortable, recently remodeled rooms, a good-size pool framed by palms, water sports at the beach, 5 lighted tennis courts, a pro shop for guests only, 2 restaurants, coffee shop, 3 bars, and exercise classes. Costera Miguel Alemán (phone: 74-842888; FAX: 74-843087). Very expensive.

Pierre Marqués – Sharing the Revolcadero beachfront (and ownership) with the next-door *Princess,* this place was constructed by billionaire J. Paul Getty and retains its authentic luxurious mien. A shuttle now runs between the two hotels. Probably the most underrated of Acapulco's accommodations, its facilities include 3 swimming pools, a pleasant, uncrowded stretch of beach, a true championship golf course (the best around), fishing, tennis, 2 restaurants, and a cocktail lounge. The only drawback: very little shade. There are 344 rooms, including junior and master suites. Rate includes breakfast. Carr. Escénica, about 11 miles (18 km) southeast of Acapulco (phone: 74-842000; 800-223-1818 in the US; FAX: 74-848554). Very expensive.

Continental Acapulco – An Acapulco landmark, it has a pool surrounding an island, and its beach is enormous. It also has 405 rooms, 3 restaurants, a coffee shop, lobby bar with live music, pool bar, and access to the 5 tennis courts at the *Hyatt Regency.* Costera Miguel Alemán (phone: 74-840909; 800-88-CONTI in the US). Expensive.

Fiesta Americana Condesa Acapulco – Next to *El Presidente* on the beach, this large (500-room) hotel — the best on the Costera — has 2 swimming pools, a social program for kids, a lobby bar where live music attracts nighttime crowds, and a restaurant with more tranquil music. Costera Miguel Alemán (phone: 74-842828; 800-FIESTA-1 in the US; FAX: 74-830575). Expensive.

Sheraton Acapulco – Set on a hillside on secluded Guitarrón Beach on the east end of Acapulco Bay, it has 17 villas comprising 226 rooms and 8 suites. Facilities include 2 pools (one with a swim-up bar), 2 restaurants, and a lobby bar with live music. 110 Costera Guitarrón (phone: 74-843737; 800-325-3535 in the US). Expensive.

Villa Vera – A glamorous jet set favorite, the place where the movie stars go and starlets follow. There are 80 spacious rooms, suites, and villas (many of which have private pools), an excellent restaurant, a large hotel pool with a swim-up bar (this is where they began), Jacuzzi, fitness center, and 3 clay tennis courts. There's no beach, but guests may use the beach at the *Maralisa.* No children under 16. In town, at 35 Lomas del Mar (phone: 74-840333; 800-223-6510 in the US; FAX: 74-847449). Expensive.

Acapulco Malibu – This smaller, circular hostelry, with its own tropical garden, offers water skiing as well as its beach and swimming pool. Though the 80 rooms are somewhat on the glitzy side, they're almost always full. 20 Costera Miguel Alemán (phone: 74-841070; FAX: 74-840475). Moderate.

Acapulco Plaza – Its exterior resembles a funnel-shaped parking garage, but it's more luxurious inside. The *La Jaula* bar hangs in the lobby gardens, seemingly suspended in midair. About half of the 1,008 rooms are small; the other half are very comfortable suites. The *Oasis Club* has a pleasant and quiet private Jacuzzi on the third floor; *Club Mirage,* on the second floor, offers more of the same, and also allows children. There's also a tennis club (4 courts on the roof of the shopping center), 2 pools, a fine beach, 50 shops in its shopping center, a health club, 4 restaurants, and a coffee shop. Service at the front desk is not always friendly. Affiliated with Holiday Inns. 123 Costera Miguel Alemán (phone: 74-858050; 800-HOLIDAY in the US; FAX: 74-855493). Moderate.

Boca Chica – One of Acapulco's older, smaller places, right on the water, with 2 restaurants (one a sushi and oyster bar) and 2 pools (one is a natural saltwater cove). Snorkeling is at its best here. Rate includes breakfast and dinner. Caletilla Beach (phone: 74-836601 or 74-836741; FAX: 74-839513). Moderate.

La Palapa – The 30 floors beneath a scalloped gold crown contain nothing but suites (335) with balconies, indoor bars, and plenty of closet space. Plants give the place an airy feel. The hotel also has a large pool with swim-up bar, water sports center, social program, live music nightly, and an electronic-game room. 210 Fragata Yucatán (phone: 74-845363; 800-334-7234 in the US; FAX: 74-848399). Moderate.

Paraíso Radisson – Right on Hornos Beach, it has 422 newly redecorated rooms with balconies and satellite TV. There's a pool, cafeteria, a restaurant on the beach, and a rooftop restaurant with a breathtaking view of Acapulco Bay. 163 Costera Miguel Alemán (phone: 74-855050; 800-228-9822 in the US; FAX: 74-855543). Moderate.

El Presidente – This rather sterile 407-room giant on the beach has 2 swimming pools, a sauna, nightclub, restaurant, 2 bars, and a social program in case you can't find enough to do. Costera Miguel Alemán (phone: 74-841700; 800-777-1700 in the US; FAX: 74-841376). Moderate.

Ritz – A modern high-rise, it has a pleasant lobby with wicker furniture, pool, restaurant, and video games. Costera Miguel Alemán on Hornos Beach (phone: 74-857336; FAX: 74-857076). Moderate.

Tortuga – This peach-colored property, with an atrium from which plants dangle impressively, has 250 large rooms, a swimming pool, sauna, 2 bars, and 2 restaurants, including *La Fonda.* Close to, but not on, the beach. 132 Costera Miguel Alemán (phone: 74-848889; FAX: 74-847385). Moderate.

Autotel Ritz – With 103 rooms, a restaurant, and pool. MAP (two meals per day included) available. Costera Miguel Alemán and Wilfrido Massieu (phone: 74-858023; FAX: 74-855647). Inexpensive.

Bali-Hai – One of the advantages of this motel is that guests can enjoy a quiet room in the back and still be right on the main strip. Restaurant; swimming pool. Room service is available. Near the *Acapulco Plaza.* 186 Costera Miguel Alemán (phone: 74-856336; FAX: 74-857972). Inexpensive.

Etel – Spotlessly clean rooms and 1- to 4-bedroom apartments equipped with air conditioning, fans, and a marvelous view. There is also a pool set in a pretty garden. Up a steep street at 92 Pinzona (phone: 74-822240). Inexpensive.

Los Flamingos – This is where the film stars of the 1940s came to frolic, and the place is alive with memories. There is a pool, restaurant, and bar. The panoramic view is a constant spectacle. Rate includes breakfast. On a hillside at López Mateos and Flamingos (phone: 74-820690; FAX: 74-839806). Inexpensive.

Las Hamacas – Across from the beach on the strip, this hostelry offers a pool with bar, garden dining room, and flamenco shows in its nightclub. Of the 160 rooms, those off the pool are nicer and quieter, though they have no view. 239 Costera Miguel Alemán (phone: 74-837746; 800-421-0767 in the US). Inexpensive.

Majestic – Up in the hills overlooking the bay, it offers 195 rooms, a pool, parking, and transportation to the Costera. 73 Av. Pozo del Rey (phone: 74-834710; FAX: 74-821614). Inexpensive.

Playa las Glorias El Mirador – People generally come here to sip cocktails at *La Perla* supper club and watch the cliff divers, but besides the dramatic view, the hotel offers 3 pools and 133 pleasant rooms with large bathrooms. It's best for those who don't need a beach at hand. 74 Quebrada (phone: 74-831155; 800-342-AMIGO in the US; FAX: 74-820638). Inexpensive.

Posada del Sol – Near *CICI Park,* this is an efficient place with an oddly American flavor. It has 232 rooms and bungalows, a restaurant, bar, and pool. 1390 Costera Miguel Alemán (phone: 74-841010; 800-445-9008 in the US; FAX: 74-840305). Inexpensive.

Sands – In the center of things, yet tranquil, it has a restaurant, 2 pools, a bar, 2 squash courts, and 59 modest but good-size rooms and 34 bungalows. The staff is pleasant. 178 Costera Miguel Alemán and Juan de la Cosa (phone: 74-842260; 800-422-6078 in the US; FAX: 74-841053). Inexpensive.

El Tropicano – Just 2 blocks from the beach, it has 127 rooms and 12 suites, cable TV, 2 pools, restaurants, a garden, and a disco. Part of the Best Western group. 510 Costera Miguel Alemán (phone: 74-841100; 800-528-1234 in the US; FAX: 74-841308). Inexpensive.

Del Mar – Almost hidden from view and tiny, with only 2 floors and 14 small rooms, this quaint lodging is surely the least expensive in Acapulco. While it's short on conveniences, there is air conditioning in some rooms and a small open-air restaurant and bar. This is one of the few budget places where you have to book ahead. 254 Costera Miguel Alemán, at Hornos Beach (phone: 74-851723). Very inexpensive.

Ixtapa and Zihuatanejo to Huatulco

Las Bahías de Huatulco, 18 miles of cove-jagged coastline on nine lovely bays, is the site of Mexico's newest — and most ambitious — mega-resort project. Upon completion (scheduled for the year 2018), this $200-million resort development is expected to surpass Cancún in size and total visitors. Although it is still in its infancy — huge construction projects are under way everywhere — its beaches are undeniably beautiful, and for those who are loath to leave the sand, this is yet another place in the sun at which to indulge yourself. Even for those who have decided to head inland, Huatulco is a perfect place for a last look at Mexico's Pacific Coast before venturing north to colonial Oaxaca.

For a detailed report on the route southeast to Puerto Escondido, and points of interest and hotels and restaurants along the way, see *Ixtapa and Zihuatanejo to Oaxaca* in this section.

En route from Puerto Escondido – Take Highway 200 east for 65 miles (104 km) to Huatulco. Exercise caution 43 miles (69 km) from Puerto Escondido at the intersection of Highway 200 and Route 175 (there are no traffic signals, so treat it as a four-way stop and yield to other cars, which often come barreling through). A right turn at this intersection leads south to pretty Puerto Angel, a small fishing village known for its outstanding beaches.

From the intersection, Highway 200 continues eastward through tropical grazing land, with groves of coconut palms and banana trees, and curves as the mountains edge closer to the coastline. About 24 miles (38 km) farther is the left-hand turnoff for the airport. The entrance to Las Bahías de Huatulco, 10 miles (16 km) farther on Highway 200, is clearly marked.

Unfortunately, once you enter the development there is a noticeable lack of signposts. Basically, the wide boulevard off Highway 200 is the main road. At the first fork, bear right for La Crucesita, a brand-new tourist town created where no town had existed before, and the hotel zone. The boulevard winds through La Crucesita and past the power plant, then continues on for 10 miles (16 km), above *Club Med,* which is virtually invisible from the road, and around Tangolunda Bay to the *Sheraton* (and the new, partially occupied shopping malls that face it), and the *Royal Maeva.* To get to Santa Cruz, a once-rustic fishing village turned spiffy marina, bear right at the second fork off the main boulevard.

LAS BAHÍAS DE HUATULCO: Known until recently to only the most adventurous travelers, tiny Huatulco was once apparently a pretty exciting place — until its decline around the end of the 16th century. It was an important Zapotec, and then Mixtec, settlement before the Spanish conquerors arrived, and by 1575 — because of its strate-

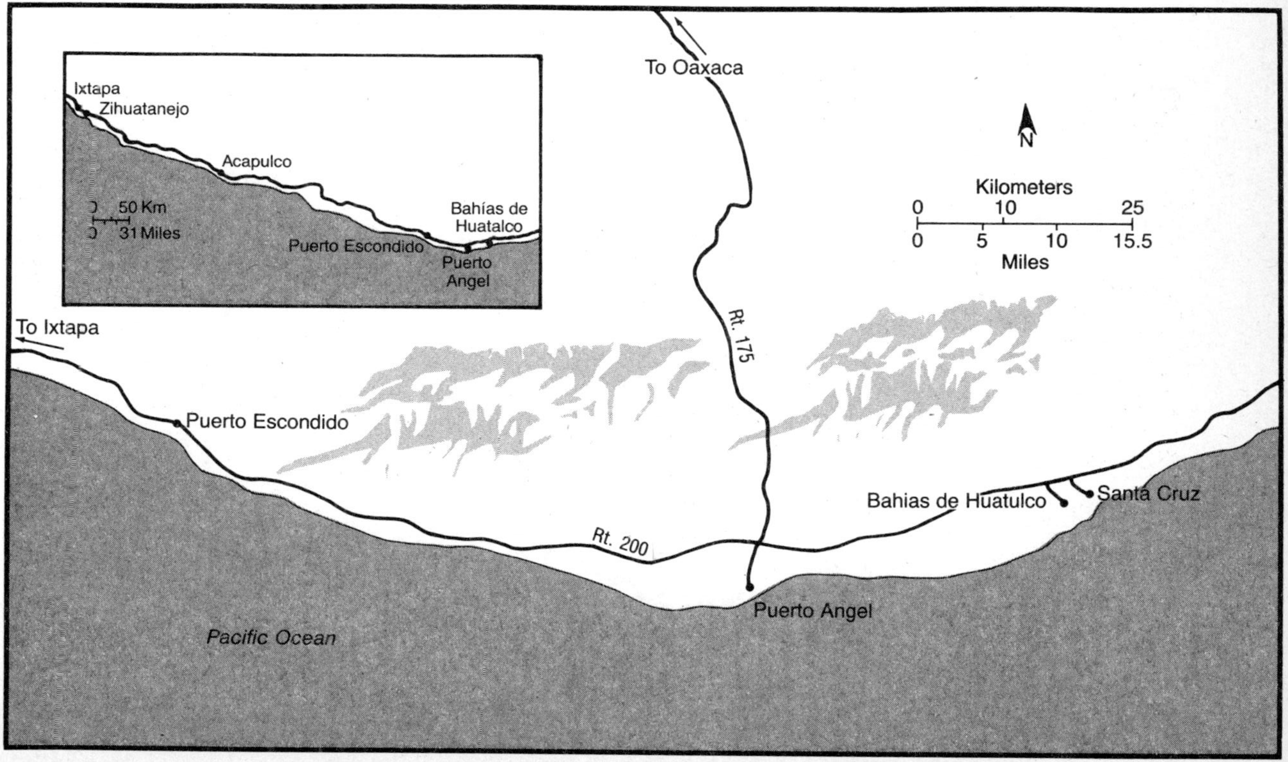

Ixtapa
Zihuatanejo
Acapulco
0 50 Km
0 31 Miles
Bahías de Huatalco
Puerto Escondido
Puerto Angel
To Oaxaca
N
Kilometers
0 10 25
0 5 10 15.5
Miles
To Ixtapa
Rt. 175
Puerto Escondido
Bahias de Huatulco
Santa Cruz
Rt. 200
Puerto Angel
Pacific Ocean

gic location — it had become the most important Spanish port on the Pacific. That was the year that Sir Francis Drake attacked Huatulco; 8 years later the English navigator-pirate Thomas Cavendish, with three galleons and 120 men, also attacked the town. Furious at finding little of value in the homes of the humble villagers, Cavendish ordered his men to remove a wooden cross that stood on a nearby beach. But the sacred cross — the Santa Cruz de Huatulco — remained mysteriously untouched by their axes and saws. When even fire failed to destroy it, Cavendish had his men tie ropes from the cross to one of his vessels and tried to haul it out of the ground. This, too, failed. Many years later, church leaders decided to remove the cross "for safekeeping," and this time it was successfully moved, to the city of Oaxaca. There it was divided up among several churches and the bishop's family. A small part was set in silver and sent to the Vatican. As for Huatulco, much later, during the 19th century, Mexican president Vicente Guerrero was betrayed by traitors in the town, and it lapsed into anonymity until it was rediscovered by FONATUR (the government agency charged with expanding Mexican tourism facilities).

At this point, Huatulco has a way to go before it becomes the sort of active traveler's destination that Cancún is. But the region is gearing up for more major development over the next 30 years. At its formal inaugural (November 1988), Phase One of Huatulco, which encompasses 1,300 hotel rooms on Tangolunda and Santa Cruz bays, was nearly complete: The *Binniguenda* was open for business, and *Club Med* was already taking in a European crowd. Now the *Binniguenda* and *Club Med* have been joined by the *Sheraton* and *Royal Maeva.* Besides hotels, the overall plan includes the construction of villas, condominiums, and homes, as well as a 100-boat marina and a cruise ship pier, and the local population is expected to exceed 300,000. Some 40,000 acres are supposed to be retained as a wildlife preserve.

For information about area happenings, accommodations, dining, and other activities, visit the tourist offices on Boulevard Chahue (phone: 958-10326; closed weekends) and in the small yellow building across the street from the *Sheraton* (phone: 958-40030), or pick up a copy of *Huatulco Espacio 2000,* a handy quarterly tourist guide, available in restaurants and shops and at the publication's helpful information booth on the corner of Bugambilias and Avenida Guamuchil in La Crucesita.

Currently nightlife remains largely confined to the hotels, although there are a few seafood shacks on the beach in Santa Cruz Bay, and a couple of discos in town. Shopping is sorely limited. But the calm waters of the bays offer excellent swimming and snorkeling, the fishing is excellent, and there's plenty of sunshine. Visually, Huatulco is absolutely stunning: Beach after beach is framed by white sands and the jagged gray-black peaks of the Sierra Madre del Sur, perfectly setting off the cerulean blue waters.The *Sociedad Cooperativa Turística de Tangolunda* rents boats at the beach of Santa Cruz for about $25 an hour. A trip on their glass-bottom boat costs about $60. And if asked, drivers will offer some local lore. The agents at the *Espacio 2000* tourist information booth recommend Captain Juan Ongiy of the boat *La Providencia* for tours of the bay.

These waters are superb for deep-sea fishing, sailing, and windsurfing. You can charter a boat from the cooperative, but it's advisable to bring your own gear. *Club Med* takes members on excursions to its own fishing spot. In addition, *Club Med* has sailboats and equipment for windsurfers, for unlimited use by members. Lessons are included in the price of accommodations. For non-guests, *Club Med* also arranges for excursions on the *Stars and Stripes,* the highly disputed winner of the 1988 *America's Cup.* A 1-hour sail, available Mondays through Saturdays, costs a hefty $70 per person, but passengers claim that it's worth the price to experience the thrill of skimming over the waves, seemingly leaping ahead of the wind.

For scuba, *Triton Dive Center* (next to the *Castillo* hotel near Santa Cruz; phone: 958-70141) offers two-tank dives that last approximately 3 hours and cost about $85 per person. Visibility ranges from 6 to 12 feet, and you are likely to see rock formations, coral, sea turtles, tuna, and bonito. *García Rendón* travel agency (in La Crucesita, on the corner of Bugambilias and Octotillo) charges about $30 an hour for dive trips to Entrega, Organo, or Maguey. Be aware that *Club Med,* which heavily promotes scuba diving at many of its oceanside facilities, does not offer it in Huatulco because of the dangerously strong currents.

Snorkeling enthusiasts should head for Tangolunda Bay, where the great reef (just below the surface) is made up partly of giant cauliflower-shaped coral, and the friendly tropical fish spatter the underwater world with color. Visibility is good down to 20 feet. Another good coral reef is at Entrega Beach. You can rent snorkeling equipment at the *García Rendón* travel agency or on the beach. *Club Med* provides gear for its members. Wherever you're snorkeling, ask the hotel or dive shop staff about sharp coral and sea urchins; both can be an unpleasant surprise for the uninformed.

The beaches outside *Club Med,* the *Sheraton,* and *Royal Maeva* are good for swimming, since all have calm waters. Maguey Bay is the only beach in the bay area with fine sand; you'll recognize it by the maguey plants jutting up out of the stone surrounding the beach. Maguey has four restaurants, one named *El Tiburón* (The Shark), but don't let that scare you. If you yearn for privacy, adjacent Organo Bay is quiet, but beware the undercurrent. There's good shelling at Conejos Bay, which is the next bay slated for development.

Reputedly named for the large population of rabbits that used to romp here, Conejos Bay is still a picturesque place where sea turtles lay their eggs in the sand, pelicans stand sentry on the rocks, butterflies flit among the trees, and porpoises frolic in the sea. It's a perfectly relaxed setting for swimming, sunbathing, and shelling. Access is by boat only.

The water spouts like a whale at Bufadora, a natural geyser between Entrega and Organo bays. Access is by boat only.

Golfers can tee off at *Tangolunda*'s 9-hole course (near the *Sheraton;* phone: 958-10059), which is open to the public. For tennis, *Club Med* has 14 courts, the *Sheraton* has 4, and *Royal Maeva* has 2.

Rancho Caballos de Mar conducts guided horseback tours over the hills to Río Copalita for a swim at Playa Magueyito. Contact *Turismo Tangolunda* (phone: 958-70024).

When it's time to take a break from the sun, first-time visitors will not want to miss the the *Chapel of Santa Cruz.* Actually a tiny open-air shack, the chapel (right across from the zocalo at Av. Benito Juárez, Santa Cruz) is a place where Huatulcans gather to worship — and to gossip.

Shopping is fairly limited to *Club Med*'s boutiques, the souvenir stands lining the zocalo, and a few entrepreneurial kids hawking black coral and turquoise necklaces and earrings at the beach at Santa Cruz. FONATUR opened a handicrafts *mercado* (market) at the zocalo, and a few shops also are cropping up in La Crucesita and at *Plaza Esmeralda,* the shopping center across from the *Sheraton.*

The zocalo in La Crucesita encompasses shops, restaurants, and a church. The zocalo in Santa Cruz has an outdoor theater, a handicrafts market, and a cultural center.

Generally, nights in Huatulco are quiet, unless you're staying at the *Royal Maeva* or at *Club Med,* where the *gentils organisateurs* (*GO*s) enthusiastically demonstrate the salsa, and a string of yellow beads buys *muchos* margaritas. At the *Sheraton,* mariachis serenade nightly. Devotees of Mexico's popular *Carlos 'n' Charlie's* party establishments will be pleased to learn that Huatulco now has a branch of its own, though it is small, located on Calle Carrizal, 1 block from Plaza Principal in La Crucesita (no phone). Otherwise, nightlife is limited to the *Magic Circus,* a disco about 2 blocks from the *Binneguenda,* and *Club Tequila* in La Crucesita. For a quieter evening, take a walk on the beach or count the seemingly endless number of stars in the sky.

BEST EN ROUTE

Expect to pay up to $250 for a double room at a hotel listed here as expensive, about $120 at a moderate place, and about $60 at a place listed as inexpensive. Note that while considered expensive, *Club Med*'s rates include most activities, and both *Club Med* and *Royal Maeva*'s rates include all meals. Opportunities for eating out in Huatulco are very limited, but the dining rooms at *Club Med* and the *Sheraton* are open to the public and offer a tasty diversion from your own hotel's fare (see below for details). Hotels and their restaurants listed below accept MasterCard, Visa, American Express, and Diners Club. Restaurant reservations are unnecessary.

Club Med Huatulco – The largest *Club Med* village in the western hemisphere, it has 500 rooms, each with a private terrace and hammock, set in casita clusters on 50 acres on Tangolunda Bay. The no-frills rooms can be divided by pulling the closets together to form a wall; marble bathrooms have two separate sink areas. The club offers a full range of water sports on 4 isolated coves, and there are 3 swimming pools and 14 tennis courts (6 lighted). Excursions are available to Oaxaca, Palenque, and Puerto Escondido. Besides the main cafeteria-style restaurant, there's an excellent Moroccan restaurant, a salmon and steaks place, a fancy Italian restaurant, and a disco. Non-guests are invited to a lunch or dinner buffet, which includes wine, beer, and soft drinks; access to the pool and other facilities during the day; and a show or entrance to the disco at night; the price is $30 per person, except Friday evenings ($40 per person) when there is a more elaborate meal and show. *Club Med* operates nonstop charter flights from some cities in the US. Rate includes rooms, meals, and activities. Domicilio Conocido (phone: 958-10313 or 958-10033; 800-CLUB MED in the US; FAX: 958-10101). Expensive.

Royal Maeva – Among the features are air conditioning in each of the 300 rooms, 2 restaurants, a coffee shop, bars and lounges, a pool, 2 tennis courts, gardens, and a playground for children. Four rooms are available for the handicapped. Rate includes 3 meals a day. Apdo. Postal 227 (phone: 958-10000/48/64; 800-GO-MAEVA in the US; FAX: 958-10220). Expensive.

Huatulco Sheraton – Set on a wide, crescent-shape beach at the end of the bay, this contemporary Mexican-style resort is furnished throughout with Oaxacan crafts; the beaded, pastel Zapotec rugs loom large in the lobby. All 346 rooms have bay views, terraces, air conditioning, mini-bars, color TV sets and radios, safe deposit boxes, telephones, and 24-hour room service; 9 rooms are equipped for the handicapped. There are also 2 restaurants, a coffee shop, 2 bars, shops, a health club, and 4 tennis courts. Non-guests are invited to the buffet dinner for $25 per person. Paseo de Tangolunda (phone: 958-40340/60/80; 800-325-3535 in the US; FAX: 958-10113). Moderate.

Posada Binniguenda – A colonial-style hostelry, Huatulco's first, set about 530 yards from Santa Cruz Bay. All 75 rooms have color TV sets and air conditioning. There's a lobby bar and a restaurant (for guests only). There's no beach, but a pool and gardens. 5 Blvd. Benito Juárez, Apdo. Postal 175, Santa Cruz (phone: 958-70077; FAX: 958-70284). Inexpensive.

Ixtapa and Zihuatanejo to Oaxaca

The state of Oaxaca is an orgy of contrasts, from cool, forest-covered mountains and lush tropical valleys to a hot, humid coastline of beaches pounded by the Pacific surf. The contrasts are cultural as well as topographical, with ancient Indian ruins lying within sight of old Spanish colonial towns. Oaxaca, the fifth-largest state in the country, also boasts more ethnic groups than any other state except Chiapas. Most of these maintain their original languages, customs, and dress, turning the villages and markets of Oaxaca into an amazing array of otherworldliness. Even geography adds to the exotic atmosphere of the state. The rivers of Oaxaca often overflow their banks during the spring and summer rainy season, minor earthquakes occur frequently, and the state plays host to a diversified wildlife population. Though tapir, jaguars, ocelots, and margays have been severely reduced in numbers by the lumber, oil, and mining industries, they can still be found in some of the forests. Alligators and boa constrictors thrive in the more humid areas in the south.

Two proud cultures dominate the many different ethnic groups in the state (including the Chinantec, Mazatec, Cuicatec, Chocho, Huave, Mije, Trique, and Amusgo) — the Mixtec and the Zapotec, whose civilizations reached great heights in architecture, sculpture, astronomy, and jewelry design long before any Europeans made their way to Mexico. In turns they built the impressive sacred cities of Monte Albán and Mitla.

The state of Oaxaca really represents three major geographical regions: the Valley of Oaxaca, the Isthmus of Tehuantepec, and the Pacific Coast. The valley refers to the part closest to Mexico City and is the cultural, historical, and economic center of the state. The isthmus is where the west coast veers northeast and forms Mexico's narrow belt. The winds of this area are treacherous and the climate is hot and humid. The Pacific Coast, lying south and southwest of Oaxaca City, is not easily accessible from the rest of the state. Thankfully, there is a modern road, Highway 200, from Ixtapa and Zihuatanejo that extends along the coast past Acapulco to the beautiful beaches of Puerto Escondido and Puerto Angel, and for those who decide to venture inland to visit the splendid ruins surrounding Oaxaca City, Route 175 is an easy 154-mile (246-km) drive north of Puerto Angel. For those who still crave more sand, the Nine Bays of Huatulco are some 466 miles (745 km) southeast of Ixtapa and Zihuatanejo on Highway 200 (65 miles/104 km east of Puerto Escondido). This route, which passes through Acapulco and Puerto Escondido before turning north to Oaxaca, can be covered in the course of a series of coastal stopovers (for further information on Huatulco, see *Ixtapa and Zihuatanejo to Huatulco* in this section).

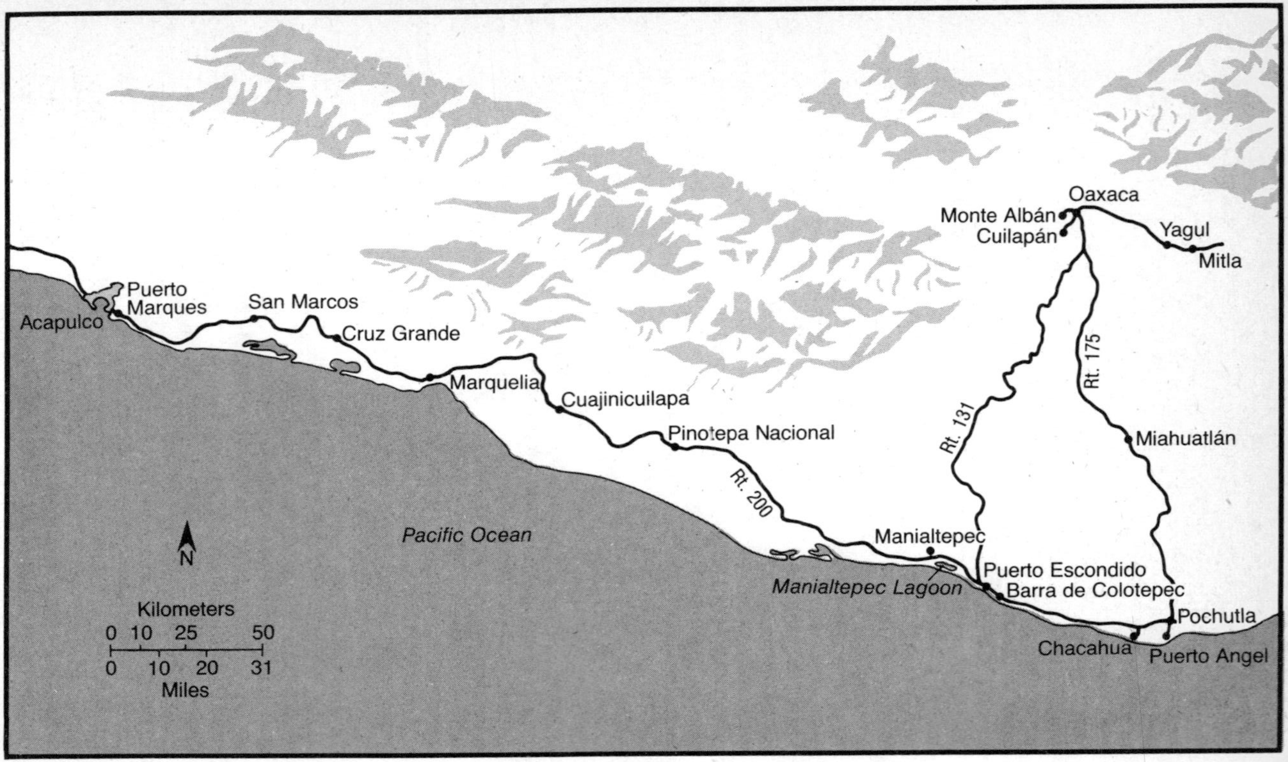

Oaxaca
Monte Albán
Cuilapán
Yagul
Mitla
Puerto
Marques
Acapulco
San Marcos
Cruz Grande
Marquelia
Cuajinicuilapa
Pinotepa Nacional
Rt. 200
Rt. 131
Rt. 175
Miahuatlán
Pacific Ocean
N
Manialtepec
Puerto Escondido
Manialtepec Lagoon
Barra de Colotepec
Pochutla
Chacahua
Puerto Angel
Kilometers
0 10 25 50
0 10 20 31
Miles

For a detailed report on the route from Ixtapa and Zihuatanejo to Acapulco, and points of interest and hotels and restaurants along the way, see *Ixtapa and Zihuatanejo to Acapulco* in this section.

En route from Acapulco – The next leg of this journey follows Highway 200 east to Puerto Escondido, 252 miles (403 km), or approximately 6 to 7 hours, from Acapulco. From town, take the Costera Miguel Alemán east (toward the airport) past Puerto Marqués, a lovely cove lined with luxury hotels and the new Punta Diamante (Diamond Point) housing development. From this point, the road leaves the coast and curves inland to the foothills of the Sierra Madre del Sur. There's a brief stretch of not-too-good road here, but it improves before long.

The stretch of coastline between Acapulco and Puerto Escondido, known as the Costa Chica (Little Coast), undergoes a subtle transformation as you head southeast. The harsh beauty of dry, desolate desert alternates with irrigated fields and orchards and tropical ranchland. While there are few settlements, dream beaches, or sites that demand a stop, the landscape and the scenes of daily life along the road are enjoyable. You are likely to see elderly *campesinos* (farmers) urging their burros along the roadside, children knocking almonds from trees with thin sticks, and women prodding herds of skipping goats across the highway. As you approach the state of Oaxaca, increasing Indian influences are visible in the colorful dress of the people, and in the mixture of architectural styles in the villages: Brick homes with red tile roofs give way to adobe houses and more primitive stick–and–mud plaster huts.

Traveling the scenic two-lane highway affords glimpses of the Pacific on the right, and the towering mountains on the left. Pass the village of San Marcos and the tiny hamlet of Cruz Grande and continue for about 24 miles (39 km) to the seaside town of Marquelia, a total of about 248 miles (398 km) from Ixtapa and Zihuatanejo (about 98 miles/158 km from Acapulco). If you travel through here on a Sunday, be sure to stop and sample the produce and handmade crafts on sale at the local market. Also worth a detour here is the secluded Pacific beach just 5 miles (8 km) south of town.

Back on Highway 200, drive about 39 miles (63 km) south to Cuajinicuilapa, a village founded in 1562 by freed African slaves; the population today — some 4,000 people — retains much of its original culture. In another 25 miles (40 km) from the state border is the Amusgo Indian town of Pinoteca Nacional, an agricultural center whose residents, a minor branch of the Mixtec, tend the land and sell their wares at roadside stalls on Sundays. The *Campestre* restaurant alongside the road into town offers good food in pleasant surroundings.

Continue east on Highway 200 for 89 miles (142 km) to Puerto Escondido.

PUERTO ESCONDIDO: A town of 45,000 people on the Pacific Coast in the state of Oaxaca, 402 miles (643 km) south of Ixtapa and Zihuatanejo (252 miles/403 km from Acapulco), this lesser-known resort is one of the most beautiful, unspoiled, and undeveloped hideaways in southern Mexico.

In fact, a lovely, sweeping view of the resort and its beaches can be seen from the Carretera Costera, the Coastal Highway. A more immediate view is afforded by the *faro* (lighthouse), which can be reached by a 15-minute walk from the main street. Look for a sign that says Camino del Faro; it points the way to the red-and-white tower.

About 95% of Puerto Escondido's population is of Indian descent, and most make their living from fishing or farming. With significant tourism just beginning to stir, it's still possible for a visitor to feel like an intruder here. Inhabitants aren't hostile or cold — it's just that they're gracious without being purposefully ingratiating, going about their lives as if no one with a foreign accent or camera had ever wandered into their midst. Service is inevitably slow (sometimes almost nonexistent), and there's little for visitors to do but enjoy the pristine, quiet beaches, snorkel over the fantastical coral reefs around the bay, and dine on fresh seafood in the town's handful of restaurants. Not yet — not nearly — the superstar resort, Puerto Escondido remains an unsophisticated hideaway; and its largely unpaved streets remain uncrowded, with brand-new cabs often cruising around empty, as though rehearsing for opening night.

Although Puerto Escondido is short on museums, historic houses, parks, and churches, it does have a handful of beautiful beaches, and quite a few lively celebrations. Its biggest bash begins on November 4. *November in Puerto Escondido* includes polo matches on burros (and using brooms), a fishing tournament, exhibitions of parachuting and ballooning, cultural events, and an *International Surfing Tournament,* in which surfers from Mexico, the US, and places as distant as Australia participate (a bikini contest, in which Miss Surf is chosen, is held on the day of the finals).

The government tourist office (120 Av. Hidalgo, next to the bus terminal; phone: 958-20358 or 958-20175) has a friendly, helpful staff and offers a very good map, as well as information on hotels and prices.

La Bahía (Main Bay), the half-mile stretch of beach (onto which the town's hotels and restaurants face), is the center of most activities — fishing, swimming, and sunning. Boats also leave here regularly for nearby, popular Puerto Angelito beach — not to be confused with the coast town of Puerto Angel, about 50 miles (80 km) away. The water at the Main Bay is so calm that locals refer to the western end of it as the "Bathtub" or "Kiddie Cove," perhaps also due to its popularity with waders under 3 feet tall.

Also worth exploring is Playa Zikatela (Zikatela Beach), at the east end of Main Bay. This 2-mile stretch of white sand and ruthless waves is considered by some to be one of the best surfing beaches in the world. From sunup to sundown, a dozen or so surfers regularly match their skills against the waves while spectators watch enthralled from the beach. (All but the best swimmers should stick to the sand, however, since the undertow is treacherous here.) Joggers and walkers will also find this beach to their liking; an hour's stroll up and down the shore, followed by breakfast at the *Santa Fe,* is a fine way to start any day. At the far end of the beach is Zikatela Point, a haven for pelicans, sea gulls, sandpipers, and other winged species, as well as for beach- and sunset-loving *Homo sapiens.*

Travel north and you'll be in Puerto Angelito. Protected from the waves by huge rock formations, the Port of the Little Angel offers tepid, tranquil water, two sandy beaches, and coral reefs attractive to snorkelers. There's easy access by boats that leave regularly from the Main Bay at Puerto Escondido; the fare is less than a dollar each way. Puerto Angelito can also be reached by car: Take the road to the airport, about 1½ miles (2 km) north of Puerto Escondido, then turn left at the sign for Puerto Angelito.

If you're in the mood for an isolated, elongated bit of beach with brilliant white sand, try Playa Bacocho (Bacocho Beach). Here is the place to wallow in solitude and contemplate the open sea. (Don't swim here; the water's too rough.) The *Posada Real Best Western* hotel provides a stunning view of this beach, as well as a path to it.

Shopping in Puerto Escondido is rather limited. There are only a few shops along Avenida Pérez Gazga, though items are also sold at the *Posada Real* and the *Santa Fe.* Most of the *artesanías* (handicrafts) for sale lack real distinction. On Saturday, the big market day, vendors stream in from surrounding communities to sell their wares downtown at the Indian market, the *Mercado Antiguo Hidalgo.*

Sports in Puerto Escondido are mostly water-related; tanks, masks, and flippers may be rented from *Transportadora Turística* (phone: 958-20114 or 958-20458). Dive trips are available for about $35 an hour, including one tank and equipment; snorkeling equipment is rented for about $10 per day. There's good snorkeling at Puerto Angelito, but the best diving areas are Puerto Angel (Vincente at the *Amigo del Mar* restaurant rents equipment) and Tangolunda Bay in Huatulco, to the southeast. Fishing boats can be rented for about $20 per hour for 1 to 4 passengers, including rods and bait.

Zikatela Beach attracts surfers from all over the world, but since the undertow is so strong only the most skillful should attempt the waves. No surfboard rentals are available.

Horses can be rented in Manialtepec, Barra de Colotepec, and in the town of Pluma Hidalgo from a man called Alejandro, "El Guapo" (the "handsome one"); inquire at the *Santa Fe* (phone: 958-20170). A typical half-day trip runs the gamut of Mexican scenery, from river crossings and thick jungle undergrowth to stark rock formations and hot springs. *Transportadora Turística* (phone: 958-20114 or 958-20458) also arranges for horseback riding on the beach, for about $15 an hour.

Puerto Escondido has little nightlife; in fact, if this little fishing village had sidewalks, they would roll up very early. But for those who aren't satisfied counting stars, there's *Bacocho* (45 Tehuantepec), *Pauline* (in the *Fiesta Mexicana*), *Macumba* (Av. Pérez Gazga), and even a show of female impersonators in *Discotheque Bahía,* on the road to Pochutla. *La Cascada* (Av. Oaxaca) has dancing and a show featuring pop music. For music only, try the *Bar Las Máscaras* at the *Villa Sol.*

EATING OUT: Puerto Escondido is not known for elaborate dinners or polished service, but the seafood is almost always good. Expect to pay up to $35 for two in those places listed as moderate, and less than $20 at an inexpensive spot. Prices do not include wine, tips, or tax. Most restaurants listed accept MasterCard and Visa; a few also accept American Express and Diners Club. Unless otherwise noted, all restaurants are open daily. Reservations are unnecessary at all places.

Cocos – Seafood and a spectacular view. In the *Posada Real Best Western* hotel (phone: 958-20394). Moderate.

Las Mariposas – Indoor or outdoor candlelight dining, an international menu, a guitarist, and a closing time of midnight (unusual in this sleepy town) are the draws here. Just up the hill from Av. Juárez (phone: 958-20197). Moderate.

La Palapa – Very attractive surroundings, good food, and friendly service. Across the street from the *Sardina Plata Beach* restaurant on Av. Pérez Gazga (no phone). Moderate.

Santa Fe – Those who are tired of *huevos rancheros* for breakfast might drop by this gracious restaurant for a vegetarian treat of homemade yogurt with granola or tofu hotcakes with fruit. The menu is basically vegetarian, but seafood — lobster, shrimp, squid, abalone, and oysters — is also offered. In the *Santa Fe* hotel, Playa Marinero (phone: 958-20170). Moderate.

Sardina Plata Beach – Well-prepared seafood and a magnificent view of the sea. There's also a swimming pool. 512 Av. Pérez Gazga (phone: 958-20328). Moderate.

Los Crotos – The service may be the slowest in town, but the prices and the food — *camarónes con frutas* (shrimp and fruit in a cream sauce) and *pescado con camarónes* (fish smothered in shrimp) — are worth the wait. On Av. Pérez Gazga next to the *García Rendón* travel agency (phone: 958-20025). Inexpensive.

La Perla – Simple and filled with plants. Seafood is the specialty. In town on Calle Tercera Pte. (phone: 958-20461). Inexpensive.

La Posada – Rustic, but serving good, basic Mexican food. Right next door to the *Macumba* disco (no phone). Inexpensive.

Rincón del Pacífico – In the hotel of the same name, with the same pleasant atmosphere and service. Seafood, naturally, and steaks. Av. Pérez Gazga (phone: 958-20056). Inexpensive.

Siete Regiones – This huge place specializes in typical Oaxacan fare from, as the name implies, the seven regions of the state. There's no extra charge for the fine view. No credit cards accepted. On Av. Pérez Gazga near *Los Crotos* (no phone). Inexpensive.

La Terraza – Seafood, as could be expected, as well as Mexican and international dishes and a lovely view. No credit cards accepted. In the *Nayar* hotel (phone: 958-20133). Inexpensive.

Da Ugo Hostería del Viandante – One of the most popular spots in town; there is sometimes a wait for a table at this little *palapa*-topped pizzeria. The menu includes a dozen varieties of pizza, as well as lasagna, spaghetti, and enormous salads. Rock 'n' roll music sets an upbeat mood. Av. Pérez Gazga (no phone). Inexpensive.

Aside from its appeal as a beach and water sports resort, Puerto Escondido is a good base from which to explore this area of Mexico's Pacific Coast. The following sites are within a short drive of the city and can be easily explored in 1 day.

DAY TRIP 1: MANIALTEPEC LAGOON

Some 15 miles (24 km) west of Puerto Escondido on Highway 200 is Manialtepec Lagoon, brimming with tropical birds and surrounded by thick, luxuriant vegetation. Boats depart from *Alejandria* and *Hamacas* restaurants for a 1½-hour excursion across the lagoon to the ocean, which costs about $6 per person. The *García Rendón* travel agency (on Av. Pérez Gazga, in front of *La Michoacana* ice cream shop; phone: 958-20114 or 958-20458) runs an 8-hour tour of the lagoon for about $30 per person, including lunch, boat ride, and ground transportation.

DAY TRIP 2: CHACAHUA NATIONAL PARK

This 50-square-mile retreat 35 miles (56 km) southeast of Puerto Escondido has fine sandy beaches and inlets and coves for fishing. Home to the myriad species of birds and fish that call the tropical Pacific home, it's worth a day trip. For those who prefer a guided tour of the area, the *García Rendón* travel agency in Puerto Escondido (phone: 958-20114 or 958-20458) offers an 8-hour tour of the park, including ground transportation and a boat ride.

BEST EN ROUTE

For such a small town, Puerto Escondido has a fair number of hotels. Expect to pay about $80 for a double room in a hotel listed as expensive; $50 to $75, moderate; $25 or less, inexpensive. During the low season, summer through fall, rates are likely to drop about 25%. Most hotels accept MasterCard and Visa; a few also accept American Express and Diners Club.

Posada Real Best Western – More typically resort-style than the others, this hotel isn't as quaint as some in town, and guests must walk down a cliff to get to the beach. But the staff is delightfully friendly and helpful. There are 100 air conditioned rooms, *Cocos* restaurant (see *Eating Out*), 3 bars, 2 pools, tennis, live music nightly, and lovely grounds. Blvd. Benito Juárez (phone: 958-20133 or 800-528-1234; FAX: 958-20192). Expensive.

Villa Sol – One of Puerto Escondido's newer stopping places, it offers 72 rooms, 24 junior suites, and 12 two-bedroom master suites with refrigerators, along with free transportation to the beach, a pool, restaurant, and bar. 2 Loma Bonita, Fracc. Bacocho (phone: 958-20382; FAX: 958-20451). Expensive to moderate.

Paraíso Escondido – This former hacienda has 20 rooms, all on the small side, but their whitewashed brick walls and tasteful furnishings are still tempting. The rooms upstairs have balconies with an ocean view; downstairs accommodations have porches and face the small pool. There's also a restaurant with bar service, *El Tecolote*. It's just a short walk to the beach. No credit cards accepted. 10 Calle Unión (phone: 958-20444). Moderate.

Santa Fe – The front door opens onto Main Bay, and the back door leads to Zikatela Beach. There are 40 air conditioned rooms, a small pool, and a fine dining area (see *Eating Out*) overlooking sand and surf. It contains authentic Mexican touches throughout: tiles from Puebla and Dolores Hidalgo, traditional ironwork and fabrics from Oaxaca, blown glass from Tlaquepaque, and furniture typical of Guadalajara and Puebla. Calle del Moro (phone: 958-20170; FAX: 958-20260). Moderate.

Loren – Simple, clean, and basic, it has 24 rooms with fans. 507 Av. Pérez Gazga (phone: 958-20057). Inexpensive.

El Mirador – Another one of Puerto Escondido's basic but pleasant places, it has 85 rooms, a restaurant, and parking. 113 Carr. Costera Pte. (phone: 958-20359 or 958-20398). Inexpensive.

Nayar – Two blocks uphill from the beach, there are 36 rooms, some with balconies, and the restaurant (see *Eating Out*) overlooks the town. No credit cards accepted. 407 Av. Pérez Gazga (phone: 958-20113). Inexpensive.

Las Palmas – It's simple, but clean and comfortable, with 40 rooms, a pleasant palm-filled courtyard, and a restaurant — an excellent place to start the day with a typical Mexican breakfast. Boats to Puerto Angelito can be rented right out front. Av. Pérez Gazga (phone: 958-20230). Inexpensive.

Rincón del Pacífico – A small place on the beach, with 26 rooms decorated cheerily in yellow and white, and 2 junior suites with air conditioning, TV sets, and refrigerators. It is well maintained, and the atmosphere is very pleasant. It also has a restaurant (see *Eating Out*). 900 Av. Pérez Gazga (phone: 958-20056). Inexpensive.

Villa Marinero – Situated close to the beach, each of the bungalows here is equipped with 2 bedrooms with fans, a small living room, and a kitchenette. Apdo. 16, Cerro el Marinero (phone: 958-20180). Inexpensive.

En route from Puerto Escondido – Continue east on Highway 200 to Puerto Angel. Those planning a visit to Huatulco should follow Highway 200 for a total of 65 miles (104 km). For more information, see *Ixtapa and Zihuatanejo to Huatulco* in this section. Just past the village of Barra de Colotepec, the highway curves for some 43 miles (69 km) to the market town of Pochutla, and the junction of Route 175, which leads north to Oaxaca. Pochutla really has little to offer, but about 8 miles (12 km) along the southern spur of Route 175, tiny Puerto Angel is worth a short detour.

PUERTO ANGEL: Though this small fishing community lacks the charm and ambience of its neighbor, it does offer visitors several attractions. Look for Playa del Panteón (Cemetery Beach), with its small graveyard with brightly painted tombstones, and Zipolite Beach, about 5 miles (8 km) out of town — one of the few nudist beaches in Mexico (beware of the undertow). Perched on a hill above town, the *Angel del Mar* offers a fine view and adequate lodging (see *Best en Route*).

En route from Puerto Angel – Rejoin Route 175 at Pochutla and head north for another 146 miles (234 km) to Oaxaca (about a 4-hour drive). The road — surrounded by the Sierra de Miahuatlán — can be treacherous here; be on the lookout for falling rocks. On the ascent are numerous signs warning "Zona de Niebla" (Fog Zone). If you do encounter fog, drive carefully and keep your headlights' high beams on.

About 85 miles (136 km) from Pochutla, past tiny little settlements and magnificent mountain views, is Miahuatlán, whose population of 10,000 makes it almost seem like a large city. Beyond this point travelers can begin to catch glimpses of the verdant Oaxacan Valley. About 52 miles (84 km) from Miahuatlán, Route 175 meets with Route 131, the unfinished roadway from Puerto Escondido. From here it's a smooth 9-mile (14-km) drive to the city of Oaxaca.

As you approach within a half mile (1 km) of the Oaxaca city limits, watch for the shop of *Alfarería Doña,* where some of the best black Oaxacan pottery is sold. Continue on Route 175 into Oaxaca.

BEST EN ROUTE

The ongoing development of Puerto Escondido and its environs is changing the face of this area from day to day. Accommodations here are varied: Near the beaches are everything from luxurious hostelries offering posh rooms and scenic views of the Pacific to inexpensive, no-frills places with no air conditioning. Visitors to the state of Oaxaca who prize comfort will be pleasantly surprised with very fine accommodations at prices considerably lower than their US counterparts. Expect to pay about $40 to $65 for a double room in these moderate places.

PUERTO ANGEL

Angel del Mar – On a cliff commanding a spectacular view of Puerto Angel, this 42-room hostelry has a restaurant, a bar, a pool, and water sports for guests. The sunsets are simply beautiful (phone: 958-40397). Moderate.

Sonaya – Across from the main pier, some of its 40 rooms have air conditioning or ceiling fans; all have terraces with lovely views of the bay. Convenient to the center of town, it boasts a restaurant and parking for guests (no phone). Moderate.

POCHUTLA

Costa del Sol – With 20 rooms (air conditioned or ceiling fan), this hotel is probably the best choice in town. 47 Lázaro Cárdenas (phone: 958-40318). Moderate.

OAXACA: High on the vast plateau of the Oaxaca Valley, Oaxaca is an Indian and colonial city surrounded, like all the valley, by the beautiful Sierra Madre del Sur. Outside the ring of the mountains are the jungles of Chiapas to the southeast, the Pacific Ocean due west, and the Gulf of Mexico to the northeast.

But within the high, protective wall of the Sierra Madre is the plateau world — 5,000 to 6,000 feet above sea level in the city and rising to 9,000 feet in the surrounding mountains. The city, the capital of the state of Oaxaca, has a population of 400,000; the state, more than 3.7 million, almost all of whom are Indians. *Oaxaqueños,* as the natives are called, are mostly descendants of the Zapotec and Mixtec Indian tribes, whose tiny villages dot the valley and mountainside. At the Saturday market, you will hear their languages spoken more often than Spanish.

As part of their legacy, these two great cultures, which first flourished in the area hundreds of years before Christ, have left the magnificent ruins at nearby Monte Albán, Mitla, and Yagul. All within a 25-mile radius of Oaxaca, these rich archaeological zones bear witness to an elaborate and highly religious civilization that was well versed in astronomy and had a system of writing that may be the oldest on this continent. In the late 15th century, however, they were conquered by the Aztec; when the Spanish arrived in the area in 1521, they found it under the grip of Montezuma's empire.

Replacing the Aztec fort with their own stronghold, the Spanish named the site Antequera. But in 1529 a city was founded and the name changed to Oaxaca, which derives from an Indian word meaning "forest of gourd trees."

The city was spared the worst ravages of Spanish rule. There was no gold or silver to be mined, so Spain's interest in it was purely aesthetic. Cortés fell in love with the area, claimed much of the land for himself, and planned to build an estate fitting his title of Marqués del Valle de Oaxaca. The estate was never built (Cortés died in Spain in 1547), but his descendants kept the property until the 1910 revolution; the name lingers on in odd places — like the sign outside an old hotel or the label on a bottle of mescal.

As with most Mexican towns today, life begins in the zocalo, or main plaza, and Oaxaca's is especially lovely, with its grand old trees and delicate gazebo-shape bandstand. The ideal places from which to view the lively comings and goings of the plaza are the sidewalk cafés under the Spanish colonnades around the square. Relax here with a drink or a cup of coffee, sit back, and let the world come to you. And it will. In the evening, from around 8 to 10 PM, the tempo picks up, and whenever there is a big band concert, it seems the whole town turns up for the show.

However, for the best view in town, head to Cerro del Fortín de Zaragoza, the hill north of Oaxaca that rises 350 feet above the city. To get there take García Vigil, cross the zocalo, and continue on Miguel Cabrera to the *periférico.* Cross the bridge and take the right fork. On its lower slope is the statue of native son Benito Juárez, the Zapotec Indian who became President of Mexico, and an open area from which to look out. Slightly farther up a short dirt road at the top of the hill is a pyramidal monument to the flag of Mexico. From both spots the view is magnificent; the hill directly south is Monte Albán, which is also a fine place from which to see the city and countryside. There you will also find the magnificent ruins of an ancient Indian community, and the present descendants walking with their goats down the hillside (see *Day Trip 1: Monte Albán,* in this section).

It won't take too long to realize that Oaxaca is an amazingly unspoiled city; rich with 16th-century architecture, 27 churches, two excellent museums, a colorful, active zocalo, a large outdoor Indian market, good shopping — and proximity to the archaeological ruins, fascinating side trips. In addition, Oaxaca has managed to conserve its traditions and customs. Known for its colorful fiestas, the town often fills to capacity during a holiday. One of the most popular is *Lunes del Cerro* (Monday of the Hill), held in mid-July. Among the festivities are the *Quelaguetza,* a celebration dedicated to the god of rain and fertility, featuring music, magnificent costumes, and dances — including the famous *Danza del las Plumas* (Indian Feather Dance); the selection of the "goddess" Centeocihuatl (not for her beauty, but for her knowledge of the customs and traditions of her region); and the *Bani Stui Gulal,* meaning "reenactment of the past," which tells the story of the Aztec and Spanish conquests and portrays the battle between the Zapotec and the Mixtec in which Donaji, the last Zapotec princess, was taken hostage and decapitated. The ceremonies are held on the Cerro del Fortín, on Route 190 about a mile (1.6 km) east of the Avenida Madero turnoff, and in the city; reservations are necessary for the main performance (book well in advance — no later than May; reservations can be arranged through US travel agents).

There is always something to see, even if it is only from an outside café along the zocalo. When you get tired of sitting, there are wonderful places to explore, and when you get tired of moving, there is always an equally wonderful place to sit. It is in many ways the quintessential Mexican city.

For information about getting around Oaxaca and its environs, there is a tourist office (Cinco de Mayo and Morelos; phone: 951-64828), and there are information booths at the airport, in front of the *Regional Museum of Oaxaca,* and at Monte Albán.

Certainly one of the gayest and liveliest squares in all of Mexico, the Plaza de Aramas (zocalo) offers a gazebo bandstand, numerous tree-shaded benches, outdoor cafés in all directions, hawkers, *evangelistas* (public letter writers), Indians, *oaxaqueños,* tourists, students, old and young, rich and poor. Musical concerts are performed evenings and on Sunday afternoons, and wandering street musicians can often be heard at random hours. It is a marketplace, social gathering, and cultural event that should not, and really cannot, be missed.

A very old and weathered church, the Basílica de la Soledad (Basilica of Solitude) is famous not for its structure (Calle Independencia, on the Plaza del Baile — Plaza of the Dance), but for the statue of La Virgen de la Soledad (Virgin of Solitude), who is the patron saint of Oaxaca and is considered to have great healing powers. The famous legend attached to her arrival in the city is prominently represented on glass panels in the religious museum at the rear of the church. In the 17th century, a pack train arrived in town with one more mule than the muleteer could account for. When the train got to the modern site of this church, the extra mule suddenly fell down and died. It was found to be carrying the incredible stone statue of the Virgin, and the people immediately decided to build a church to commemorate this miraculous event. The church was built in 1682. The statue is robed in a jewel-encrusted black velvet cloak, with a large pearl hanging on its forehead. It also has several changes of clothes for various religious occasions.

The Cathedral of Oaxaca, built in 1553, was a gift from the King of Spain to the city of Oaxaca. Situated on the north side of the zocalo, its original lovely baroque façade remains intact in spite of various alterations. The clock, although several hundred years old and made with all wooden works, still keeps good time.

Founded by the Dominican Fathers in 1570, the Church of Santo Domingo is an exquisite example of baroque art and a favorite with the natives of Oaxaca. While the outside is certainly worth a close look, it is the interior that stands out as a truly exceptional work of art: covered in gold scroll and polychrome reliefs set against a white background, with paved tile floors, massive gold chandeliers, and incorporating 11 chapels, including the lovely Chapel of the Virgin of Rosario (off to the right as you enter). The church, located at Gurrión and M. Alcalá, is one of a kind and should not be missed.

Step into the converted convent attached to the Church of Santo Domingo (Calle M. Alcalá) and you'll discover the *Regional Museum of Oaxaca,* with its series of rooms quietly arranged around an open courtyard. There are themes for each space, including regional arts and crafts, costumes, and archaeological artifacts. On the second floor, behind a heavily vaulted door, are the incredible, priceless jewels found at the excavation sites at Monte Albán in 1932. These objects, which date back to AD 500 and display considerable technical sophistication, include ornate filigree work, alabaster vessels, and jade and bone carvings of an earlier Indian culture, either Zapotec or Mixtec. Closed Mondays. Admission charge (phone: 951-62991).

The spectacular *Rufino Tamayo Museum of Pre-Hispanic Art* (usually called the *Rufino Tamayo*) traces the development of art in Mexico from 1250 BC to AD 1500. The 2,000 art objects that make up this collection were donated to the city by native *oaxaqueño* muralist and painter Rufino Tamayo and his wife, Olga. They are exhibited in a beautifully restored colonial mansion (at 503 Morelos) redesigned by Tamayo. Each gallery is arranged to represent a specific culture: Olmec, Totonac, Zapotec, Mixtec, Maya, Nayarit, and Teotihuacán. Closed Tuesdays. Admission charge; Sundays no charge (phone: 951-64750).

Driving along Porfirio Díaz (named after another native son who became President of Mexico), past the *Misión de los Angeles* hotel, stop at the impressive Fuente de las Siete Regiones (Fountain of the Seven Regions). A tribute to the natives of the area, it includes six statues of Indian women in regional garb and is topped by a figure of a male dancer from Teotitlán del Valle, wearing a plumed headdress.

Standing 4 miles (6 km) east of Oaxaca in Santa María del Tule is the Tule Tree, a huge ahuehuete cypress tree estimated to be over 2,000 years old. Some 140 feet high, with roots buried more than 60 feet in the earth, the tree (on Tehuantepec Highway, en route to Mitla) is the traditional sentry for the town of Santa María, and is larger than the church in front of which it stands.

As for shopping, there are a number of items that are unique to Oaxaca, and a number of places where they can be purchased. The famous dark green pottery of the nearby village of Atzompa is available at excellent prices in Oaxaca, as are the Miró- and Picasso-inspired wall hangings from Teotitlán, and the black unglazed pottery of Coyotepec. Cotton and woolen shawls, blouses, bags, blankets, heavy serapes, and hammocks are all well made in this area, as are baskets and fine steel hunting knives and machetes with ornate hand-carved handles and engraved blades. Many pieces of jewelry on sale in Oaxaca are reproductions of pieces found at Monte Albán — including necklaces, earrings, and pendants of gold, jade, and seed pearls.

For a true shopping experience, make Saturday your market day. This is when merchants from all the neighboring communities come in, wearing their native costumes and speaking their various dialects of Zapotec, to sell their wares at the arts and crafts *tianguis* outside the *Central de Abastos.* All the different types of mole (sauce) are available in the *Viente de Noviembre* market (at Viente de Noviembre and Aldama). Behind the market is a chocolate mill, *Mayordomo,* where Oaxacan chocolate can be specially blended to taste with almonds, sugar, and cinnamon. Considered one of the most colorful and interesting of all Mexican markets, it is worth a visit whether or not you are interested in buying anything.

Alfarería Jiménez – Carries mostly pottery, brightly colored and handmade, including pitchers, plates, serving dishes, and vases. It's possible to watch the artisans at work here. 402 Zaragoza (phone: 951-62102).

Aripo – Ten rooms are filled with rugs, pottery, weavings, and ornaments, primarily from Oaxaca. You can watch craftspeople at work on wooden looms. 809 García Vigil (phone: 951-69211).

Artesanías Cocijo – Pottery, wood, tinware, and textiles. At several locations, including 521 García Vigil (phone: 951-68081).

Casa Brena – This textile store and weavers' workshop sells pottery as well. Walk to the rear — listening for the slapping of the looms — to see people spinning yarn and dyeing cloth. 700 Pino Suárez (phone: 951-50222).

Copel – An elegant shop with a wide selection of antique and contemporary masks. Talavera pottery from Puebla and crafts from all over Mexico also are available. 303 M. Alcalá (phone: 951-67302).

El Diamante – A selection of tinware, pottery, jewelry, and other local crafts. Behind the cathedral, at 106H García Vigil (phone: 951-63983).

FONART – Clothing, metal ornaments, and ceramics are the wares here. The selection and prices are quite good. In a red-and-white building at 116 M. Bravo (phone: 951-65764).

Joyería y Artesanías – One of the few fine jewelry stores in town carrying silver pieces and precious and semi-precious gems. 226 M. Alcalá (no phone).

Mercado de Artesanía – A clean market with well-displayed crafts, where weavers can be seen at work, it's open daily. Some items are 50% less than at other places, but bargaining is a must. Corner of J. P. García and Zaragoza (no phone).

El Oro de Monte Albán – Reproductions of pre-Hispanic jewelry made on the premises. Plazuela Adolfo C. Gurrión (phone: 951-64523).

El Palacio de las Gemas – Regional gold jewelry with pearl and coral inlays, as well as a large collection of semi-precious stones. Morelos and M. Alcalá (phone: 951-69596).

Productos Típicos de Oaxaca – Though unimpressive from the outside, this group of shops set around a sculpture garden is packed with quality pottery, textiles, handmade toys, and tin figures. They will ship items too big to carry home. 602 Av. Belisario Domínguez (no phone).

Taller de Artes Plásticos Rufino Tamayo – The exhibition and sale of paintings, sculptures, and graphics produced by local artists in a workshop bearing the name of one of Oaxaca's most famous native sons. 306 Murguía (no phone).

Tianguis – A wide selection of native textiles, as well as other native handicrafts. Portal de Clavería, on the zocalo (phone: 951-69266).

Victor's – In a 17th-century monastery, it carries crafts as well as woven clothing. 111 Porfirio Díaz (phone: 951-61174).

Yalalag de Oaxaca – A tasteful selection of Indian and contemporary crafts, native clothing, and Josefa designs. 104 M. Alcalá (phone: 951-62108).

Sports fans should not leave Oaxaca without attending the Mexican-style rodeos. *Charreadas* are held in the *Lienzo Charro.* There is no schedule, but events are always well posted around town.

Swimming pools in Oaxaca are available at most of the large hotels and at the few resorts just outside town.

And tennis facilities can be found at the *Misión de los Angeles* (phone: 951-51500) and the *Victoria* (phone: 951-52633).

Although the city closes down early, it hardly means the people retire. Most of the hotels have cocktail lounges. In particular, the *Victoria,* on the edge of town (at Km 545, Rte. 190), has a lovely piano bar that looks out over the city. Discos include *Yonke Video Disco* (at the *San Felipe Misión*) and *Chaplin's Disco* (508 Av. Independencia). *El Corsal Negro* (at the *Fortín Plaza*), *Kaftan*'s (102 Porfirio Díaz), and *Tanilaoo* (at the *Misión de los Angeles*) have live music for dancing. And as expected, there is the nightlife on the zocalo, where music is heard from 7:30 to 8:30 PM nightly. People promenade and lively socializing continues until 11 PM. *El Sol y La Luna* (Sun and Moon) restaurant and coffeehouse (105 Murguía) is a lively gathering place with music every night. At *Los Guajiros* (302 M. Alcalá) there's dining and dancing to salsa and Latin American jazz nightly from 8 PM to 1 AM. The *Monte Albán,* on the plaza, has a very fine nightly show of regional dances; it's free to guests. On Thursdays at 8 PM the *Misión de los Angeles* (105 Porfirio Díaz) features folkloric dancing.

EATING OUT: There are three specialties for which Oaxaca is known: mole sauce, tamales, and mescal. Mole is a spicy, multi-ingredient sauce made with chocolate, and served with chicken and pork. It can be found throughout Mexico, but in Oaxaca it is made darker, thicker, and usually tastier because Oaxacan chocolate is very special. Local tamales are even more special. Moister than elsewhere in Mexico, flat and rectangular, they are wrapped in a banana leaf rather than the usual corn husk. The most common fillings are chicken and mole sauce, and it definitely should be sampled. Mescal, the local alcohol, is made from the maguey cactus (as is tequila), but with a different distilling process and altered taste. The bottle often contains a dead worm; aficionados eat bits of it while drinking the mescal, not unlike the way tequila drinkers lick salt. When eating in restaurants, expect slow service and a bill of around $40 for dinner for two in places we call expensive; about $25 in the moderate range; and under $15 in an inexpensive place. Prices do not include drinks, wine, or tips. Most restaurants accept MasterCard and Visa; a few also accept American Express and Diners Club. Unless otherwise noted, all restaurants are open daily.

El Refectorio – The refectory of the original convent and the adjoining patio have been combined into a charming setting for continental and Oaxacan dishes. Fridays in the chapel there's a *quelaguetza,* at which a Oaxacan buffet is served. Reservations advised. At *Stouffer Presidente* (phone: 951-60611). Expensive.

El Tule – This hotel dining room serves excellent continental and Mexican food (chicken in mole sauce is a specialty), and offers a fascinating view of the city below (mist-shrouded in the morning; streetlight-sprinkled at night). Reservations advised. At the *Victoria* hotel, Km 545, Rte. 190 (phone: 951-52533). Expensive.

Del Vitral – It's a lovely mansion complete with European chandeliers and stained glass windows. Specialties include the traditional Oaxacan moles and such exotic regional specialties as *nido de grillo,* a basket of tortillas, fried grasshoppers, and guacamole. There's live music in the afternoons and evenings. Reservations advised. 201 Guerrero (phone: 951-63124). Expensive.

Ajos & Cebollas – Although the name of this popular restaurant and bar translates as "garlic and onions," these aren't the edible items for which it's known; chicken curry and veal parmesan are more likely choices. There are three separate dining areas whose ceilings grow increasingly low as you move from one to the next — part of the strange and appealing decor. The intimate bar boasts a peppery house cocktail made with mescal, and live music is provided by a trio. Reservations advised. 605 Av. Juárez, across from Paseo Juárez (phone: 951-63793). Moderate.

Antequera – Set in the *Misión de los Angeles* hotel, it features a pleasant dining room with music provided by local musicians. Dinner is finished by 10 PM. Reservations advised. 102 Calzada Porfirio Díaz (phone: 951-51500). Moderate.

El Asador Vasco – Try the Oaxacan version of mole sauce here — steamy, black, and marvelous on chicken, or the *cazuelas* — small casseroles of baked cheese, mushrooms, and shrimp in garlic. It's easy to order too much. Dining is elegant and the bar comfortable, but the waitresses can be dour. There's a show every night at 9 PM. Reservations advised. One flight up at Portal de Flores on the zocalo (phone: 951-69719). Moderate.

Mi Casita – Many consider this the best place to enjoy true Oaxacan cooking. The actual dishes are displayed here, so you can see what your food looks like before you order it. It is especially famous for *chapulines* (grasshoppers), but there are also more conventional Oaxacan dishes such as enchiladas with chicken and spicy mole sauce. Try to get a table by the window (*Mi Casita* is 1 flight up). Closed Thursdays. Reservations advised. On the south side of the zocalo at 616 Hidalgo (phone: 951-69256). Moderate.

La Morsa – A large, open-air *palapa* (thatch-roofed tent) serving excellent seafood and steaks, with live music on Sunday afternoons. Reservations advised. 240 Calzada Porfirio Díaz (phone: 951-52213). Moderate.

El Sol y La Luna – This lively spot is a combined restaurant, coffeehouse, and gallery, with only 10 tables inside and another 5 on the terrace. It's worth the wait for an inside table to hear the music that begins at 9 PM every night. Pizza, salads, Italian dishes, and good chocolate-covered crêpes are on the menu. Open from 7 PM to 1 AM. No reservations. 105 Murguía (phone: 951-62933). Moderate.

Catedral – A local favorite, it is nicknamed the "House of Filets," with no less than 11 tenderloin cuts from which to choose, as well as regional dishes, hamburgers, sandwiches, and a variety of soups. Guadalajara artist Miguel Angel España's paintings fill one of the pleasant dining rooms. Live entertainment at dinner. Reservations advised. A block from the zocalo, at the corner of García Vigil and Av. Morelos (phone: 951-63285). Moderate to inexpensive.

Alameda – The good food (mole and Oaxacan-style stuffed peppers), service, and decor (especially the indoor patio), as well as the reasonable prices, make this a very agreeable place to dine. Reservations advised. Two blocks from the zocalo at 202 J. P. García (phone: 951-63446). Inexpensive.

El Biche Pobre – The hands-down favorite for local dishes (there are about seven types of mole) and Oaxaca's famous tamales. Closed Wednesdays. Reservations unnecessary. Mártires de Tacubaya and Abasolo (no phone). Inexpensive.

La Flor de Oaxaca – One block from the zocalo, this is where many *oaxaqueños* come for breakfast, lunch, or dinner — or simply for a cup of hot chocolate. It's an especially good place to sample a typical Oaxacan breakfast. 311 Armenta (phone: 951-65522). Inexpensive.

Los Guajiros – An offshoot of *El Sol y La Luna* (see above), it serves the same type of food, but the real specialty here is the music: salsa and Latin American jazz. There's dining — salads and Italian dishes — and dancing from 8 PM to 1 AM. Closed Sundays. Reservations advised. 302 M. Alcalá (phone: 951-65028). Inexpensive.

■ **Note:** Many cafés line the zocalo; among the best are *El Jardín* and *Del Portal.*

Oaxaca is an excellent base for exploring the nearby ruins at Monte Albán, Cuilapán, Yagul, and Mitla. Travelers can take guided tours, or visit on their own at their leisure. Each of these tours can comfortably be covered in 1 day.

DAY TRIP 1: MONTE ALBÁN, CUILAPÁN

Overlooking the Oaxacan valley from a flattened mountaintop 5½ miles (9 km) southwest of Oaxaca (follow Miguel Cabrera to the *periférico;* cross the Atoyec River bridge, then take the right fork) is Monte Albán, once a Zapotec holy city of more than 40,000 people covering 25 square miles, and now one of the most magnificent archaeological ruins in all Mexico. The Zapotec leveled the area in about 600 BC. The buildings are carefully arranged on a perfect north–south axis, with the exception of one structure, thought to have been an observatory, which is more closely aligned with the stars than the poles. The oldest of the four temples is the Temple of the Dancers, so named because of the elaborate carved stone figures that once covered the building. They are naked and distorted in strange positions, and have since come to be thought of not as dancers but as patients in what might have been a hospital or school of medicine. Then, sometime around 1,000 years ago, the Zapotec were conquered by the Mixtec, an enemy tribe. These new inhabitants never lived in Monte Albán, but used it as a city of the dead, a massive cemetery of lavish tombs. More than 160 have been discovered, and in 1932 Tomb 7 yielded a treasure unequaled in this hemisphere. Inside there were more than 500 priceless Mixtec objects, including gold breastplates; jewelry made of jade, pearls, ivory, and gold; and fans, masks, and belt buckles of precious stones and metals. All are now on view at the *Regional Museum of Oaxaca.* The ruins are open daily until 5 PM (until 4 PM during the rainy season); most of the drive is straight up, tortuously slow, and splendidly scenic. Return over the Atoyec River bridge, then take the left fork to Cuilapán.

Another very different type of ruin is located at Cuilapán, a Mixtec village about 3½ miles (5 km) southwest of Monte Albán. Here, in 1555, a group of Dominican friars began work on a massive monastery, but the project was never completed. Today, it has deteriorated into an odd combination of functioning parts and crumbling ruins. The walls of the basilica (which is in use) hold the tombs of what was perhaps the last of the Zapotec and Mixtec royalty, the Mixtec Prince of Tilantongo and his wife, Cosijopi, daughter of the King of Tehuantepec.

In its heyday, Cuilapán was the hub of the cochineal (red dye) industry, so important in the development of Mexico's traditional textiles. Long before the Spanish invasion, the Zapotec Indians used this dye, which is derived from the fried female cochineal mite. After they laid their eggs on cactus pads, the mites were gathered and dried for marketing. And it is from them that the rich and enduring scarlet dyes are obtained. During the colonial period, the Spanish crown had a monopoly on cochineal, and vast Oaxacan haciendas were built during the heyday of the industry. The Spanish took their monopoly so seriously that anyone caught removing the cactus from Spanish territory was sentenced to death. Only the Spanish were allowed to export it, which they did, and scarlet soon became the rage in Europe. Even the resplendent red coats of the British army were dyed with cochineal.

In January 1979, Pope John Paul II made this stop one of the most emotional of his 8-day visit to Mexico. Hundreds of thousands of barefoot peasants trekked into the town to get a glimpse of the pontiff, who put on a native hat and picked up a little girl in a moving scene captured by news photographers and sent around the world. Local officials welcomed the pope with a *quelaguetza,* a traditional ceremony in which natives don 3-foot fan-shaped hats decorated with streaming ribbons and dance to the haunting beat of a single drum.

Three miles (5 km) farther down the same road is Zaachila, a rustic, pastoral village — and the last capital of the Zapotec nation. There is an archaeological site at the edge of town that is only partially excavated. What has been unearthed so far in the way of clay figurines, gold plate, carved reliefs, and royal remains is quite fascinating, and much more is yet to be revealed. Reverse the route for your return to Oaxaca.

DAY TRIP 2: YAGUL, MITLA

About 19 miles (30 km) southeast of Oaxaca on Route 190 is the group of ruins at Yagul. Not as elaborate as Monte Albán, but set in a lovely spot on top of a hill, Yagul is certainly beautiful and interesting enough to make it worth the trip. This city is predominantly a fortress that's set slightly above a group of palaces and temples; it also includes a ball court and more than 30 uncovered underground tombs. Continue on Route 190 to Mitla.

Plan to spend most of the day at Mitla, 5 miles (8 km) southeast of Yagul (24 miles/38 km from Oaxaca). These fascinating ruins are a complex of ceremonial structures started by the Zapotec but taken over and heavily influenced by the Mixtec. The name, derived from an Aztec word, *mictlán,* means "place of the dead." The architecture here is totally different from that seen at any of the other ruins in the area. The walls of stone and mud are inlaid with small stones cut into geometric patterns, forming a mosaic that is Grecian in appearance. Unlike other ancient buildings in North America, there are no human figures or mythological events represented — only designs. Another unique feature of Mitla is the fact that it was still in use after the Spanish conquest of Mexico. A trip here can be nicely combined with a stop at the famous Tule Tree mentioned above, just 4 miles (6 km) east of Oaxaca, and the *Frissell Museum of Zapotec Art,* just off the plaza in Mitla. This museum, which is also a regional research center of the University of the Americas, is in an 18th-century hacienda and houses a fine collection of Zapotec artifacts, labeled in English, that clearly trace the development of the Zapotec-Mixtec empires. It also houses the rustic *La Sorpresa* restaurant, which serves hearty country cooking (marinated, tender, and pungent lamb and chicken) and mescal cocktails. (The restaurant is open daily from 8 AM to 6 PM; the museum is open daily from 9 AM to 6 PM.) Adjoining the ruins is a small handicrafts market. About a half mile (1 km) from the museum, the ruins can be reached by following the main, paved street, which is lined with small clothing shops. Return to Oaxaca on Route 190.

BEST EN ROUTE

In Oaxaca, expect to pay $90 to $125 for a double room in the expensive category; about $40 to $65 in a moderate hotel; and up to $35 in the inexpensive range. Most hotels accept MasterCard and Visa; a few also accept American Express and Diners Club.

Stouffer Presidente – Beautifully restored, this unexpected jewel was formerly a convent, originally built in 1576. A monastic air still lingers in the form of breezy patios and small enclosed gardens. There is, however, now a reasonable complement of modern conveniences in the 91 rooms, including TV sets, plus a heated pool, dining room, and cocktail lounge. Stop by for a drink and look around even if you don't stay here. Jazz is played in the bar every night except Tuesdays, from 9 PM to midnight. On Friday nights there is a buffet of traditional Oaxacan dishes in *El Refectorio* (see *Eating Out*) and an excellent performance of regional dances. 300 Cinco de Mayo (phone: 951-60611; 800-472-2427 in the US; FAX: 951-60732). Expensive.

Fortín Plaza – Located on the Cerro del Fortín, this modern, 6-story hostelry affords a magnificent panoramic view of the city. Each of the 100 pleasant rooms has a TV set and a telephone, and there's a pool, bar, coffee shop, restaurant, and live music and dancing at *El Corsal Negro.* Av. Venus and Calz. Héroes de Chapultepec (phone: 951-57777; 800-826-6842 in the US; FAX: 951-51328). Moderate.

Hacienda la Noria – A 72-room hostelry, 13 blocks south of the zocalo, it has 2 swimming pools, a restaurant, and ample grounds. *Periférico* at 100 La Costa (phone: 951-67555; FAX: 951-65347). Moderate.

Margarita – About a mile (1.6 km) from downtown, this motel offers 60 units, a swimming pool, garden, dining room, and cocktail lounge. 1254 Madero (phone: 951-64100; FAX: 951-61133). Moderate.

Marqués del Valle – Right on the plaza and in the middle of things, with 95 rooms. The ground-floor restaurant serves a good breakfast, from bananas and cream to hotcakes. 1 Portal de Claveria (phone: 951-63295; FAX: 951-66294). Inexpensive.

Mesón del Rey – A nice little surprise of a hotel, only a block and a half from the zocalo, it offers 22 rooms, a cozy lobby, and cordial staff. No credit cards accepted. 212 Trujano (phone: 951-60033). Inexpensive.

Principal – Modest with only 17 rooms, it charms with geranium-filled clay pots on the balconies and skylights in the bathrooms on the top floor. The lobby has an excellent map of the town. No credit cards accepted. 208 Cinco de Mayo (phone: 951-62535). Inexpensive.

Señorial – With pool, roof garden, and cocktail bar open until 10 PM, this is one of the most conveniently located hostelries in Oaxaca. The one drawback is the thin walls separating its 127 rooms. 6 Portal de las Flores (phone: 951-63933; FAX: 951-63668). Inexpensive.

Trebol – The entrance to this property, set amid some rather shabby shops, belies the sparkling cleanliness within. The 14 rooms are small but comfortable, built around a sunlit patio, and there is a restaurant and laundry service. No credit cards accepted. 201 Flores Magón (phone: 951-61256). Inexpensive.

INDEX

Index

NOTES

NOTES

NOTES

NOTES

NOTES

NOTES

NOTES

NOTES

NOTES

NOTES